THE $8 MAN

THE $8 MAN

FROM INDIA TO NORTH AMERICA, IMMIGRANTS WHO
CAME WITH NOTHING AND CHANGED EVERYTHING

EDITED BY BRENDA H. CHRISTENSEN

Published by Redtop Publishing, Woodside, CA
The8dollarman.com

The phrase "The $8 Man" is trademarked by Brenda H. Christensen

Edited and Designed by Girl Friday Productions
www.girlfridayproductions.com

Editorial: Emilie Sandoz-Voyer
Interior Design: Rachel Christenson
Cover Design: Debbie Berne

Image Credits: cover photograph courtesy of Suhas Patil, used with permission;
all interior photographs owned, controlled by, and used with permission from
the individual contributors.

ISBN-13: 978-0-692-84798-5
ISBN-10: 0-692-84798-7
e-ISBN: 978-0-692-84799-2

First Edition

Printed in the United States of America

*To my husband, Thomas W. Barry, who never wavered
in his support and belief that storytelling about people who
do good is critical to creating a just society.*

*To all the people in Canada and America who have openly
welcomed immigrants throughout our histories.*

To those people who act on the belief that we are all equals.

*To the immigrants who assimilated and brought their ideas and
philanthropy to make communities richer for all.*

TABLE OF CONTENTS

FOREWORD

The diverse cultural fabric of the United States is often described as a mosaic, the design of which has been shaped by the successive generations of immigrants who came from across the globe to put their indelible imprint on the country. A nation of immigrants, ours has been immeasurably enriched throughout its history by the contributions made by those who began their lives elsewhere, their additions enhancing the United States' social, political, economic, scientific, and cultural landscapes. The American spirit has provided opportunities, education, and freedom to those who graced our shores, and they, in turn, have served to make the United States the strong, pluralistic, inclusive society that it is today.

I am the son of immigrant parents from India. My father came to the United States in the 1960s with little more than dreams of a better life for his family and a few dollars in his pocket. Because of his and my mother's sacrifices and determination, and because the nation that welcomed them set no limit on what they could achieve or what roles they could hold, I was able to write my own chapter in the continuing story of the United States. It is a source of great pride that our family's story began in Jalandhar in the North Indian state of Punjab and is written today in the office of the US ambassador to India. But I do not fool myself into believing that our story is unique. Indeed, my pride of country is greater for knowing that I am one of many whose story started in a distant land and progressed to a point where we have been able to meaningfully contribute to the country that has made it possible.

Investing in education, hard work, talent, and a never-say-die spirit have been the hallmarks of the many Indian Americans who have made immense contributions to the United States, to India, and, indeed, to the entire world. From the innovative technologies developed by Silicon Valley entrepreneurs to research conducted by NASA astronauts, the Indian diaspora in the United States has led by example. Today, many of America's leaders in nearly every field, from business and finance to government, from the arts and humanities to the ever-expanding frontiers of the IT world, are Americans of Indian descent. It is not hyperbole to say that the story of the Indian diaspora in the United States encapsulates the essence of the American dream.

The $8 Man includes the stories of the founding of TiE (The Indus Entrepreneurs) and is being published at the time of TiE's twenty-fifth anniversary. It is in this spirit that I heartily congratulate all those who founded TiE and continue its mission. TiE is an amazing organization, established by Indian Americans not only to inculcate and nurture an entrepreneurial spirit, but also to give back to the society that enabled its members to realize their potential in countless corners of America. TiE's constant grooming of young leaders through its various activities will ensure continued US leadership in the world in entrepreneurship, civic engagement, and philanthropy. TiE projects help uplift the lives of entrepreneurs around the world by providing mentorship and guidance to talented youth. The work of TiE serves to share the American dream with rising entrepreneurs around the world and help empower them to realize their dreams. TiE is in its own way writing a new chapter in the American opus, and Americans of every heritage are richer for it.

Richard Rahul Verma
Former United States Ambassador to India

INTRODUCTION

In the early 1990s I started working with a computer industry colleague from Canada who had invented a new technology. His name was Kumar Malavalli. I was an industry marketing professional who understood the value of this new technology and was eager to help it succeed. Kumar and I started traveling together to promote his ideas, and I soon joined his start-up company as VP of Marketing. While traveling on business, you get to know a great many stories about your colleagues' lives, and Kumar shared much with me about his journey to North America from India, where he had grown up and gone to college. Later, in the early 2000s, we started a storage networking conference business in India. I came to appreciate the country, the people, and the history of India. In addition to Kumar's story, I learned more about the journeys of others who emigrated from India to Canada and the United States in the 1960s and '70s. One shared detail in their stories stuck with me: When they left India, the Indian government gave these immigrants some money to help them get to North America. It amounted to eight US dollars. How, I wondered, could you get to the US or Canada with only eight dollars?

Thus began my interest in the lives and stories of Indian immigrants to North America during the 1960s and '70s. I was curious to understand their motivations for leaving India. What inspired them to leave in the first place? And how had they navigated the new food, the unique customs, the diverse cultures, and the language style of North

America? How had they managed with no communication with their families back home except for postal mail that took weeks? Did these immigrants always plan to return to India? Would jobs be waiting for them in India once they completed their advanced degrees? What led them to stay and assimilate? During their arrivals in the 1960s and '70s, the United States was in the midst of tremendous change and chaos with the Vietnam War, the civil rights movement, the change of presidents, and the recession. How had these events impacted their lives and their decisions?

With our twenty-first-century familiarity about India and its people, we may not know or remember that following WWII, and through to the 1960s and '70s, there was a great deal of tension between the United States and India. India cultivated relations with the Soviet Union in the 1960s for both strategic and military purposes, while the United States was simultaneously aligning its policies with Pakistan. India publicly stated it was nonaligned, but the government's close relationship with the Soviets was in response to US ties with Pakistan. The United States was brought somewhat closer to India during the rise of Communism in China in the 1960s, but during Nixon's time in office, the tension between India and the United States continued.

During these decades, there nevertheless remained a particular bright spot in the relationship between the United States and India. Through a consortium of leading universities in the United States, India established several India Institutes of Technologies (IITs). The IITs included professors from Canada and the United States, as well as some other countries, who helped set up the academic programs and development of laboratories for research and teaching. Many of the eight-dollar men in this book attended the IITs or similarly rigorous engineering institutes in India for their undergraduate degrees. The US government offered hundreds of doctoral fellowships to IIT graduates under a technology cooperation program meant to assist the development of India post-partition.

Because the rupee still wasn't convertible, the Indian government gave out their limited foreign reserve to assist people who were mainly leaving India to go to graduate school. People who left to pursue advanced education out of India generally got what amounted to eight dollars, although it varied somewhat. Often their families paid their airfare to major US and Canadian airports, and then the immigrants had to make it to places such as New Brunswick and Spokane and Houghton with the money exchanged from the Indian government. Occasionally a relative might give them a bit more—what they could spare—but there was never much money to make the journey and start a life in North America. Fortunately, airlines were still serving food in those days. Money continued to be a problem for these young immigrants once they settled in North America. These students got through school on scholarships or burdened themselves with loans. They stayed in dorms or lived frugally with other students. When they got to college, they became teaching assistants or found other ways to earn money, often doing work that wasn't attractive to a person who had already completed their undergraduate degree.

Over the years of our work and friendship, Kumar Malavalli introduced me to many of his peers and friends who were fellow immigrants. Like him, they had come to North America during the 1960s and '70s. Also like him, most had done it with eight dollars from the Indian government and very little else. I did not meet any women who immigrated alone during these decades—mostly because women didn't leave India without their family or husbands at that time. The men I met through Kumar were instrumental in the computer industry, inventing technologies and building or creating companies. Through another connection, I met some of the immigrants who lived in Minnesota. That is where I first met the two women whose stories are included (even though they didn't receive the eight dollars when they departed India). The immigrants I connected with in Minnesota were not involved in high technology. They assimilated through graduate schools and the India Association of Minnesota, and they were instrumental in designing organizations and methods by which both Indian immigrants and Minnesota natives could appreciate and learn from each other. One of the other immigrants in Virginia has made his life work building low-income housing and inspiring communities of people with considerably different backgrounds—racially, financially, and educationally—to connect and improve the quality of life for everyone.

In creating this book, which is a compilation of first-person interviews with a wide variety of those whom I have dubbed "eight-dollar men," I hoped to showcase stories of hard work and triumph. But I also imagined that we would learn something about what an effective immigration policy would look like from the perspective of those who have been through the process. As this book took shape, I came to appreciate how much these men and women valued education and took ownership of their *own* education. Even today, children in India know how important it is to be educated and do well if they get the chance to go to school.

Following this introduction, I have included two graphs used with permission from the book *The Other One Percent: Indians in America* by Sanjoy Chakravorty, Devesh Kapur, and Nirvikar Singh (see pp. xvi and xvii). These graphs support the profiles of the eight-dollar men in this book. Here we see the improved outcomes that result when people assume full responsibility for their education, even when considerable barriers exist to achieving that goal. These graphs demonstrate why we need a strong immigration program for people who are educated in this country and have the skills to help Canada and America continue to be countries of innovation. To make that a reality, we need the continued assimilation of diverse ideas, people, and ideals. Today we may be familiar or associate with many people of Indian ancestry in North America, but as we see in the graph this wasn't always so. In fact there was clear legislation in the United States barring people emigrating from Asia until President Johnson, in 1965, proposed a new strategy for US immigration. Canada had a similar program. (See the Appendix, p. 307, for excerpts from President Johnson's special message to Congress on the matter of immigration, as well as for details on Canada's policies.) Opening immigration from India to the United States was in many ways a response to the Cold War and the space race with the Russians. America didn't have enough engineers. An unintended consequence of the Vietnam War was the drafting of the American men who would have been eligible to fill graduate colleges in engineering and medicine. The colleges had the faculty and the institutions, so they looked to India as a source of qualified candidates for these programs.

My grandfather was an economic migrant from Norway at the turn of the twentieth century. He wanted to become an educated man, but he and my grandmother had many children to support. Every one of their eleven children desired an education but were almost exclusively denied it because of the demands to go to work and support the family. I found in these stories of Indian immigrants that same quest to become an educated person. My grandfather never wanted to return to the harsh conditions of a North Sea fisherman. Did these immigrants from India expect to return to India after their master's degrees or PhDs? India as the Motherland has a strong pull for émigrés. What was different for them than for my immigrant grandfather? Was it just the times? Why are these immigrants to North America generous in their philanthropy to Canada, the United States, and the people in Mother India?

In this book, I consider myself an enabler for storytelling. I listen and ask questions that allow people to describe their life journeys, complete with the dreams, disappointments, surprises, intersections, mentors, losses, and aspirations that form the story of their lives. The stories of these eight-dollar men don't follow a question-and-answer format. They are not my interpretation of their stories. Instead, I listened to them describe their life journeys and recorded these details. I allowed them to review the transcripts for additions and deletions. I wanted them to say, "Yes, this is my story."

These are inspiring and engrossing stories of leadership and assimilation, of personal resilience and professional vision, of the willingness to make sacrifices. These stories tell us that what America and Canada espouse as values come naturally to Indians. *The $8 Man* is for anyone concerned about motivating and teaching children individual responsibility for their own education, and for anyone who seeks to foster a love of learning as an essential element in lifelong development. *The $8 Man* sheds new light on why we need an immigration policy that encourages the best and the brightest to come to our shores and stay as citizens. And most importantly, *The $8 Man* introduces successful entrepreneurs and community leaders who have quietly become major philanthropists, enriching both India and North America.

Indian immigrants came to America in the 1960s and '70s with eight dollars in their pockets. How did they make it? *The $8 Man* tells you their stories.

Brenda H. Christensen
Woodside, California

BRENDA H. CHRISTENSEN

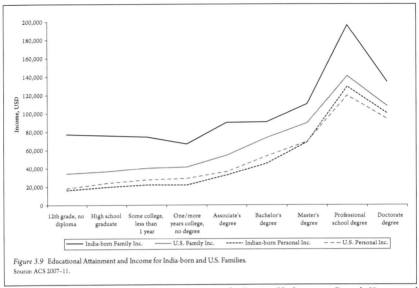

Figure 3.9 Educational Attainment and Income for India-born and U.S. Families.
Source: ACS 2007–11.

From The Other One Percent: Indians in America *by Sanjoy Chakravorty, Devesh Kapur, and Nirvikar Singh. Oxford University Press, 2017. Page 106. Used with the permission of Oxford University Press and the American Community Survey, United States Census Bureau.*

We argue that there were three distinct periods or phases of Indian immigration to the United States in the nearly five decades after 1965. Figure 2.1 shows the broad outlines of this periodization, which we name as follows:

Phase 1—The Early Movers (1965–1979)
Phase 2—The Families (1980–1994)
Phase 3—The IT Generation (1995 to date)

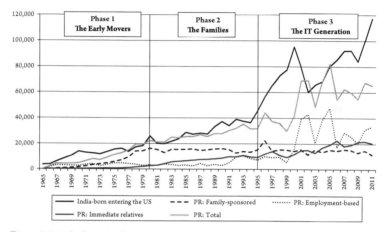

Figure 2.1 India-born Settler Streams in Three Phases, 1965–2011.
Notes: PR: Permanent Resident (or Green card). The PR Total does not include the data for refugees/asylees (see Figure 2.8 for details). The Indian-born entry numbers reflect individuals who were alive and present in the U.S. for the ACS 2007–11 or PUMS 2012 (see below). The original numbers would have been higher, especially in the early years, because the recent estimates do not take account of mortality in this population nor the returnees. For the PR data: before 1977, the year end was June 30 and it became September 30 in 1977, which means that the 1977 data is reflective of 15 months.
Sources: The Indian-born entry numbers in 1965–2006 are from ACS 2007–11; the data for the last five years (2007–11) are from PUMS 2012.

From The Other One Percent: Indians in America, *by Sanjoy Chakravorty, Devesh Kapur, and Nirvikar Singh. Oxford University Press, 2017. Page 28. Used with the permission of Oxford University Press and the American Community Survey, United States Census Bureau.*

KUMAR MALAVALLI, SILICON VALLEY

BORN IN MYSORE, INDIA

EDITOR: *Kumar experienced being a guest worker in Germany and a citizen of Canada before his final immigration to the United States. Kumar's story includes a brief introduction about the founding of Brocade Communications, highlighting the circuitous path and unique approach that led to its founding and formed the basis of the company's technology and start-up. Brocade's beginning was a significant milestone in Kumar's eight-dollar-man journey as well as in the computer industry. During the interview process for this book, I had the privilege of interviewing Kumar's parents, Narayanaswamy and Indiramma Malavalli. They provide a unique perspective on Kumar's story through their reflections on his influences as a young man, his immigration, and his personal attributes. They visited the United States frequently and were able to enjoy Kumar's life transitions from an eight-dollar man to a founder of a new technology and several companies. The interview with Kumar's parents can be found at the conclusion of this chapter.*

KUMAR: Before I tell my story I do have thoughts on what the US immigration policy should be. I have worked in four countries (India,

Germany, Canada, and the US) and have experienced being a working immigrant in Germany, Canada, and the US.

THOUGHTS ON AN IMMIGRATION POLICY

I have five points that I would recommend to be considered for a US immigration policy. (1) There are millions of undocumented immigrants in the US, and we should follow the German program, registering them and legalizing them as guest workers. They can then pay taxes and can get a driver's license. They don't live in secrecy. The guest worker card doesn't give the person the right to be a citizen. If they want a green card, they need to get in line like all others applying, but they have a guest worker status. (2) Any of the undocumented immigrants who have criminal records must be immediately deported. (3) The H-1B visa program is broken. The system should be like the Canadian program, which is based on national supply-and-demand needs and not a quota system. In the quota system big companies like the ones from India and China grab the visas and smaller companies and individuals are left behind, and yet they may be very qualified and have a talent we need. (4) The US is now lagging behind in technology and other sectors because there are not enough people coming out of the universities in engineering, science, and medicine who are allowed to stay after their master's degrees, PhDs, and post-doctoral-level studies. They should be given green cards immediately upon completion of their degree rather than being forced to return to their home country and have

Kumar Malavalli
(photo courtesy of Kumar Malavalli)

their talent wasted to the US. (5) DREAMers [those young people registered under the Development, Relief, and Education for Alien Minors (DREAM) Act], because they are born here, raised here, and educated here, should be given citizenship immediately. Why would we punish these people who have lived their entire lives in this country? There is no benefit to America.

DECIDING TO LEAVE INDIA

After I finished my graduation in engineering in Mysore, I went to work as an installation engineer for AEG, and I learned German technology. At that time I wanted to migrate to the US. In 1969 if you passed the interview at the US consulate, you could get a green card. I applied for

the green card and was invited to come to the American consulate in Calcutta, where I passed the test but had to come back for the medical test. At the same time I had learned from some of my friends who had migrated to the US that they had problems getting engineering jobs although they were qualified. They had to take jobs in gas stations and

Kumar as trainee engineer in Germany
(photo courtesy of Kumar Malavalli)

doing manual labor. This discouraged me so I didn't go back to the US consulate, even though I was young so I wouldn't have any problem passing the medical test. So I bypassed the opportunity to immigrate to the US, and instead I took the chance to go to Germany.

GETTING THE EIGHT DOLLARS AND DEPARTURE TO GERMANY

I did get the eight dollars the Indian government was offering us as support on our emigration from India. I think I bought a beer and some magazines with the funds. It is easy to forget that India in the 1960s was a very different country than it is today. My first professional job was working on Siemens control systems at Mannesmannröhren-Werke in Düsseldorf. I worked in the special measurement and process control area. This was the first time I was exposed to design and process control systems.

I was a trainee. If I wanted to recommend something, I had to organize the idea and put it on paper first, get my hands dirty by building a
model, and try it in the production environment. There was really no
one to help. I got the approval to do all this because it was not a critical area to the factory so they allowed me to do it. I was very excited
about the idea of using an electronic device to measure the pressure
and, accordingly, deciding how much pressure is needed to hit the
target. I don't remember how I came up with the idea. In Germany I
had two bosses and four colleagues. They all liked my idea and no one
objected. This small-scale idea continued on when I went to work later
in Canada.

LEAVING GERMANY FOR CANADA

I left Düsseldorf to go to Canada. I had to leave Germany because I
wanted to pursue my career in electronics and control systems, and,
as I was not able to get a stay permit, I was asked to leave. In Germany
you needed both a work permit and a stay permit, which gives you the
right to work and live there. For a limited period of time (two and a half
to three years), I was under a training program. The stay permit goes
along with the training program. I got an extension of the training,
but the two departments didn't talk with each other. I got my work
permit to extend my training, but the stay permit was not given to me.
I knew I had only six months before I had to leave Germany. I applied
to US immigration and was refused. In 1974 there was a big recession
in the US, with the oil embargo, and lots of bad things were happening economically. I could not get a US green card. I wanted to work
in something related to electronics, in either the US or Canada. For
me, electronics meant either process control or telecommunications;
both of these matched my skill set. At that time I knew I could develop
something electronic and make something happen from not only
building the hardware but also writing the software directly related
to the hardware. That was what I did for the very first product that I
developed for another company.

When I was in Germany, I went to Bonn, and the Canadian coun-
sel general told me there would be no problem getting a job in Canada
and they would welcome me. I came to Canada with that in mind. I

chose Toronto because I had been told it was English speaking, and it had the most industry, and therefore the most jobs and more chances for getting a job. That was my rationale.

I arrived in Toronto with no job, the little money I saved in Germany, and two suitcases. My first day in Canada was Thanksgiving weekend, and I didn't know about this Canadian holiday. I arrived the day before the holiday, and I couldn't go to any employment agencies. I asked at the arrival area for someplace inexpensive, decent, and clean to stay in Toronto. I had to stay in the hotel while I waited for the Thanksgiving holiday to end. When the workday came, I went to register with the Ontario Welcome House, which welcomed new immigrants. They gave me the addresses of employment agencies, and I went there to register. They found me a job within three days at Thermo Electric as a technologist. They didn't trust my background as an engineer so they made me a technologist. I wanted a job so I took it. A technologist versus an engineer was a status thing—the job was up from a trainee but not quite an engineer. It was a class-system difference.

It was a mundane job with no chance for innovation. You had to do whatever you were instructed to do. It was a confined, constrained job. Do the job and leave at five p.m. I told my boss after fifteen days that I wouldn't be coming the next day. I said, "I am sorry, I just don't like this job." He said okay but he was surprised. He just called the employment agency to retrieve the commission because I left the job before three months, which was the condition of the company using the employment agency.

In another week I got another job at Pilkington Glass. It is a famous English glass company, making sheet glass for automobiles and construction. I got a job in control systems. There I developed a few control systems to use in-house. I wanted to start a company in process control while I was working at Pilkington, but that didn't work out. I worked for Pilkington for five years. I became fascinated with telecommunications. I read up on my own and went to the University of Toronto. I took night classes because I had to work during the day. As this was a totally new area, it wasn't something Pilkington was going to fund because it wasn't part of their business.

BECOMING A COMMUNICATIONS DESIGN ENGINEER

In the meantime, the association of professional engineers in Ontario asked me to take some exams. I took the exams, passed, and then was certified as a Professional Engineer in the province of Ontario. Then I got a job at ITT as a communications design engineer. ITT was a big American conglomerate, and it had a private branch exchange (PBX) division that I joined as a junior design engineer. I designed features for the office telephone exchange. This was in 1979 and was the beginning of my communications experience.

After two years at ITT, I went to Amdahl. Amdahl Computer Systems had a branch in Mississauga, Canada, that worked with Wide Area Communications products (T1-T3, ISDN). I was so lucky to transition from PBX to wide area networks (WAN) communications. I was hired as a senior architect. I did well in the interview, and I had the ITT experience. I developed a couple of features for the PBX that was sold worldwide. ITT was really research and development (R&D). I took it upon myself to find a way to better the products, such as I did for process control at Pilkington. At Amdahl I got to be a real architect. I knew that I belonged in this job and area. I was excited to be an architect because I could create something and make it useful. R&D is okay, but if it isn't tangible, and beneficial to the customer, then for me it was no good. Amdahl had worldwide T1, T3, and ISDN product sales. There were meetings of international standards bodies, but I didn't attend. The senior people went to special ANSI committee meetings. I hoped to join this kind of work someday.

WORKING IN FIBER-OPTIC LANS

After two years, I left Amdahl and joined Canstar Communications to work on fiber-optic-based local area networks (LANs) they were developing. It was similar to but different from Ethernet. It was called Hubnet, a technology from the University of Toronto. At Canstar I got involved with the high-speed LAN design that proved to be very interesting. We developed the product and had several installations—one at the University of Illinois, several in Europe, and one at the US Naval Defense Lab managed by Dr. Hank Doherty.

I joined Canstar as a manager, having moved up from a technologist at Pilkington Glass, a design engineer at ITT, and an architect at Amdahl. I was manager of hardware and software systems, serving as an architect and a marketer. I was in charge of the entire product experience. We wanted to connect computers because, in 1986, routers were already making big headway. I wanted to link Canstar into one of the routers and link T1s and T3s into the routers, which were doing the T1, T3, and FDDI routing. At this time Cisco had this business.

We identified two companies we wanted to work with in 1984, Wellfleet and Cisco, and we met with them at a conference in Washington. We went to their booths to determine who would be the best to work with. At this time, there were tabletop exhibits with the founders of Cisco, Len Bosnack and Sandy Lerner. At Canstar my group did the hub and another division did the star coupler LAN interface. Cisco and Wellfleet wanted the interface with other networks. Both companies looked good, but Cisco looked more interesting. We met with one gentleman, from Stanford, who was the CEO of Cisco, Bill Graves.

When we came to meet with them at their office on Willow Road in Menlo Park, there were fifteen people at Cisco. We spent two days discussing how to integrate. There were no standards for 100 Mb LANs. Cisco did not like FDDI, and there was no standard for it. Ethernet was there but at 10 Mb. Canstar had 100 Mb fiber-optic LANs before FDDI. The University of Toronto (UT) had developed the technology for royalties. It worked and we adopted it. But we did poor marketing. We didn't follow up. Cisco developed the Multibus. We developed the user interface for the Multibus Cisco chassis, and they did the software for routing Hubnet to Multibus. We didn't have the expertise. After the development, we made some big mistakes, our marketing did not follow through, Cisco got frustrated, and finally they decided to go with FDDI.

LEARNING FROM FAILURE AND
BECOMING AN INDUSTRY ARCHITECT

I learned much from the failure with Cisco. When you partner with another person or company, you have to make it a win-win. I knew that Cisco put in more effort than Canstar. Silicon Valley companies were more aggressive than others. We were a small division of a big conglomerate (Alcatel). You have to move fast and we didn't. My failures became learning experiences that I can apply to the start-ups and new technologies I work with today. I learned a great deal about what not to do.

While at Canstar, to understand what FDDI was doing and to understand the differentiation, I started going to ANSI meetings. During that time I came to know Dal Allan, Roger Cummings, and others I met at SCSI meetings (the SCSI and FDDI meetings were happening simultaneously). At dinner we all agreed that SCSI has lots of loopholes and FDDI has bandwidth problems. We wanted to come up with a new protocol to take on the SCSI data and increase the speed, connectivity, and distance of the network and make it agnostic to transfer protocol. We needed some protocol that could run anything (SCSI, IP, etc.).

It was 1987 when we started talking about a new protocol, and even though SCSI was in its infancy, we wanted to change it. The first meeting was hosted by Advanced Micro Devices (AMD) in Sunnyvale. Eight to ten people attended (Rich Taborak, Horst Truestedt, Roger Cummings, Dal Allan, and a few others), and we came up with high-level project plans. Because we had hallway interchanges, we could meet and discuss. This is the first time I was really providing a contribution to the industry standards. We applied to ANSI to take it as a project and got approval. In 1988 we got approval for Fibre Channel. (We all came up with the name Fibre Channel, which is spelled in the Queen's English, hence the *re* instead of the *er*.) Dal Allan wrote the project proposal, with Roger Cummings' help, because they had expertise in writing these types of documents. We then selected two types of switches to create a Fibre Channel network. One was connection based, which ANCOR led, and I developed the connectionless; we became coauthors of the switch document.

At that time, I was promoting Hubnet, through which Canstar could be the connectionless fabric. If you go to old (archival) standard documents, you will see that Hubnet was the basis of the Fibre Channel fabric. Fibre Channel had two sections: host interface and fabric. For the fabric side, we identified the necessary connection based and the other connectionless. Hubnet was the candidate for the connectionless protocol. When we started developing Class II and Class III, we realized Hubnet could not take care of certain requirements in the data center, and we started developing the fabric document based on Class I, II, III, without Hubnet. I became the author of the switch document in 1988 and 1989. It took until 1993 for Fibre Channel to be ratified as a standard for the host-side interface.

The IBM engineers were working on the host side. We had to develop several more documents: one physical layer, one for data link and transport layer, one for common services, one for IP mapping, and one for mapping of SCSCI and then the switch standard. After that we introduced the services, such as management and name services. In 1989 it evolved into a group of standards. To develop the switch standard, we had lots of input from the host and services sections.

To be an architect requires creativity. I could understand technology and convert it into useful products. I could look from different angles—what we now call "outside the box." If you can change your perspective, it really helps not to be limited by obvious results. At Canstar, Bent Stovehase and I gave this perspective to the Fibre Channel standard. An architect must be creative, to read between the lines and to translate feature to benefit. If you just develop a feature, it can be good technically but may be useless. When you sell systems versus components, it is totally different. There are great philosophical differences between these ideas. Canstar had about two hundred employees. My Hubnet group had five people. We had a little bit of marketing, but it was almost like a pet project. We didn't develop as a full-fledged product organization. Cisco was the first one who could have become an OEM [original equipment manufacturer]; the others were all end users who were purchasers of 1s and 2s. Cisco could have been a volume customer.

CONNECTING WITH CUSTOMERS AND MARKETING

I wished that I had more marketing expertise. I needed to know more about product requirements for our partners and channels. We needed to do joint marketing. We just thought we'd give our hardware to a company, they would write the software, and they would sell it.

Today I try to tell all the engineers I work with that they must understand the market. If the customer wants to buy a donkey, you don't want to "build an ass." I found I could, and needed to, connect with the customer, connect with engineers, and become a liaison between the customer, engineering, and marketing. I certainly was excited to not repeat those mistakes.

When my group at Canstar was bought by HP, we got a new discipline. The odds were against me to create the Fibre Channel industry. There are people out there like me who have great talent but need to be able to work with marketing and discover what ticks at the business level. The customer writes the check and uses the product.

I developed the skills to organize people and technology. It is like swimming in the ocean—you have to know how to be in the wave to get to a safe place. If you listen a lot, you will know where people are coming from. Listening is more important than talking. Talking is pushing. When I worked with Brenda Christensen, who was VP of Marketing at Brocade, we had a good balance, a counterweight. She wasn't designing a product, but she listened and she could ask the right technical questions. I had the technical depth, and now was attuned to marketing, and we deliberated between the customer business needs and what we would develop for a product that met technical requirements. We worked together in evangelizing, and we could listen to customers and know what was important for them. Companies put millions of dollars into products that go nowhere. But there is often no balance between marketing and engineering. For me, the timing was perfect. I had the opportunity to understand what was lacking in the I/O (input/output) world, and I could influence the standards, the prototypes, and the early-stage companies. My company could be a leader in that specific technology with their product. All components had to be together (host, switch, services) to make a network, and then it would be a real solution for a market that was ready to accept it. Interestingly, the fabric was the most stable and mature of all the components necessary for a solution, and yet the host took the longest time to get to market in any robust way. Switch companies made multibillions from Fibre Channel switches. The odds were against my ideas. Those ideas had the minimum investment proportionally to all the components but have paid off the most.

FOUNDING OF BROCADE

At Canstar, I was working on the quarter-speed Fibre Channel switch product. We went on a roadshow to prospective customers, such as IBM, Sun, and HP. In 1993, the HP division manager and executives decided, instead of signing up to buy the product, to purchase our group and the technology that was at Canstar. HP created a new division near Toronto called Canadian networks operation, working on the Fibre Channel switch project. Although we were part of HP Canada for administration and salaries, we reported into the HP group in Cupertino, California. Ed Frymoyer was a great internal promoter at HP for the work that the former Canstar was doing. At that time, HP was looking at a storage network but didn't call it that. It was simply a network made of storage, inside the main data center, and it would be the next generation after SCSI. HP Roseville was looking at Fibre Channel as a private network, and it was, at a much later time, to be called a storage area network (SAN). After our acquisition by HP, we developed the prototype switch based on quarter-speed Fibre Channel.

I felt there wasn't the progress I wanted in promoting Fibre Channel switches in the industry while working at HP—we only had quarter-speed, and we needed to be full gigabit speed. I was also trying to promote the fabric of switches, and not just a switch, in order to have a meshed network. We were developing an E-port for switch-to-switch connection in gigabit networks. I tried very hard to get HP to understand switches. HP's Canadian Networks Operation had to compete with all HP R&D organizations for money and resources, and the bureaucracy caused delays. That created a lot of my frustration in moving my ideas forward. So in

Kumar at Brocade with his parents
(photo courtesy of Kumar Malavalli)

1995 I began looking for some funding sources to start a company to develop Fibre Channel fabrics that became Brocade.

Ed Frymoyer and I communicated on a regular basis in the standards committees. I, of course, spoke with him about the frustration of HP not understanding the potential of Fibre Channel fabrics. He was trying to help me get funding, and we just couldn't find the support in Canada from venture capitalists (VCs), who were rare or nonexistent. In a meeting in Monterey, California, for Fibre Channel standards, Ed mentioned he wanted to arrange a meeting with Seth Neiman, who was a new venture capitalist. I went to India in June 1995, and during my stay in India, Ed called me saying that Seth wanted to meet with me in California. When I returned, Ed connected me with Seth for a dinner at Gaylord Indian Restaurant at the Stanford Shopping Center. We discussed putting storage on the network and the potential business and market opportunities to create a non-disruptive way to connect storage. Seth understood the ideas immediately. He confirmed his interest and said he'd get back to me in a few days. Then I heard, after coming back to Canada, that he wanted a reference for me. I gave him the name of my former boss at Canstar, Dr. Colin Baron, who was still disappointed that Canstar "gave our group away" to HP for little value. He was a PhD and had good grasp of technical problems.

We had introduced Seth to some of the key technologists for Fibre Channel at various companies. Ed was the program manager for the Fibre Channel System Initiative (FCSI), composed of HP, Sun, and IBM, and both Ancor and Canstar represented switches in FCSI. We needed someone with product development experience. Ed had tried to recruit a well-regarded engineering manager for the engineering position, but he wasn't anxious to go to a start-up. After all, there weren't any successful start-ups in Fibre Channel at that time. That eventually led to Ed introducing Seth to Paul Bonderson, who had storage products engineering experience at Sun. Following that, Seth invited me to meet Paul, and we had a second meeting when I came down from Canada, along with Seth's boss Rich Shapero, who was a partner at Crosspoint Venture Partners. After this meeting, Seth said he was going to give us initial funding of $1.3 million dollars for a company in Silicon Valley. We decided to form the company, and I called for a meeting to discuss the go-to-market strategy. Ed organized a meeting in Toronto with Seth, Paul, and myself. We named the company Brocade (after fabrics) and developed the first go-to-market strategy and high-level description.

FUNDING THE COMPANY AND MARKET CHANGES

Seth understood the importance of storage and changing the architecture of how storage was connected. Paul understood implementation. I understood networks and the architecture of Fibre Channel fabrics and had leadership within the standards committee and the market arm of the industry, the Fibre Channel Industry Association (FCIA), so I had close contact with potential customers so I knew where the business could go as Brocade developed a sales and marketing strategy.

There were three things happening in the market: disk prices were falling, which allowed for more storage; the Internet was becoming popular and everyday people could access it, requiring more storage; and with this network, architecture storage could now be distributed but appear local. These three factors in the market created a lot of potential for Brocade.

All of us supported the use of Fibre Channel. There was no other technology alternative. At the time the FCA was hosting meetings about how to deploy the technology, and Seth attended one of those events and supported Fibre Channel. The $1.3 million Crosspoint gave us to start the company had to be used just to work on the prototype, not for the product. There was no concept of angel investors at that time, as there is today, or even institutional funds. Crosspoint was really an angel investor. It was an unusual scenario that a VC gave seed money to write the business plan after starting to work on the prototype.

We started the company with nine people who focused on the architecture, concepts, prioritizing the features, and the high-level features for the customer. We spent lots of time on the whiteboard and in discussions that took about two to three months. Bent Stovehase and Kha Sin Teow came from HP (Canstar group) with me. It wasn't easy to face the risks of joining a start-up, in a company where there was no real industry at the time. Dave Banks and Paul Ramsey came from Sun and joined Bonderson's team.

We arrived at a top-level plan—a gigabit speed switch with E-port. The only contention was over implementing virtual channels between E-ports. Seth made the first call to resolve the disagreement between Paul and myself on this issue, in favor of the (presumed) future marketplace. Virtual channels on E-port were to provide separation of data and control paths between the switches within the fabric. Without the E-port with separation of control and data between switches, we could have never made a fabric. The standards committee had already started work on the E-port within the standards document for fabric, but we moved ahead before the standard was ratified, with the firm belief that the committee would accept our proposal for the virtual channels between the E-ports. This gave us a leg up in the industry, having a product that met the fabric standard. Brocade would later receive a patent for the E-port virtualization channels for control and data. This was in the very early stages of virtualization.

MEETING OUR CUSTOMERS
AND HIRING THE ENGINEERING TEAM

While the engineers were working on the architecture, Seth and I went out in the field, traveling around the country. We went to HP, DEC (Digital Equipment Corporation), and others to give a presentation, including to McData, who would later be Brocade's competitor and would eventually be purchased by Brocade. During my presentation, we got the market input of what features were urgent and what we could delay. Bonderson was only able to join us for a few of those meetings, but we got the data back to the engineers. Dave Banks was really extraordinary in executing the design as an ASIC engineer leader, and Paul Ramsey had extensive system software expertise. Craig Martin, Ezio Valdevit, Jieming Zhu, and others were hired and executed their work beautifully. We all agreed that unless some customer came with money to fund a change or addition of features, we would focus on the list that was market tested. One aspect of the use of funds that really made a difference, in getting a quality product to market initially, was that each engineer was given powerful workstations and the best-in-industry tools. Seth never skimped on the tools or the verification process. He knew that investing up front would allow the company to scale.

Roy Sardiña was hired as the VP of Business Development and Sales, and he secured angel investments from Sun founders Bill Joy and Andy Bechtolsheim, who were friends of Roy's from his work at Sun. Seth also knew Roy from their Sun experience. Seth was very involved in the company as neither Paul nor I was keen on, or experienced at, being CEO. Seth became interim CEO and, after about ten months, he interviewed candidates for CEO. The first was the CEO of a big storage company who declined. There was a second candidate who also declined, and finally Bruce Bergman was selected as CEO. Bergman had no experience in the storage industry, but at that time the industry was ready to commit to using Fibre Channel to develop a storage area network (SAN), creating an entirely new industry—the networking of storage. Trudy Selkirk was the office manager. At the end of the first year, Brenda Christensen came on as VP of Marketing, and she also brought to Brocade her leadership as chair of the global Fibre Channel Industry Association (FCIA).

CREATING A NEW INDUSTRY: STORAGE NETWORKING

In 1995, there was a critical industry meeting hosted by the FCIA and funded by HP with the consultant Geoffrey Moore, who wrote the book *Crossing the Chasm*. Moore led this industry meeting of forty-seven competitive and cooperative companies. This was an extremely unique experience in the history of any industry. It was at that meeting that the industry aligned around the SAN and the use of Fibre Channel. Moore's public and private position was never supportive of Fibre Channel, which isn't surprising because Cisco and others were saying that there would never be a storage network outside of one based on Ethernet. There were lots of consultants hired to give advice about the death of the separate storage network and certainly the death of Fibre Channel as the technology of choice for the storage network. The FCIA meeting with Moore was truly an historic industry meeting. There has probably never been a group of individual, competitive companies that have applied their talent to building a new industry. The multiple components that had to be brought to market were vast—from copper and fiber-optic connections to host interfaces to ASICs to disk drivers. All of them had to be consistent with the standards. Simultaneously, multiple companies were created. It all became a multibillion-dollar industry with some of the biggest players actually refusing to participate. At one point, some groups within Adaptec, Seagate, and IBM tried to stall the industry by promoting disk technology as a substitute for networking storage. Fortunately, a wise executive at Seagate understood the impact of the entire investment to date and once again got behind the initiatives. Much of this had to do with the lack of understanding about networks. The fact that gigabit Ethernet and gigabit Fibre Channel shared the same core components at the launch stage of both technologies is lost to history.

CHALLENGE OF STANDARDS DEVELOPMENT VERSUS PRODUCTS TIME-TO-MARKET

Ed Frymoyer helped get Brocade started, created interest with the initial VC (Seth Neiman), and was an early-stage advisor. Greg Reyes came on as CEO and helped Brocade take advantage of the IPO financial bubble in the technology industry. Fortunately, the product and the company were sound investments. There was always a rift between the engineers and technologists, based on the implementation and future product needs that had to be built initially into the product. There are some features that have to be designed into the architecture and deployed in ASICs, rather than software, to meet performance criteria. The engineers frequently had the attitude of "let's not worry about that now." Those of us involved in the standards work and with the market contact had a longer-term vision. We wanted the engineers to look at what they were implementing as something other than just hardware and software. We wanted a more integrated view of the applications and how a real network would be created. Bent and I had more information about how customers would use the product. It was a difference between the designer-view versus the user-view of the product. When we introduced zoning, Brocade charged a very hefty price, and it created a substantial multimillion-dollar revenue stream, but the engineers were very exhaustively against this feature set. The framework by which we viewed making decisions was very different. Those of us with the vision for the product had the users, the user interface, and applications in our minds and plans. The engineers had another view based on just moving data—more bits and bytes. Two groups with two different visions had to work together. The tension between the technology group and the engineering group did resolve itself in an excellent product. Fortunately, we aligned on common goals and made it happen.

Now, when I work with start-up companies, I want to know how the features will be useful to the end customer, not just meet the need of engineers to get a product to the market. The engineers had very limited field contact. I am not saying every engineer has to have customer contact, but the CTO, VP of Engineering, and VP of Marketing have to have common and frequent contact with each other and with customers. It's easier to make product road-map decisions based on technical contact with customers.

CRITICAL EVENTS THAT IMPACTED SUCCESS

There were three critical events and circumstances that impacted Brocade's early market success. One was the direct relationship with LSI, the semiconductor manufacturer, who took Brocade as a direct customer. This is highly unusual, but it allowed Brocade priority access to LSI's manufacturing engineers, planners, fabrication, and even the corporate executives. The Brocade engineers had an excellent track record in the industry, especially at Sun, and LSI was anxious to keep in tight contact with these engineers for products they were developing to be sold outside of Brocade. As a result, Brocade got a very quick time-to-market and LSI received best-in-industry engineering guidance. LSI was also an early corporate investor. From 1995 to 1996 there was a substantial demand for ASICs, and Brocade received priority. This made a time-to-market difference. LSI was in fact being very close to its customer—Brocade.

The second factor was Sequent (later purchased by IBM). Sequent had chosen Anchor for Class I switches. Anchor had some difficulty fulfilling the feature set. Brocade's Class II and III switches offered Sequent features it needed. Sequent offered a challenge to Brocade to produce a prototype and test it in the lab. Sequent was the first to produce a storage area network by connecting multiple switches in the same network, although at the time it was all local under the NUMA-Q architecture. At that time they were buying more hubs than switches, and the price of switches was very high ($3,000 per port). But due to the architecture of the hubs (loop), Sequent was not meeting its service level agreements (SLAs), costing them money and customer satisfaction. With switches there was fault isolation and the ability to operate even under degraded conditions. One operations manager at Sequent did an analysis and determined it was in fact less expensive to use switches than loops due to the fact that they could keep their customers operational. This changed the future of Brocade.

Third, Dell, as a commodity producer who was cost sensitive, told Brocade to reduce the cost per point by one-third. This was achieved to Dell's satisfaction, and this became the basis of the volume business.

INDUSTRY COMPETITION AND COOPERATION: DEFINING THE PROBLEM AND DEFYING THE BIGGEST COMPANIES

One of the major turning points for Brocade was when we had to make a decision, because the SSA Group at IBM, along with Seagate and Adaptec, all wanted Brocade to support the loop technology (FC-AL). A company called Gadzoox had all their strategy in the hub line. We decided to go into switches and switch fabrics. We protested that we were in a different market and hubs offered no fault isolations. Data centers could not tolerate technologies that could not isolate faults and remain operational. If one link failed in the hub, all links failed. Brocade had three choices: (1) a hub only, (2) a switch only, and (3) offer both a switch and hubs. Hubs were much less expensive. At that time, no one knew how important switches were going to be. We had the same customers as hub vendors. The industry analysts all projected that hubs would oversell switches as the volume product. We reminded them that Ethernet was not a great example. Storage networks were not the same as client networks in Ethernet. The demands were much higher in the data center and couldn't accept failures or faults.

We defied the biggest companies in systems and networks. Brocade made it from launching on August 18, 1995, to IPO on May 24, 1999. That is only four and a half years. There was a small core of us (people and companies) who worked very well with each other. [*PC Week* once did a feature story on the thirty people who were making the technology and the industry happen. While there certainly were more than thirty, the number wasn't much larger. Seagate and a few other companies sent their best technology developers on airplanes around the world, working tirelessly to make Fibre Channel disk technology available.] We worked together as an industry to continually evolve the standards and create an ecosystem to provide solutions that resulted in new multibillion-dollar businesses. The most well-known and highly paid analysts and consultants, globally acknowledged technologists, and even early individual investors and top-named venture capitalists protested that Fibre Channel was never going to succeed and that Ethernet would be the single technology for the data center. They didn't whisper this opinion—it was shouted. Even to this day, they won't really acknowledge what has been twenty years of real benefits to customers—Fibre Channel as the basis of the storage network. Wall Street was able to operate its data centers within a small window of time after the 9/11 events in the US and the disruption to its data centers, because Fibre Channel allowed the servers and storage centers to operate at substantial distances. Before networked storage, it would have been another element of disaster for the financial and most other industries that rely on immediate access to data to recover their businesses after natural and national disasters. Ours wasn't just a blind, bigoted attitude toward Fibre Channel being all things to all people. It was a sensible understanding of technology and some fundamentals that had to be provided by *any* technology for networked storage to succeed. Technologies evolve, but data centers and especially storage technologies and products enjoy a long, profitable life.

LESSONS LEARNED FROM PUSHING DREAMS AGAINST ALL ODDS

I've learned some good lessons along the way. If you believe in something, if you understand the true fundamentals of customer needs and applying technology to those needs, and if you are willing to work tirelessly, you can succeed. When Brocade went public, I was fifty-six years old. I started the company in my fifties and was an immigrant from

Canada. Everything was against the outcome of Fibre Channel and Brocade offering benefits to global customers and to employees and shareholders as it does today. There are very smart people who wanted the protection of a large company and didn't want to take the risk of a start-up, and a start-up with an untested technology and nonexistent industry. And many good start-ups fail, but so do giant corporations. If you want to have intellectual satisfaction, you have to sometimes buck the odds. You have to believe in yourself. You have to create wealth for others and it will come to you.

I believe my success came from my direct relationship with customers, the industry, and standards bodies. I could integrate the various segments that became the basis of products. I was comfortable cooperating and competing, and I always respected the competition. I had an excellent marketing partner at Brocade, and she (Brenda Christensen) and I were willing to put in long days and hours to become the industry educators. Brenda came from Digital Equipment Corporation (DEC), so she had both systems and networking background. Brocade's brand was built by the education we provided to the end user and the industry itself, long before the product was launched, even though it was a quality product from the first release. We had to move the entire industry from point-to-point storage/server connections to understanding what it meant and to ultimately experience the power of networked storage. We had to connect the technology to the customer. We had to work to keep the standards process an open process. Industry heavy-weights were busy trying to "standardize" proprietary technologies. The launch of a new industry meant that an industry that based its entire product history on propriety-technology-based products had to move to compete in an open marketplace. This was essential for the end users, and what it took to break this proprietary stranglehold is very underestimated. Many people don't want to spend the kind of time we invested to create and move the industry, and even internally at Brocade this was true. When I was inducted into the Silicon Valley Engineering Hall of Fame, I was mindful of the indispensable technologists who haven't received the attention or acknowledgement they deserved for being tireless pioneers for the storage networking industry. There weren't that many of us, but we stayed together pushing our dream against all odds—and it worked.

REFLECTIONS FROM INDIRAMMA AND
NARAYANASWAMY MALAVALLI

The storyteller is Narayanaswamy Malavalli, Kumar's father, who was the chief administrator for the maharajah of Mysore.

When I went to Germany with the maharajah of Mysore, we were guests of Baron Thyssen, of Thyssen Industries. The maharajah and I went to his estate, which was a castle, and saw the landing on the moon [in 1969] from the top of the castle where they had a TV set. The maharajah asked the baron to come to Mysore as his guest. The baron came, along with his fifth wife, and we of course tried to treat him very well. One day he said, "I would like to come to your house." They came, and Kumar and his two brothers, Seetheram and Shivaram, were all there. The baron asked me, "What is your son [meaning Kumar] doing?" I told him, "I don't know what to do. I am trying to get him a job." The baron said, "What is the matter? Why don't you send him to Germany?"

Kumar went to Germany and got into a company in Düsseldorf. The government of Germany wouldn't give him a work visa. I told this to the baron, and he said, "Forget all this chatter. We'll put him on as a trainee, and that will get around the visa limitations." That is how he got to Germany first. For two years, he stayed in a room in a house in Düsseldorf owned by two women. Vijaya and Ranjini [Kumar's wife and daughter] stayed with us in Mysore until Kumar could get settled in Canada, after Germany. Because of work permits and travel costs, it was four years before Kumar could see his daughter. We forget how easy it is to travel now. Ironically, it was years after Kumar started Brocade that he was finally able to get his US green card.

Kumar always wanted to be an engineer. This is in contrast to his brother Seetheram, who didn't want to be a doctor, but his mother forced him into it. Seetheram wanted to be anything but a doctor, but today he is a pediatric neurologist. Shivaram is a computer scientist. All my children were obedient children, and Kumar had good analytical skills. He had no dream to be a designer when he was younger. He wanted to be an electrical engineer. He took some tests and knew he wanted to be in that area. The schools, administration, education, and governance in India were good because of the British. The French could not give the same to the provinces they controlled in India. The English were forced to develop these institutions because there were not enough English people to work in India.

Kumar as a student at Taj Mahal
(photo courtesy of Kumar Malavalli)

They liked Kumar very much in college. When he graduated from college in India, he wanted to go to work right away. There were jobs in India, and we didn't want him to leave. AEG (the German company) was doing heavy electrical gear installation in steel plants as part of their India operations. Kumar worked as a junior installation engineer at AEG, but he did not like that kind of work—it was all process control. Communications jobs didn't really exist on any large scale, even in the US, except for at a few very large companies. I didn't want Kumar to work in that India operation because it was a dead-end job. It had very little dignity and didn't match his qualifications. There were options available to Kumar in India. There was an electric factory that built transformers and similar products in Mysore. There were hydroelectric schemes that wanted electrical engineers in the 1960s and '70s. There were very big textile companies requiring electrical engineers. AEG assigned Kumar to work in the steel plant in Rourkela in Orissa [now Odisha] state. As Kumar was an electrical engineer, I could have gotten him a job in the electric department for the city of Mysore. His mother wanted him to work in Mysore but at a different company. She was not happy that he left for Düsseldorf. Once Kumar met the baron, he was inspired to leave, as they had companies all over the world, and his going to Germany happened very fast.

Kumar has good perseverance, and people like to work with him because he has big ideas. Kumar likes to control circumstances and knows how to work with both the good and bad sides of people. He knows his subjects and therefore can guide people because he knows enough to correct mistakes. Kumar came to success from companies that didn't have a big brand name, and he didn't have big staffs to get things accomplished. He had no "big stick" to administer from, and he wouldn't do that anyway because that isn't Kumar's personality. Therefore, it was important that he inspire people to work with him and build on the ideas he had.

EDITOR: Kumar was awarded an honorary doctorate of science from California State University, East Bay in 2013.

RAM AND NEENA GADA, MINNESOTA

RAM BORN IN MUMBAI, INDIA; NEENA BORN IN KUTCH, INDIA

EDITOR: *This interview was with both Ram and Neena Gada of Minnesota. They played a unique role in the development of Indian communities and organizations in Minnesota and have helped educate people in the state about the culture, contributions, lives, language, religions, and music of people who have emigrated from India or are persons of Indian origin (PIOs). Neena founded the School of India in Minnesota, and Ram is now director emeritus of the Minnesota Historical Society. When Ram came to Minnesota in 1965, there were fewer than a thousand people of Indian origin in the state. In 2014, the estimate was more than forty thousand. Ram and Neena Gada have contributed their leadership skills to the assimilation of Indians in Minnesota.*

RAM: More than fifty years ago, in 1964, I put my feet on the shores of New York, in the United States of America. It was an exciting thirty-day voyage on cruise ships sailing from Bombay [now Mumbai] to London via Aden, the Suez Canal, Naples, and Gibraltar. After three days of staying with a friend in London—and wonderful chilly sightseeing there—I boarded another ship from Southampton to New York. At the New York port, I boarded the Greyhound bus for Fargo, North Dakota, where I was admitted at North Dakota State University for my master's degree in engineering. This was a journey that changed my entire life. But first let me tell you about my childhood and education, leading up to my arrival in the US for higher studies.

Ram at immigration
(photo courtesy of Ram and Neena Gada)

I was born in Bombay, now called Mumbai, in 1940. In a year or less, my mother moved to our ancestral home in the village of Bada, located in Kutch [in Gujarat], three hundred miles north of Bombay. Bada, with a population of two thousand, was a village with no electricity and no connected water/sewer, with dusty, narrow streets and no medical clinic or doctor. Later I was told that our move was due to World War II and the fear of bombing on Bombay. My father stayed in Bombay, performing an administrative job, and visited us once a year during his vacation or leave. My [paternal] great-uncle lived with us, as he did not have any of his family members around. He and my grandfather had a coal distribution business in Bombay for a long time; however, it declined with the increased use of kerosene and natural gas. Later my father moved to Kutch, due to his weak health in Mumbai with its humid weather. He did various jobs in Kutch, which did not pay much. He was well educated (he had matriculated at that time), but that did not translate into a good-paying job.

I was the oldest child, with one brother who was two years younger than I and one sister who was four years younger than I. My youngest [one-year-old] sister died during a smallpox epidemic in Kutch. Another sister was born in 1955, when I was away from home, during my high school years. I went to a one-room/one-teacher government school in Bada from kindergarten to second grade. I studied well from third to seventh grade in a private school run by Jain Mitra Mandal. Even with one teacher teaching all subjects, I was able to do well in all grades and maintained a number-one class ranking. As a result, the teacher trusted me to instruct lower-level students as an aide. This was a great experience and honor for me. The last teacher for two or three years in the higher grades (Ranchhod Das) was one of the best teachers I had. He gave us so much personal attention and discipline. He not only taught us what was in the books, but he gave us life's ethical lessons, such as how to behave and work hard to achieve goals. He tutored us at his home, even after school hours. He drilled us in English and math fundamentals, which helped me tremendously in high school years. I learned English and English grammar even before learning Gujarati grammar in the higher grades. He was in his heart a true teacher/guru and has left an everlasting imprint in me to do my best, whatever I do in my life. He advised me to study further, at least to complete high school.

I had nobody who could advise or help me regarding action to take after seventh grade. My family's poor finances might have forced me to take a job in Mumbai. I wrote a letter to my stepbrother in Mumbai and expressed my desire to continue studying. He helped me apply to a free boarding school at Shree Mahavir Jain Charitra Kalyan Ratnashram at Songadh, Saurashtra, 150 miles southeast of Bada and three hundred miles north of Mumbai. After they looked over my academic records and poor financial conditions, I was admitted with a very nominal monthly fee, which was paid by my stepbrother. I lived and studied for four years (eighth through eleventh grades) in a charity hostel and completed high school. The hostel had one hundred students in different grades and from different family backgrounds. It had two to three large rooms where we stayed in a group residence, and we had to make our beds every night with something like a sleeping bag. We had a very disciplined hostel life. We got up at five every morning and went to bed at nine p.m. After a morning bath, we studied for ninety minutes in a very quiet atmosphere. After lunch, we walked twenty minutes to school, which went from eleven a.m. to five p.m. Math, science, social studies, and civics were taught in my mother tongue, Gujarati, and our second language was English. Hindi and Sanskrit were additional languages. At the hostel, many extracurricular activities were planned, such as morning exercises, sports, yoga, music, debates, and folk dances.

Gurukul High School was a public school with students from all sects—Hindus, Jains, Muslims, and Harijans. There were about eight hundred students. Several high school teachers not only taught the subject material but also life lessons. One of the teachers who was our hostel superintendent had a tremendous impact on me during my four years at the hostel. In ninth or tenth grade, he started saying, "Ram, you have to go to college." I couldn't imagine how I would afford college, with my parents' financial condition. He told me about various scholarships and loans available for bright students. He boosted my morale, saying that I was the most brilliant in the class, maintaining number-one rank, and that I would have a great future ahead with a college degree. My internal conversation, with his inspiration and moral support, started changing from "How can I?" to "Yes, I can."

COLLEGE OR A JOB?

After SSC (Secondary School Certificate) exams, I moved to Mumbai with mixed feelings of hope and despair. Indirect pressure from elder family members was mounting to take a job and forget about college. My parents were not able to say anything, as they were back in Bada, Kutch, and did not have enough money to take care of the family. My older brother clearly said that he could not afford my college expenses. I was on my own for college if I decided to go. I told him I would still look into all the possibilities and make a choice. The words of my teacher/mentor were rumbling in my head. I started searching for scholarships/loans, getting applications, and applying. College-bound cousins and friends encouraged me about college and about scholarships and loans. But I still had to wait for the final SSC exam results. [The night the results were published] I waited anxiously at my cousin's place in Mumbai until two a.m. for the newspaper publishing the results. I got a first class, with distinction, at 76 percent marks, which was considered excellent at that time. My cousin told me that I could get into a top college with this ranking. At eight a.m. we went to Elphinstone College—a very prestigious college in downtown Mumbai. I was accepted right away in a meeting with the principal. I was advised by the college office that I would be eligible for full tuition, considering the low income of my parents. Well, the first hurdle was tackled. The second problem was solved for my room and board when I was admitted at Shree Mahavira Jaina Vidyalaya on an interest-free loan program. This was a big help. I did pay back the loan within two years after I started earning money in the US and got a congratulatory letter thanking me for paying back the loan in such a short time.

The third hurdle was a dire need of living support for my parents in Bada. My parents blessed me for my success in the SSC exam and getting into college. They accepted that I would not be able to support them while going to college for five to seven years. They assured me that I didn't need to worry about them if I could manage my own expenses. My mother was a brave woman who worked very hard for many years. She would grow crops on our farm to sustain the family. One of her cousins promised to help the family in case of emergency. Kutch was an inexpensive place to live. My brother, after seventh grade, joined me at the same institution after my two years in Songadh for high school. So at home, only my younger sister was able to help my mother. My mother had a great influence on me in helping others and working hard. These were her ideals that I still live by. I never got to see my mother's joy over my college acceptance and scholarship in person because she was in Kutch and I was in Mumbai, so she had to learn by letter. I was overjoyed and relieved.

My school dream was to be a doctor, to serve others. One of the founders of the hostel where I was living was a Jain monk, Shree Kalyan Chandraji Maharaj (we called him Bapa—grandfather), who devoted his life to educating young people. He went into social work and helped many poor people. He was an expert in Ayurvedic medicine and treated many patients free of charge. In the first year of college, I still had this dream to become a doctor. This required a biology class and lab, which required the dissection of fish, frogs, and insects in formaldehyde, and I could not bear the smell of the lab. With deep regret, I changed my mind from medicine to engineering, with my math and science background. The college teachers were professionals in their own subjects, but they weren't like high school teachers who gave you life lessons. There was one Gujarati language professor who would impart some life lessons while discussing many books, poems, and essays of famous writers of the time. At this point in my life, I had already formed my living credo from my mother's life, schoolteachers' inspiration, and the Jain monk's life of service to others.

DECISIONS AND CONSEQUENCES

I learned earlier in my high school years that any decisions that I made were my own, with consequences that would impact my life. One of the many activities at the hostel was debating—public speaking. I took part in a debate competition for the first time and won first prize. This showed me the value of public speaking to impart your ideas and views to others. The debate coach helped me more. I fully engaged in every extracurricular activity at school, without missing my prime studies. We had exams every week, every three months, every six months, and the final one at the end of the year. We were always being reevaluated for ranking, and I didn't want to miss being number one at the top of the class.

After two years in the science program at Elphinstone College, Mumbai, I entered Lukhdhirji Engineering College at Morbi, Gujarat, 350 miles north of Mumbai, and received a bachelor's of mechanical engineering in three years, in 1963. After five years of college, I got my first job as a development engineer at Premier Automobile Company, which assembled Italian Fiat cars in Mumbai. At that time, in 1963, engineering jobs were hard to find—with India just getting independence in 1947—and there weren't many industries that were flourishing. But for your first job, you had to take it wherever you could get it, and I took the job at Premier. I needed the income. In those days, bureaucracy and chain of command in the company kept things bottled up, even though my boss was a US-educated and -trained executive. I was frustrated and didn't see how I was going to get a chance to move ahead.

Within three months, I realized that I did not have much future there. When I was in my final year at engineering college, my classmates were applying to colleges in the US for their higher studies. At that time, I had no inclination or interest in this, given my situation. As a matter of fact, I was happy just to finish high school and college against all odds.

I asked for guidance from my friend who had worked at Premier and was working for GM in Michigan. He encouraged me to seek admission for my master's, borrow the money if I had to, come in the spring quarter, and work summer quarter to save money for college expenses. I was able to raise the funds for only two quarters, from loans from community charity organizations and one relative. There was no scholarship or loan available from the Indian government. The Indian government did give us some American dollars in exchange for rupees. I think it was two hundred dollars as an education allotment for the first quarter. But I am not sure whether I received the eight dollars that other students got later.

CHOOSING A COLLEGE AND SELECTING NORTH DAKOTA STATE UNIVERSITY

I was accepted into two colleges to study industrial engineering—one in Fargo, North Dakota State University (NDSU), and the other in Raleigh, North Carolina. The question was, where to go? The choices were all ten thousand miles away and unfamiliar to me. My parents and other elders advised going to the place where there was someone I knew. I knew no one in Raleigh. Fargo was the choice, as a person from our community was studying there. At the college, I learned I could finish my master's in mechanical engineering in one year or nine months, compared to two years for a master's in industrial engineering. With my lack of finances for two years, I switched to mechanical engineering as a practical solution. After studying in spring quarter, I worked during the summer for a consulting engineering company in Minneapolis. I fell in love with the green parks and streams and lakes of Minneapolis in summer. I enjoyed Minnesota farm life and the hospitality at my coworker's parents' home near Mankato. I completed my master's in the next two quarters at NDSU. The firm Michaud Cooley Erickson, the Minneapolis consulting engineering firm where I had the summer job, was happy to hire me as a permanent employee. I did engineering design for heating, ventilating, and air conditioning (HVAC) for buildings, hospitals, schools, and shopping centers. I worked for them for fifteen years (1965 to 1980). In those fifteen years, I worked my way up to vice president and started a new energy management department.

In 1974, with the Arab oil embargo, people started to seriously look at saving energy, so I changed directions and started the department, which took me into building systems to save energy. I had a desire to be a partner in the company for a better financial position and more responsibility. When my immediate boss told me to wait another three to four years, I was disappointed. However, this inspired me to take a major challenge to excel in my profession. My consulting engineering company, Gada & Associates, Inc., was founded in February 1980 and has served the industry for thirty years. We've had great success with clients and their projects. They've appreciated our expertise, integrity, personal attention, and on-time completion of their projects. Our company received several awards in energy management and conservation projects.

One thing about coming to the United States, and especially Minnesota, is that I had a great deal of support and acceptance from our clients and the professional community. I always had a desire to give back to the community, both professionally and socially, as they have played a very important role in shaping, supporting, and nourishing my life. Even when I came to NDSU, the mechanical engineering department was considerate enough to give me a small loan in the last quarter, to be paid back over time. I was grateful for their support in my time of need, and I paid back the loan to the department within six months. The department head sent me a congratulatory letter and appreciated that I paid back the loan so fast.

GAINING PROFESSIONAL ENGINEERING EXPERTISE

I joined the American Society of Heating, Refrigerating, and Air-Conditioning Engineers (ASHRAE) a professional organization that advances science, research, and technology in the area of the environment. I chaired the Energy Committee of the Minnesota chapter, which helped to develop the first Minnesota energy code in 1978. We started giving lectures on the energy code. I was elected as secretary of the Minnesota chapter, which had seven hundred members at that time, then I became vice president, and eventually I became president of the Minnesota chapter, from 1981 to 1982. With my interest in history, I also served as chapter historian for two terms, during which time we won several awards at the regional level. To stay on top of my practice, I regularly attended professional workshops and seminars.

On a student visa, the US allowed eighteen months for a training-period job. To stay longer at the job, I applied for a green card, which took three to four years for approval. During this period, you cannot risk leaving the US, in case you are denied reentry. Thanks to President Johnson, who liberalized the green card quotas for non-European countries such as India, on January 4, 1967, I received a New Year's gift of a green card from the INS.

RETURNING TO INDIA FOR A LIFE PARTNER

This expedited my visit to India to search for my life partner. Without a girlfriend waiting, this was a difficult mission. However, my family was able to ease the process through what is called an "arranged marriage." They had circulated my matrimonial data with a photo in our community news bulletin. It said, "Our son is coming from America for a short visit—a professional engineer with an MS in mechanical

engineering and a good job." My family received about thirty-seven proposals from girls' parents. The family had a system to determine who would qualify. They wanted an educated girl who had been brought up with good family values and a good background. The short list of five girls was prepared for the next stage. I had no idea in whom I was interested until I had seen and talked with each of them. Once you get a short list, the boy's side of the family, which consists of the boy and some family members, visits the girl and her family at a suitable place. Sometimes it is a

Ram and Neena's wedding
(photo courtesy of Ram and Neena Gada)

teahouse or other relative's home. Both sides of the families would talk with each other, have tea, and then there would be a meeting between the boy and girl in privacy.

I was impressed by Neena Gala, with her personality, presence of mind, presentation, and beauty, of course. We chatted about her education, hobbies, and interests. I talked about general life in the US. I made her aware that she would be going ten thousand miles away from her family to a place with harsh winters and none of the Indian groceries she was familiar with. We, of course, couldn't make eye contact right away, in typical Indian modesty and shyness. During the meeting, I did not tell her that she was beautiful and I liked her, even though I was 95 percent sure in my mind that she was the one I would like to spend my life with. There was a second meeting with her and her family. After our engagement, Neena and I started going out together, sort of dating, to learn more about each other before getting married in a month. I was sympathetic to Neena, as she was going to make lots of adjustments in her life in America. As a student, I had gone through my frustrations with cooking and the reality of harsh winters.

I was lucky to get ten weeks of leave from my job, considering two weeks' vacation is standard in the US. My boss was nice to grant me such a long leave when I told him that I was going to get married in India. I had saved six weeks' vacation after three years of working, and took four weeks' leave without pay.

There were specific family customs and information about what gifts our families would exchange for the wedding. Each family would decide what to buy. The boy's side is organized by the boy's parents, and the girl's side by the girl's parents. It is all traditional. I arrived at the wedding place in a Chevrolet Impala, decorated with flowers. It was a modest wedding, even though I was working in the US. I always believed in simplicity, and I did not have much money in the bank. I had paid all my college loans and family debts in my first two years of working, as my first obligation and duty.

My parents didn't mention in words anything specific about my progress or achievements. I noticed their blessings through their eyes and expressions. Parents in India don't express their inner feelings like we do in the West, but one can feel in their eyes their happiness and contentment to see your progress. They don't very often say, "I love you." I had sent money to my mother to settle all the debts when there was no income from me. My parents were able to pay off the house mortgage and became completely debt-free. I helped my younger brother buy his own house in Baroda [now Varodara], where he had started his own business.

FAMILY LIFE IN MINNESOTA

After our first house purchase in 1971, we invited our parents to stay with us and see what life was like in the US during the summer of 1972. For me, this was the best time spent together with my parents since I'd left home in 1954 for high school. My daughter, Lisa, born in 1969, loved her grandparents very much. My father spoke English well so he enjoyed watching TV and reading books. My mother had the handicap of not speaking English. Lisa played a very important role as the interpreter between my mother and her friends, even though she was only three years old. My mother was curious about how things were done or worked in the US. She would observe all the phases of a new house being built across our street, and she would report to us all the progress made for the day. She would help Neena in our garden patch. Even though she didn't have a formal education, she devoted her life to be of service to her family and community. She was a woman of organization, compassion, and action, and the community considered her smart and wise. People came to seek her advice. My father would never interfere with her activities.

Even though we were poor financially in earlier years, she was always generous. She would distribute free extra buttermilk to people who did not have animals. We had our cows. She knew Indian medicine and would help sick people in need. She had the capability of massaging people to eliminate their headaches with the technique of acupressure. In the early morning she could do healings, anything that could help someone, with this massage. Her name was Ganga, like the Ganges River. Sunderji was my father's name, which means "beautiful." My father died in Mumbai in 1976, and my mother died in Baroda in 2010 at the age of eighty-eight.

NEENA: I spent my early years in Bombay [now Mumbai], even though I was born in Kutch. I studied Gujarati medium [of instruction] in our community schools with both boys and girls. I was not at as high a level in class as Ram, but I did well. I was also very busy in all types of extracurricular activities, such as running races, sports, drama, and dancing. My ninth-grade Parsi English teacher really boosted my morale and self-confidence. He would encourage others by my example, saying, "Look at Neena,

Neena at immigration
(photo courtesy of Ram and Neena Gada)

how well she is doing." I think it was his words and power of suggestion that helped me excel. He made me feel special. I always had good reviews from teachers, even though I wasn't number one academically. I didn't have the distinct teacher experience that Ram had. Homework was something I did myself, but my family provided a private tutor for math. In India it was common to have a tutor. English was easy for me, but math wasn't. I had my own discipline to study and didn't have others to supervise my work. My first goal was to go to college. None of my older sisters went to college. My older brother went to college and became a lawyer. He was my inspiration and mentor. I admired him. My brother was very much a community service person. He is well-known and admired in the community, due to his progressive social activities.

I attended Wilson College in Mumbai after SSC and received a bachelor of arts in sociology and political science in four years. Our family had migrated from Kutch one hundred years earlier. My father was a businessperson in the wholesale grain commodities market. My mother managed our joint family. She wasn't educated, but, like my mother-in-law, she was very capable.

My uncle passed away at a very young age. My father had promised him that he would take care of his family. My mother took care of his widow, including her four sons and a daughter, along with our family of seven. My father was a progressive leader in our community. Due to this, I was exposed to many social issues as I grew up.

Before I met Ram, I had already made up my mind about the person I wanted as my life partner. Ram and I were both products of the joint family system and governance. I wanted a self-made man who had moved ahead with his own determination and efforts. I wanted to be like that myself, even though I was dependent on my parents for financial needs. Even within the joint family system, I had my own ideas on many things. My mother and I discussed many issues. My elder sister and I were very close. I had met two boys previous to Ram, but I was not impressed with them. At age twenty-four, I was very idealistic. In those days you grew up on your own, and you decided many small things on your own. Sometimes my brother and sisters helped me more than my parents. I was the youngest one in the family, so everyone was eager to help me. That is the way I grew up.

DECIDING ON THE MAN FOR MY LIFE PARTNER

After Ram and I met the second time alone, I was convinced that he was the man I was looking for. His family was supposed to contact us in a couple of days after our meeting, but the phone rang on the same night to confirm. This was joyous news for me and my family. Ram and I went out daily to different places in Mumbai before our wedding on April 2. I had my own ideas for the activities we did. Our main purpose for dating was to know each other better. I wanted to know more about the US, its geographic and climatic variations, and life in general. My conception was that the US was the richest country in the world.

I loved to read English detective books by Erle Stanley Gardner with my favorite hero, Perry Mason. I was able to borrow them from my brother's lawyer friend, who had a large library collection. Once I came across a book about statistical data for crimes of passion in the US. I got really scared reading about the rapes and cruelty done against women. Once I came to America, all my preconceived fear and notions of insecurity disappeared, seeing normal family life in Minnesota.

With Mumbai's temperate weather, I had never even owned a sweater. [Before we left for the US], Ram's friend in Minneapolis advised that you did not need any warmer clothes now as they were having a wonderful early summer. Ram said we would buy warmer clothes when we arrived in Minnesota. After four short airport stops from Bombay to Paris, London, New York, and Milwaukee, when we landed in Minneapolis it was 32 degrees Fahrenheit on May 1. I was freezing in my Indian sari and sleeveless blouse. London airport ramps were very cold, without any heating in those days.

In the early years, I did not work, so I was ready to explore new things and activities. (After our children were grown, I helped Ram in his office with all his administrative tasks, including phones, billing, banking, payroll, etc.) My first priority was learning to cook Indian food. Back in India, my family never taught me how to cook, as I was studying in college. Another hurdle was finding Indian groceries and other ingredients that were not available in Minnesota in 1967. I spent lots of time learning to cook and finding substitutions for Indian cooking. There were seven or eight newly married couples from India, like us, in our social group. My neighbor Indian lady was a very friendly woman who invited over any new Indian families she met in the Twin Cities. At her place, we had lots of fun activities and celebrations of Indian festivals, like Diwali, Holi, New Year's, or birthday dinner parties. That is how we came to know many other Indians.

THE SCHOOL OF INDIA FOR
LANGUAGES AND CULTURE (SILC)

In the '60s, the University of Minnesota was very generous and active in helping foreign students' wives. I learned a lot from ten-week home economics seminars they offered. Once a month, the Junior League of Minneapolis would give us a guided tour of many interesting and educational sites in the Twin Cities. I enjoyed a festive Christmas party at the Minnesota governor's mansion on Summit Avenue in St. Paul. Those social and community activities widened my horizons. I was accepting new things and challenging old things, and was getting ambitious for new horizons to reach.

Some of the ladies and I started volunteering at an Indian weekend school, originally called the Bharat School, in 1976. With our disagreement on the nonprofit status of the school, five of us mothers founded a new school—the School of India for Languages and Culture (SILC)—in 1977. Every Sunday morning, teachers, students, parents, and volunteers met for three hours. In the first hour, several Indian languages were taught, and the second hour was devoted to Indian general knowledge about history and geography. The last hour was all elective activities, such as yoga, cooking, Indian music, and dance. Ram helped us draft the SILC constitution and bylaws to operate the school as a nonprofit secular institution. Our school was open to everyone interested—Indian or non-Indian—regardless of race, religion, or color. My primary aim for this school was to impart our Indian cultural heritage and values to our children, who were growing up in two cultures—one Indian, at home, and the second outside with the community at large. The community at large didn't know much about foreigners in general and Indians in particular. Prejudice or misunderstanding is easy when one does not know about another person or another culture. Once, my daughter returned home from school complaining about her classmates calling her bad names. The next day I volunteered at her school with other parents and developed relationships with other parents. I became part of the system to show them that we are no different from them, hoping for the same progress for our children. These were the humble beginnings of our SILC, which is still serving well after thirty-seven years. Our children could experience Indian culture with other Indian youth and were able to educate others about who we are.

Our school had a lot of projects that encompassed the community at large. We invited everyone to come and learn about India and its culture. There is a law in Minnesota that ethnic-diversity education has to be part of the curriculum at each school. SILC sent out letters telling Minnesota schools that if they needed classes on India, SILC would come and volunteer. We were able to organize information seminars and workshops. One year, I facilitated a ten-week seminar series on Indian culture, customs, music, and child-rearing for parents who had adopted Indian children through the Children's Home Society of Minnesota. In our community, we had several experts in many fields who could impart their expertise to a diverse group of organizations.

My goal was to be a resource for information about India. Ram and I had a part in founding, organizing, or volunteering for most of the Indian organizations in Minnesota. The children coming to SILC gained self-confidence when they met children of Indian descent who looked like them. Maybe they went to schools where they were the only ones, and when they

Neena and Ram
(photo courtesy of Ram and Neena Gada)

came to the SILC, they could say, "Oh, there are others just like me" and "I am not alone." They would discuss their issues and concerns; this interaction had a positive effect on their morale and self-confidence.

When we started this program, the University of Minnesota International Center became the main activity place for the majority of Indian students on campus. On Saturday nights, Indian Hindi [Bollywood] movies, regardless of the image quality, were the main attraction for social get-togethers at the Bell Museum of Natural History on campus. Under the Indian Student Association at the campus, I and other ladies who came from India in 1967 performed the Diwali celebration program. I was thrilled to be part of the Brides of India show in downtown Minneapolis, put on by the university. What a cultural shock it was to have fresh snow on the ground, and we were walking around with sandals and thin bridal saris. Another culture shock was the food. One time we were on a trip to Fargo, North Dakota, and Ram ordered a McDonald's hamburger without the meat patty. The server was surprised at this request. Being a vegetarian, I was able to eat only french fries.

I was somewhat homesick for my family and familiar companions, even though we made social contacts and friends on my arrival. Ram worked long hours, including Saturdays, and went out of town for projects. One activity that really helped me was writing letters. As soon as I received a letter from my father in India, I replied right back to him. Our letter exchanges were regular every week. My father always kept me informed of what was going on. He was the biggest source of family news. Recently I revisited my collection of forty years worth of letters and enjoyed sweet memories of the past.

My parents visited us in 1973, a year after Ram's parents came. My brother always addressed me as his "little sister." He was amazed to see me managing my house without any outside help and all the activities I was doing. In India, it was and is still common for a household to have outside help for the house chores. My father, having a business, would periodically send staff people to our home to do some things.

CITIZENSHIP AND ASSIMILATION INTO MINNESOTA LIFE

RAM: I became a proud citizen of the United States in 1984, and Neena did so in 1992. Since our arrival to the US, things have changed immensely. We have become an integral part of Minnesota, and we call it our home. We have had the great opportunity to establish several Indian organizations and to participate actively in several others. In 1976, we founded Gujarati Samaj of Minnesota to celebrate and preserve the Gujarati language and the cultural heritage of Gujarat—the western state of India. Several of us had migrated from Gujarat and from places around the world where Gujaratis had settled many years ago. Over the years, Gujarati Samaj has grown from forty families to about five hundred families, providing many cultural activities for youth and adults. Summer picnics and Navratri, Diwali, and Holi celebrations are very well attended. At Diwali in 2014, attendance exceeded over eight hundred people. I have learned many good things about the US, especially about its constitution and the democratic governance of nonprofit organizations. From the inception of Gujarati Samaj and its bylaws, we have ensured that everyone knows and follows its rules for transparent governance. We have followed similar bylaws in the other organizations we founded or actively participated in.

I founded the Jain Center of Minnesota in 1989 to spread the message of *ahimsa* (nonviolence), *anekant* (diversity), and *aparigraha* (self-control) taught by Jain's last teacher, Shree Mahavir. I represent our Jain Center as a director of the national organization Federation of Jains in North America (JAINA). The Hindu Society of Minnesota and Hindu Temple were started in 1978. I gave Sunday *satsang* talks once a month at the temple. Now there is a new large temple, built in 2006, in Maple Grove, and we continue to be trustees and donors. Neena was one of the founders of SILC, where I taught Gujarati language and social studies classes for several years. This was a great experience, and it was so rewarding to interact with young minds who have now become successful individuals in their professions. Many of them are leaders performing social community services, thanks to SILC culture and its inspiration of service for others.

Neena and I were active in the US political system and were able to form the Minnesota Asian Indian Democratic Association (MAIDA) in 1994, a chapter under the Minnesota DFL party. Our main purpose was to involve new Indian American citizens in the political process and to let our elected representatives know our conditions and concerns. We felt strongly about participating in a democratic process, where everyone learns to accept others, regardless of color, creed, religion, gender, or national origin; to respect different points of view; and to promote equality among women and men. Every year we fully participate in political campaigns, fund-raising for the candidates, phone calling, and educating Indian communities about their rights. We present our issues and interests to the candidates. We also encourage Indian youth to participate in the political system. This year there was a national movement to get young Indians, both Republicans and Democrats, to participate and run for office in the state houses and US Congress. Now the governors of South Carolina and Louisiana are of Indian origin, and the first Hindu, from Hawaii, was elected to the US Congress.

In 1983, Neena and I were instrumental in revitalizing an all-India secular organization, India Club, which had not been very active since its inception in 1973. We created new bylaws, expanded the activities, and coordinated with all the other linguistic, cultural, and religious groups for wider participation. Every year, India Day has been organized to let the community at large experience Indian culture, food, and people. The annual event was so successful that the India Association of Minnesota (IAM, formerly India Club) now celebrates it at a large, open mall at the state capitol grounds in St. Paul. In August 2014, the governor of Minnesota was the chief guest and hoisted the flags of both countries in the presence of more than twenty thousand people.

THE INDIA DIASPORA AND THE
MINNESOTA HISTORICAL SOCIETY

In 1992, the Minnesota Historical Society (MHS) had an exhibit on recent immigrants to Minnesota, and we began to seek out missing data and stories on the new vibrant community of Asian Indians. My good friend Godan Nambudiripad, myself, and some other members met at my office, and the idea for the Indian Oral History Project was born. With mentoring from Polly Sonifer, the narrator, and James Fogerty of MHS, the first Indian Oral History Project under IAM was completed in 1994 or 1995. It included oral interviews with sixteen Indian immigrants who arrived in Minnesota in the early '60s, recording their life experiences. We had a very careful selection process to identify the interviewees, considering the diversity of Indian languages, religions, and cultural traditions. We wanted to tell the story of our past and our present aspirations as Minnesotans. We are just like Swedes, Norwegians, or Northern Europeans, with an emphasis on family, education, and hard work. We have settled here to be part of Minnesota, contributing our knowledge, experience, talent, and resources for the betterment of the people. From 1994 to 2014, IAM has completed more than eight Indian Oral History Projects with the Minnesota Historical Society. Some of these projects were for IAM; others were for SILC, the Indian Music Society of Minnesota (IMSOM), Ragamala Dance, or the Hindu Society of Minnesota. IMSOM was able to digitize Indian classical music performed by visiting guest artists of the last thirty-plus years. These histories will be preserved at the Minnesota History Center for education and research by present and future generations.

The Minnesota Historical Society was impressed with all the projects we were doing for the community. When asked about my motivation for these activities, I humbly stated that I was paying back my debt to the society that has helped me to be the person I am today. Since my childhood, people and organizations in India and the US have helped me with my needs and development.

In 2003, I was elected as a director of the Minnesota Historical Society Council. I enjoyed this position and learned a lot during my three terms over the course of nine years, serving on finance and program committees and as vice president for the last term. At present, my relationship continues as director emeritus of the society. The society dates back to before Minnesota became a state in 1858. It is a premium state organization with more than twenty-five thousand members, preserving the state's history, maintaining state monuments, and educating the people of Minnesota about their past and preparing for the future.

The MHS has developed the curriculum for school history classes and organizes history day for Minnesotan high school students. Minnesota students have competed for and won several national awards in various categories of history every year. In oral history, it was very important to share our experiences, trials, and tribulations, as well as the contributions we've made since our arrival. I told the MHS that the success of Asian Indians is due to our strong family ties and values, stressing good education. We can be part of the Minnesota history and legacy by spreading education and the practice of yoga and meditation at all levels of daily life for good physical and mental health. The world needs real peace, with nonviolence and tolerance and respect for each other. We remind ourselves of what Mahatma Gandhi said: "Be the change you wish to see in the world." I am hopeful about all the changes taking place in India right now. I hope that the leadership of the country can change the people's minds and hearts. There is a great deal of creativity and enthusiasm for change in India. If you can change people's mind-set of blind habits just a small amount, it will multiply geometrically for a billion people.

THOUGHTS ON IMMIGRATION POLICY

Our US immigration system is too complex. I would tell the INS to welcome the people who can contribute to the advancement of the country with simpler and faster visa granting. This would put the United States at a greater advantage to attract creative and bright people from all over the world. America has a system in place that helps to create and bring out new energy from immigrants who want to work very hard to succeed. America has become richer in science, technology, business, and art because of all this new, fresh talent. America is ahead of Europe and Japan because of this diversity. Now it is very difficult and expensive to get a visa to come to the US. America is still a new world, and you have to look to people who want to put in their own energies and want to succeed. People who come to the New World want to make their mark and contribute. Immigrants have a desire to get ahead, and they have the energy to support that desire. If you look at the history of immigrants from old to new—whether they came from India, China, South America, or Europe—they have worked hard to succeed, maybe harder than the people who are already here. Maybe it would be a good idea if, at age 18, everyone had to be like all immigrants and learn the Constitution and other things that immigrants have to learn, and if everyone had to declare their desire to stay in America. It may be a good idea for all of us to take a refresher course in civics, just like we have to renew a driver's license or, for physicians and engineers, a professional certification. Becoming a good citizen requires solid commitment and a strong desire to serve your country. We can't have a strong society when its citizens become careless about their rights and responsibilities, including voting. This country is a melting pot of many nationalities and cultures. Everyone has to contribute to keep it growing and prosperous. We have to tell these stories of "Yes, I can" and "Yes, we will."

RAM AND NEENA: This broad base of organizations and their sustained activities have brought satisfaction to us. We have created a small mini-India here in Minnesota. While visiting SILC, an Indian ambassador commented that our SILC is unique and that there is nothing like it in India or elsewhere in the US. SILC is not like a regional one-language school and is not a religious school. It is a secular school teaching many languages, the history and art of India, and religious philosophies, under one roof, and it is open to everyone. SILC's biggest impact is what it has done for children in building their character, self-identity, and self-respect. SILC has a very good name as an organization in this community and has worked with adoption agencies such as the Children's Home Society and Parents of Indian Children.

Maybe we should export some of these ideas to India to help them get along with each other. When we used to visit India, we used to bring back many Indian textbooks. None of us were teachers when we organized SILC. Everyone was an immigrant with different languages and customs, so we tried to bridge our differences, which is a unique American experience. The children with SILC experience have gone back in their professional lives and are volunteering their time, talent, and resources to help others. Here we see the fruits of our small beginnings of SILC.

THOUGHTS ON EDUCATION IN AMERICA

NEENA: If I were to get in front of a random group of parents in Minnesota and talk about the education crisis in our country, I would encourage them to teach the fundamentals to their children, starting at a very primary grade level. I'd encourage them to read books aloud with them. I'd tell the parents to be part of the child's education and his world. Create curiosity and let them ask questions. Have conversations with your children. Ration their idle time wasted on TV or social media. As children get older, it seems they have less communication with parents or adults. Indian parents in Minnesota are well educated and are ready to help their children achieve excellence. In India we grew up never challenging our parents or elders. Modern parents have to be extra vigilant regarding the education and overall development of their children.

PHILANTHROPY AND MOTHER INDIA

RAM: While building community in Minnesota, we have not forgotten our responsibility or obligation to Mother India. We try to collect funds for the education NGOs (nongovernmental organizations) working to teach children in very rural and poor areas of the country. Our largest funds go to the communities devastated by natural disasters. After the terrible killer earthquake of 2001 in Kutch, Gujarat, we adopted an entire village, Vijaypar in the Rapar district, by paying for sixty-five houses, the village hall, a primary school, and a children's playhouse. We had a gathering of Gujarati people to raise funds to rebuild the homes. People started with $100 or $200 donations, which were not sufficient to overcome the massive damage that Mother Nature had dealt to such poor people. I spontaneously came up with a scheme to "Adopt a House for $2,000." Neena and I pledged the first two houses to get the ball rolling. One house was a lifetime of blessings for the people who were going to live there. Our community rose to the occasion, and we had pledges for fifty homes that night, with $100,000. We carried the same message to other Indian communities with the India Association of Minnesota, and to the community at large, and were able to raise $365,000 to cover home expenses. We contracted with the CARE organi-zation responsible for

The Gada-Norton Families in 2016
(photo courtesy of Ram and Neena Gada)

the planning and supervision of that village's reconstruction. We had some money left over because one project couldn't be done. The villag-ers told us to just give them the cash, which we were not going to do. We found a better use for the cash—helping village women with their medical care. We contracted with the Bhojay Sarvoday Hospital to buy a medical van to travel from village to village, instead of the village women traveling to the hospital. This van carried a doctor and nurse to these villages each week. Some of these people had never had vaccines. Some women in male-dominated societies had never even seen a med-ical professional. We named that van the Minnesota Medical Mobile. It was a great humanitarian success. We no longer support that van, but medical supplies are still donated, so the program continues. Neena and I went to the inauguration of the Vijaypar village and the Bhojay medical van.

NEENA: I was able to talk to the women who came to the medical van inauguration. Many of these women were Muslim, and they could not get out of the house due to poverty and social customs. Many of the women had borne eight to ten children. Frequently, there was a lack of nutrition for their children. I heard stories of how one woman's uterus was so loose that it would fall out. The local women's organizations were happy to deal with these women now, as the van was able to travel to the villages. One woman who'd never spoken in public before came to the podium to speak about her experiences, which were very sad, and it was hard to imagine and feel her pain. This was perhaps the beginning of women's empowerment in rural India. Education, and especially girls' and women's education, will be the only way to solve many of India's ills and problems.

RECOGNITION FOR CONTRIBUTIONS

RAM: This life journey has been very rewarding in networking with so many people. We hope our efforts have helped to create the right environment to preserve our cultural heritage; to spread values of cooperation, trust, and understanding; and to become good citizens of Minnesota and the United States. I am humbled and grateful for receiving recognition and lifetime achievement awards from organizations such as IAM, the Hindu Society, SILC, JCM (Jain Center of Minnesota), JAINA, KOJAIN (Kachchhi Oswal Jain Association in North America), and ASHRAE. In my acceptance speech for receiving the 2014 Lifetime Service Award from the Council on Asian Pacific Minnesotans, I dedicated the award to my mother, who was my mentor for serving others. Her life lessons are alive in me all the time. I feel happy and satisfied if any of our activities have made a positive constructive change in one person's life or any organization's progress. We are very grateful to the many people, volunteers, and organizations who have given us lots of support. I am proud that together we have accomplished a lot and set the strong foundations to excel at higher levels.

In October of 2016, I was elected to the Honorary Council of the Minnesota Historical Society. The honorary council is "a group of special people who are recognized for their distinguished service to Minnesota History." I am honored as the first Indian American to join with these distinguished Minnesotans.

EDITOR: Neena received the IAM 2016 lifetime achievement award for her dedication to SILC and IAM.

EDITOR: From the *Times of India* November 12, 2016, reporting on Ram's distinction as a member of the Honorary Council of the Minnesota State Historical Society:

Gada deserves the lion share of credit for bringing the Smithsonian travelling exhibition, "Beyond Bollywood (BB): Indian Americans Shape the Nation" to Minnesota, although it was truly a collaborative effort. Three years in the making, this exhibit highlighted numerous contributions of over 40,000 NRIs [Non-Resident Indians] in diverse fields—social, cultural, political, governance, business, entrepreneurship, scientific and economic. It made people aware of facts such as the earliest known Indian to set foot in Minnesota was Swami Vivekananda in 1893. . . . Gada's leadership in the oral history project allowed the Indian community to re-imagine, recast, and flirt with its own history in the context of Minnesota. Future generations will forever be grateful to this "history buff" for his efforts to preserve more than 100 years of the history of the Indian community in Minnesota.

PRABHU GOEL, SILICON VALLEY

BORN IN MEERUT, INDIA

EDITOR: *Following Prabhu's graduation from IIT Kanpur, he immigrated to get a PhD at Carnegie Mellon University. After summer jobs at IBM, he gained full employment and was awarded an IBM corporate award for solving the problem of testing of very large integrated circuits. He went on to found Verilog, a software that became the gold standard for the development and testing of ASICs. Prabhu and his family have changed the lives of thousands of very low-income families in India by financially supporting their children through engineering and medical school. This scholarship program should be considered the model for focused philanthropy.*

I was in born in Meerut, a city near New Delhi, but for most of my childhood, I was raised in Nainital—a beautiful city in the Himalaya Mountains with a beautiful lake. It is also the summer capital for Uttar Pradesh. I lived there from age 1 through age 11, when we moved to a city called Allahabad, which is more of the educational city of Uttar Pradesh; I completed my high school equivalent in that city, then I went to IIT Kanpur, which is also in Uttar Pradesh, and from there to the US.

Prabhu Goel
(photo courtesy of Prabhu Goel)

My father had a diploma in engineering. He was a civil engineer and had gone to what is now called IIT Roorkee, which was a very prestigious university in India at the time for civil engineering. His position for the government was in the area of civil works, meaning roads and buildings. Most of the time my father was at home, although certain times, when he worked about twenty miles away, we didn't see him every night because it was difficult to get home. But before we went to the university, we saw him every day.

My mother was only educated to the sixth grade. She was one of fourteen children, and her father was highly educated—with a master's—and had studied law. All her other siblings were highly educated except for her oldest brother and herself. It makes no sense that the two of them weren't educated, and I suspect that her parents held her back at grade six. I have never been able to understand the reasons and never asked—and of course it is too late to ask my grandparents—but my sense is that there were too many children and her mother needed help. My mother was quite smart and picked up English, and was involved in teaching us children when we were little. We were seven children—I think birth control didn't work well in those days—and I was the second. She didn't supervise our homework, but certainly my early education. When I was two through five years of age, she was teaching my older brother, and I got involved studying along with him. As children we did not have much responsibility around the house or for the other children, as we had help in the house. My grandparents did not live with us because we lived in government housing because of my father's job. But both of our sets of grandparents visited us in the summer because they lived near Delhi and it was very hot. In the winter, when it was snowing, we went to visit them. My parents had an arranged marriage, and, in fact, they never saw each other before they got married.

ATTENDING SCHOOL

We had fabulous teachers in the private schools we attended. I attended a preparatory school where the principal and the owners were Christian, although there was no affiliation with any religious type. My elder brother and I both attended that school. We were not being taught any religion, and I had the best education at that school until I was in grade five. The teachers were phenomenal. I remember one winter, for three months when I stayed behind and lived in the dorms, they treated me as if they were my parents, and I was probably three or four years old. I still remember a boy, a boarder, who was in my class, and when his parents came to pick him up he ran away and hid so his parents couldn't find him. He was a boarder whose family lived in another place, and he would hide from them because he didn't want to go home, as he was very happy there. My family lived in the city where the school was located, so I lived at home.

The school was lots of fun. I don't remember a situation where I thought it was a burden to study but instead had great fun learning. We always spoke English at school, and at home we spoke both English and Hindi, with our mother mostly speaking Hindi. Both languages were easy, although I thought I was better in English than in Hindi when I was growing up. From grades five through nine, I went to St. Joseph's, an Irish Christian Brothers Catholic school, and it was excellent. The fees were not large, and I lived at home so there was no boarding expense. My father believed that education was so important that he would sacrifice anything that was necessary for us to have a good education. The Brothers were strict, and I started to recognize that there were such things as grades and merit certificates. There were these gold, blue, pink, and white cards given to scholars that would indicate your level of academic ranking, the gold card being the highest. The entire school assembly would watch as the teachers gave out these cards. The gold was first, then blue, then pink, and finally white. Everyone knew how you performed. The parents would not come to the awards ceremony, but when I came home I gave the cards I received to my parents. I didn't need my parents to supervise my homework. Just the pressure of knowing that I had to submit the homework the next day was motivation enough.

From there my father got transferred to Allahabad, which was in mid-India and much hotter in the summer. In this city, I went to three schools, the first being a boys' high school operated by Christians and with instruction in English. A year and a half after that, I transferred to another St. Joseph's, and I finished my Senior Cambridge exam in that school. Then, after the Cambridge exam, I found myself too young to go to any of the IITs, which had a lower age limit. I was fifteen years old when I finished the equivalent of high school, as I had started studying when I was three, so I went to a couple of colleges locally. One was a government college, listed as the best in that region, that was based on a different system and in which the school year ended in March rather than December. So I had to fall back into the grade I was already out of. Because I didn't take my annual exams for the same grade that I got pushed into, the principal was so upset he kicked me out of the school. I went to what was considered a third-rate school, and that was the first year that I, as a scholar from that school, topped the entire district, beating out the other schools that were always at the top. My father met the principal of the government college at another meeting related to schools where he was citing how well his scholars performed. My father told him that it was relatively easy to take top scholars and have them perform, but the trick was to take poorly performing scholars and have them perform. He then reminded the principal of how he had expelled me from his school.

In the three-month intervening period when I was repeating the grade, I entered a military academy that was the equivalent of West Point in the US. They wanted me to have surgery for a deviated septum so I could qualify for military service. I was not convinced I wanted to do the surgery and, at the same time, I got admitted into IIT, so I abandoned the military academy and went to IIT. I had a high rank entering IIT.

ENTERING IIT

The IIT I attended started in 1965, and was funded by a program set up by the United States based on a consortium of nine universities, including Stanford, MIT, Princeton, and others. They actually provided faculty, financial assistance, and curriculum. We had professors from these universities regularly. I lived in the dorm when I arrived in 1965. Because of the environment I'd grown up in, I was adaptable, so there was no big deal in anything that I had to do, including going to a dorm. The years before, during, and after I attended IIT, they had some of the best faculty in the world. Besides the visiting professors, there were Indians who had gone to the US to get PhDs and came back to India to teach. I can't think of any better teachers than undergraduate teachers. However, I don't remember any specific inspiration, as it was a very competitive school. Every scholar had been top in his college before coming to IIT. There was this expectation that it was going to be tough to bubble to the top. I set myself a goal to absolutely be the top in the school, and thinking back on it, I am not sure it was all that relevant. That became a passion and drove me to be sure I excelled at academics. Stacked rankings from the school were published by GPA priority. I think out of 10, my ranking was 9.95 over the five years, and we all knew who the other guys were in the rankings. Two of us shared the gold medal when we graduated from this five-year program. The other guy, Sartaj Sahni, received his PhD at Cornell, taught at Minnesota, and is now at the University of Florida. He has written a large number of books on computer science. I don't think prior to this time anyone had shared the gold medal.

I was not thinking of going to the US when I entered the engineering institute. I was fascinated by the idea of going overseas but didn't think anything in particular about the United States. At the time, there were four scholarships for apprenticeships being awarded by Rolls-Royce. I believe Indira Gandhi's son Rajiv got that scholarship and apprenticeship. I applied and got selected, and then the question came about what I should do. One of my chemical engineering professors, who had been educated in the US, introduced me to Professor Smullen, who used to be the head of electrical engineering at MIT. He told me, "Prabhu, you don't want to go to Rolls-Royce." Smullen asked me why I wanted to go to London with the scholarship and come back to India with the requirement of working for five years for Rolls-Royce in the factory that made airplanes. He told me going to the US was much more interesting. In India, the level of awareness about what was going on in the rest of the world was not that high. This was 1965 to 1970, with some relative awareness in our communities, but there was no discussion about where to go and what careers we might consider. On day one I picked electrical engineering, but it was not because someone was coaching me on what to do; it was because it was what I liked. When I was small we used to make little crystal radios and other physics projects. India did not have many jobs in those days except for civil engineers, power engineers, and the like. Decisions were made in an impromptu manner, not with any guidance. You faced a decision and you made a judgment—that was how things happened.

GETTING A PHD AT CMU AND TRANSITIONING TO FULL-TIME WORK WITH IBM

Based on my discussion with Dr. Smullen, I stayed back in IIT and got accepted at many US schools, such as Stanford and MIT—but not all of them offered scholarships for a PhD. And I remember, when I came to America, my father didn't even have enough money for my ticket. It was tough. I had scholarships at Brown and Carnegie Mellon University (CMU), and, with a full scholarship, I went to CMU, even though the weather was atrocious in Pittsburgh. I decided I needed to get my PhD finished as fast as I could so I could go to work. When I was in India, I did work on computers and software programming. With my friend Sartaj Sahni, who shared the gold medal with me, I wrote India's first FORTRAN compiler as a scholar project. This program got used by other scholars after us, on the school's IBM 1620, which did not have a FORTRAN compiler at that time. This exposed us to programming. Even though we were in electrical engineering, software programming was part of the curriculum, and every scholar had to do some programming, even with the limitations of systems in the 1960s.

At Carnegie Mellon, I did a joint electrical engineering and computer science program, with some classes in each department. After the first year, which was the master's program, I got a summer job in an IBM-sponsored research program at CMU in Pittsburg. As part of that program, they gave us summer jobs at IBM to help us understand the problems IBM had. This started me on summer jobs at IBM. That is also how I ended up choosing a thesis subject on testing very large-scale integrated circuits. After you manufactured these circuits, you had to know what was working inside, and if there were manufacturing defects inside, and what tests and measurements you could subject the device to so you could certify at the end of manufacturing that the device was good and not defective.

For the next three years, I had summer jobs at IBM. I finished my thesis in 1973, three years after I arrived. I turned in my thesis and left the university for IBM. I finished my thesis in August but did not receive the doctoral degree until June of the following year, the standard time for it to be awarded. IBM sponsored me for the work visa I needed, but 1974 was a very tough year, and they told me they were only hiring four people that year. There had been a very bad recession in 1973, and I think President Nixon was not making life easy for immigrants. IBM put in a great deal of effort to help me. I was now in East Fishkill, New York, and had a fabulous manager and teammates for colleagues. When I was growing up in India, nothing that I was doing taught me how to work with professionals or how to communicate. There was no guided program on how to manage your career and build your network. You had to learn this on your own, and I wish I had known this earlier; in hindsight, I would have done a better job.

DEVELOPING THE ALGORITHMS TO TEST LARGE CIRCUITS AND WINNING THE IBM CORPORATE AWARD

My natural curiosity drove me to look for problems that IBM needed to be solved in the electronic design automation group. I came up with ideas, published, and filed for patents and invention disclosures, as IBM had a system of rewarding innovation through giving you points. I was happily doing this work. I was in contact with IBM Fellows who were working on the same problems, and on those areas we collaborated. There was a very interesting problem IBM had with their 370 not being able to test particular chips that incorporated error-correction circuitry because the standard methods of generating needed tests would not work. The algorithms they used would get lost in the circuitry because the number of decision points was too large and it took forever to figure out what test to apply. I came up with a simple algorithm that helped test those very large circuits and helped IBM solve a major testing problem with the thermal conduction module in the 370. A thermal conduction module would have as many as twenty to thirty of these chips on a single module. By the time they put them all together, they would have to test the combined group of connected chips externally, but they couldn't test it because it was too large in complexity. My algorithm helped them come up with tests effectively. As a result, I was given an IBM corporate award in 1980 and I got $50,000 from IBM, which was several times my annual salary. I didn't apply; they picked me. It was a great deal of money and it was tax-free.

IBM TO WANG

I was now a first-level manager at IBM. I started to think about what opportunities were available to me at IBM. There were many layers of management above me, and I started to ask myself serious questions after this significant change in my life from the award. If the award had not happened, I don't know if I would have been thinking about these questions. I had to ask myself, between the politics and the ethnic issues, where would I end up at IBM? A fourth-level manager of mine left IBM and went to work at Wang Laboratories. He called me to come interview. Inside IBM, one never thought of leaving IBM, which was so secure. I wonder if they intentionally made you feel that way so you wouldn't consider leaving. But I was a risk taker and liked the idea of a smaller environment and more decision-making opportunities. So I moved to Boston to work at Wang and run part of their design automation function. My IBM colleagues and bosses assured me that I was crazy. The plant manager doing an exit interview asked what they could do to keep me. I couldn't think of anything that would be possible for them to do that would make sense. They did give me a checkmark on my exit papers that they would rehire me. It was unusual, at that time, for IBM to do this. This gave me a lot of relief knowing I could go back to IBM if things didn't work out. I liked the situation at Wang, where Dr. Wang was trying to make his own chips and set up his own semiconductor center, which I was part of. There weren't many people in my group at Wang. Unlike IBM, with a huge number of people in semiconductors, design, and its automation, this gave me a ground-level opportunity in which I could grow significantly.

Wang was a highflier in those days. A year into the program, I was starting to see that Dr. Wang did not have the support of his management team for the semiconductor program. They did not see the value of the semicustomizable ASIC chips. So I saw the handwriting on the wall and, after speaking with other people, understood that this was not going the way I thought it would. In my one year at Wang, since we didn't have enough time to write our own design automation software, we used what was commercially available. In the process, I got to know about the commercial design automation industry, which I would not have known about otherwise. At IBM I never bought any design tools externally. I got to know some people in the United Kingdom— some very interesting people (one of whom I eventually hired back into my own start-up company)—and acquired the high-level simulation tools for the design of chips that were then available. In the process, I spent ten days in England at a university that had produced a program called a HiLo (high level, low level) simulator and a few other tools, and I acquired them for internal use at Wang. I was one of Harvey Jones' first customers. He was the founder of Daisy and Synopsys, and I remember him giving me a demo on Daisy. I was so fascinated with Daisy, I bought it for Wang also. In the process, I was really exposed to commercial design automation, and I realized that one of the tools we needed and did not have was test generation, which was an area that I knew. I knew there was nothing available commercially for test generation for certain design styles. At this point, I understood that Wang's internal chip design efforts were not going to go anywhere.

DEFINING AN INDUSTRY PROBLEM
AND CONSULTING TO SUPPORT MY IDEAS

I was never a marketer of any sorts, but I saw this hole in the commercial market, for test software, as an opportunity. In the meantime, I started to talk with the other vendors, and I decided I wanted to do something. I had $100,000 in the bank—$50,000 from the IBM award and $50,000 that I had saved. I decided to quit my job. There weren't many people at Wang who could say that I was crazy to quit. Fortunately, my wife didn't know any better at the time so she couldn't complain. So I quit and started out working in one of our bedroom suites that I could convert to an office as we had a large house. I started to develop the software program myself. I knew I was a good software developer and even had experience at IBM writing assembly-level code. I consulted with companies like AMD, National Semiconductor, and Digital Equipment Corporation (DEC). I went around giving lectures at these types of companies on how to design for testability, as it was a hot area in those days. They gave me $1,000 a day plus travel expenses. DEC would give me $1,000 even if I came in for an hour, as they were just in my backyard. This allowed me to break even, since I could feed my family without having to break into my $100,000. I worked sixteen-hour days writing my software for test generation on a VAX 750 time-shared machine, which was forty miles away. I used a TRS-80 Model II as an intelligent terminal, saved the software on a floppy, and transmitted it to the VAX machine on a 300-baud line. I used this system to develop my software and started calling on Texas Instruments, DEC, and Raytheon. They acknowledged that they had a hole in some of their product offerings, in that they did not have a reliable method to generate tests to help screen manufacturing defects in their chips. They started listening.

SELLING MY FIRST SOFTWARE LICENSES

I knew I could figure out licensing because I was on the other side of buying software at Wang. Also, I had taken a business law class while I was at IBM, so I understood contracts and had a very good understanding of business law. As I started calling these guys, I found these companies would listen. The product was ready in about five to six months after starting—it was not that complex—and I made it as simple as I could. Simplicity is essential for high quality. It took me almost eighteen months from when I first started writing the software until I got my first contracts. I sold two licenses for my software product, for a total of $300,000, at almost the same time. Raytheon and Texas

Instruments (TI) both issued purchase orders in December of 1983. I knew how Teradyne was pricing their so-called test generation product, which was for a different area, and I priced mine exactly the same. No one else had my product, so I knew I could charge enough for it.

In those days $300,000 was a great deal of money, so I was able to start recruiting others to my company. I recruited another colleague from IBM about six months before that date. I was sure I was getting the contract, but it took me the additional six months to actually negotiate the contract. Raytheon would sit me down in a conference room, and there would be ten of them and I was by myself. They would negotiate the contract with me, although they never asked me to negotiate or change the price. They were asking me for terms and warranties. Thank goodness I had taken the course in business law, so I knew at least how to approach the issues. I was still one person doing coding, selling, and every day calling forty to fifty people on the phone. Typically, I was calling managers, directors, vice presidents. I didn't know how to sell, so my approach was that I just picked up the phone and contacted them. I understood the problem the other person had, but I didn't understand the politics of the organization or other issues in selling. I had a reputation in the industry, with papers published, and the fact that I was from IBM really helped. I was one of the first people from India who actually started a high-tech company on my own, as there weren't that many people from India who were into business at that time. I started with no venture financing, and I actually bootstrapped it with my savings from IBM and the lucrative consulting contracts from DEC's manager, Prakash Bhalerao.

NO OPTION TO FAIL: I HAD TO SUCCEED

With Texas Instruments, in Dallas, the guy I was speaking to gave me visibility at the vice presidential level for what I was doing. They said they would run a benchmark. They knew I was working out of my house and I couldn't take a meeting anywhere else. We agreed to meet in a hotel near my house in Boxborough; they stayed at this hotel and took a room. Up until that time, my test product was working at the gate level. TI told me they wanted transistor-level test generation because they had MOS, PMOS, and CMOS devices. I had started to figure out how to do it, although I didn't think anyone else in the industry had done it. I came up with a way to generate tests in mixed environments of gate and transistors. They didn't tell me that TI would be benchmarking on the transistor level; I was led to believe the benchmark would be at the gate level. The transistor level had not been tested with production software, and I was still in the process of developing it. When they came, they gave me twenty-four hours to run a benchmark, which was unheard of. They gave me the tape with the net list, and I had to get it to the VAX machine, which was forty miles away, and in twenty-four hours get the results and go back. I stayed up all night doing this and sent them back the results. What happened was that night I found thirty-five bugs in my software tied to the transistor level because I had not exercised it. I fixed the bugs, and, in the morning, I gave them the results, and they had no idea I had bugs in the software. They took the results home and verified them and I got the order. The way I wrote the software it could trap errors. It could help me find the errors quickly. I used decision trees and captured decision states that were out of bounds and could tell me where I was in the software. Interactive debugging was not easy in those days. That is how I got it resolved. There was not an option to fail. I had to succeed. At Raytheon it was easier because the benchmark was at the gate level. The difficult part was trying to negotiate the software and get past the legal team.

I now had $300,000 in the bank and called Phil Moorby, the guy I had spent ten days with in London who was one of the principal developers of HiLo, and recruited him to work for me. He was on his way to work for another company in the US; he abandoned that and came to live in our home for a few months, in the same suite because we couldn't afford another place for him, he didn't have a place, and his wife was still in London. Phil was a world-class software developer and had developed a mixed-level simulator before, which was the one I had acquired at Wang.

DEVELOPING A NEW LANGUAGE AND SIMULATOR

Phil had this idea to develop a brand-new language and a simulator behind it. I gave him a clean sheet of paper and told him to do whatever he wanted. If anyone could do it, he could do it, and he came up with a language we called Verilog, which is now an industry standard. I hired another guy who was a synthesis expert, and between the two, we made sure the language was synthesizable, which was something Phil had not done before, and he probably wasn't paying attention to it. That is how the language got developed and how we got the first customer for this product, which came out in early 1985. He started with me in December of 1983, so in about a year and a quarter, the product was starting to work. We started with companies such as Motorola, Sun Microsystems, Silicon Graphics, and National Semiconductor. I was the sales guy, marketing head, VP of Engineering, and CFO. All of those jobs.

My father was alive at this time, and he came to visit in 1982, just as I was starting the company, and it was a tough thing for them to come at that time because we were tight for money. We were buying cheap groceries in limited quantities. My parents wanted to shop and travel. I remember telling my mom when she came on that visit something she never forgot—about cash flow. I said that a penny saved was a penny earned. We were trying to save so I didn't have to earn that penny. We still traveled and took them to Niagara Falls and Washington, DC, but mindfully. It was still a pleasure to have them. My father was not a businessman, so he didn't really understand what I was doing or the risk and other issues involved in starting a company.

STARTING VERILOG

I called the company Advanced Interactive Design Systems. Of course, of all the names we could have picked, it turned out to be AIDS. There was also a weight-loss candy called AYDS, which was marketed by a very large company. They ran into the same problem that we did. What do we do with this name? With the rise of the illness AIDS, we decided to change the name of our company after a few years to Gateway Design Automation. But no one remembers that name, and it was better known for its product, Verilog. We spent too much time on sales calls explaining our name, AIDS. The first product I developed, for which I wrote the software, ended up selling close to $10 million over the life of the company before we sold it to Cadence. The benefit of the sales revenue from my product was that it funded the development of Verilog.

At this point, I owned 80 percent of Gateway. The first guy I recruited from IBM, I gave 10 percent of the company, and Phil Moorby had 6 percent. The guy I recruited for synthesis, I gave another few percent, but basically the company was self-funded. Fast-forward, we are in 1985, with money in the bank, and I was thinking of how I could grow the company. We had two products—Verilog and a simulator and test generation product. No one had a vested interest in our success other than the team. No one was telling me how to sell or market. On the East Coast, I was relatively isolated. I was not networked with enough people. I was looking for venture advisors, and, as no one gave me venture money when I started, there was no expectation that they would give me money now. A contact, Bill Kaiser, who worked at Apollo and was their marketing manager who covered their design automation, was seeing how we were doing. We had asked for free Apollo machines to port our software. He saw what was going on and told Greylock (the venture firm) about us. At that point, we were contacted by a few venture firms—the Sprout Group in Boston and Fred Nazem, who had also invested in Cirrus Logic. We received three unsolicited venture offers. They approached us and gave us term sheets. We took the lowest valuation term sheet because we wanted the highest-quality venture firm, which was Greylock.

I still remember Nazem's term sheet had me revesting my stock all over again after I had run the company for almost three and a half years. He wanted me to revest my shares. Even when Greylock invested, I still had almost 50 percent of the company. They had three board seats, as Fidelity and Greylock came in together. They wanted Bill Kaiser to be a board observer, and I gave him a board seat. I wasn't aware of board dynamics, and I gave them board control without them asking for it. My condition was that every manager I hired had to be interviewed by them. I knew that as VCs, they must have judged people well. So everyone from manager level and above had to interview with them. I think they helped me tremendously. They helped as great coaches and helped me recruit the CFO at the right time, as well as the VP of sales. I finally had an advisor—my board of directors—someone I would report to at the end of the day, saying, "These are your goals, this is your performance, this is how you are doing." Internally, whom do you report to? It actually worked out very well.

ADDING INVESTORS EVEN WITH MONEY IN THE BANK

We started to take off like a rocket. We didn't use the money we'd raised because we had a $1.5 million in the bank. We only took the money because we wanted someone with skin in the game to associate with us. It helped that we had more money in the bank and that we had Greylock as an investor. It raised our credibility, and then we had the Motorola microcontroller group in Austin starting to use our product. Word got around Motorola that it was a great product, and someone in the ASIC group—Fuad Musa, head of the ASIC group in Motorola—asked if he could use our simulator for ASICs. He offered to teach us how they did simulation. ASIC simulation is a very different story, because they have to characterize every gate and cell. They needed to track each gate's (or cell's) load and how the delays get affected

Prabhu receiving the New England Entrepreneur of the Year award
(photo courtesy of Prabhu Goel)

because of the loading from each gate. They also simulated with pin-to-pin delays on the gates rather than just the block delays we were using. In exchange, they taught us how to properly model the blocks and gates for ASICs.

BECOMING THE INDUSTRY STANDARD: THE GOLDEN SIMULATOR FOR ASICS

We became the golden simulator for the ASIC world. The golden simulator meant that if someone was using that simulator, Motorola would accept test vectors and guarantee the silicon to those vendors. We impacted the time to delivery of Motorola's suppliers. At that time, Motorola was one of the most prestigious ASIC vendors. When everyone else found out what Motorola was doing, National Semiconductor and AMD got into it, AMI got into it, then Toshiba and NEC got into it. We would still sell to these companies and had a large sales team of several hundred individuals, with representation in Japan and Europe, along with the US. I was president and CEO at this time. Meanwhile, Harvey Jones and Aart de Geus of Synopsys got together with me and asked why we didn't combine the two companies. I didn't have enough understanding of the implications of combining Synopsys and Gateway, and it would have been an incredible combination. But they proposed a three-man CEO team. Three men "in a box" to be CEOs, and I would run engineering, Harvey would be the administrative CEO, and Art would run marketing. That didn't make sense to me. If there had been a single CEO, it might have been different, as they offered a merger with us owning 60 percent equity and them owning 40 percent. I did not take that seriously.

IPO OR ACQUISITION?

We were now close to an IPO situation, and Alex Brown was taking us public. We were halfway to an IPO. Then I ran into Joe Costello from Cadence, and he charmed the hell out of me. We started talking about the companies merging. It had been almost eight years since I started the company, and it was taking its toll on the family. You don't get to know your kids too well. I was traveling two to three weeks per month. At that stage, I decided that rather than run a public company, I would sell the company. The board accepted this idea because they supported my strategy. If we went public, it would require a different strategy and probably a different leader than me. I am not sure if, at that time, I could have grown it to the size that was the true destiny of a company of that sort. Had I agreed with Harvey and merged Synopsys and Gateway, I think that would have been the right thing to do. Maybe Harvey should have continued as CEO, but I probably wasn't mentally prepared at that stage to give up the CEO position. We were so focused on our own company, it was difficult to tell what was happening with other companies.

In 1985, Mentor Graphics was having internal discussions on buying us, and Gerry Langeler, who was their president, was pushing very hard to buy us. The Mentor CEO, Tom Bruggere, pushed back and they did not buy us. Gerry Langeler said that was the most expensive mistake that Mentor Graphics made, because they could have dominated that space. At that time in 1985, we were not large enough, so they could not have made a decent enough offer that we would have accepted—all this while we developed the language that became a worldwide standard. Every ASIC designer was using it. Our competitors had VHDL, which was government sponsored, and an IEEE standard, but it was so difficult to use that no one was seriously using it. We had quite an advantage. Ours was a de facto market share industry standard. Everyone was pushing VHDL against us. They couldn't play in Verilog's space otherwise. We had licensed Verilog to Synopsys for synthesis purposes. We wanted customers to have the best simulation and synthesis combination, but we had not licensed it to anyone else yet. Synopsys couldn't make a Verilog simulator out of it. They could only do the synthesis, so that is why they pushed a competitive simulator with VHDL.

Those were the dynamics I was facing, along with relentless sixteen-hour days and no time with the family. So I decided to sell the company. Along the way, I hired my former boss Manny Correia, who had taken early retirement from IBM. He was an incredible guy who came in as VP of Marketing and Customer Service. He was a top-notch manager and leader. He knew how to manage people, and I learned much from him after he joined the company. He had great communication and customer service skills. I couldn't be the only person doing this, and I needed him. He was incredible with customers. He came in 1987, after we had venture funding.

VERILOG'S MERGER WITH CADENCE

In 1990, we merged with Cadence. We exchanged stock, and I owned 7 percent of the company at that time and was on the board of Cadence. It was hard to be second fiddle in a company after you have made all the big decisions. At a communications meeting we had, I asked Joe Costello to clarify a question from one of the employees. I made the mistake of being politically incorrect, as there were five hundred people in the meeting; he was upset, and that blew my relationship with Costello. I left six to nine months after that. He begged me to stay on, but my passion was gone. It is not easy to stay on. When decisions get made, the CEO rightly has to rely on his gut and make judgment calls; even if you disagree with the call, you should back it—whether you like it or not. If you experience enough of those calls, it is frustrating. If I'd been in an environment where it didn't matter, and if I hadn't been in a position of previously making those calls, it would have been different. Today start-up CEOs know the customer problems in most start-ups, and they get involved. But I was the CEO for almost eighteen months at the start of the company. I had a broad level of knowledge that most people take longer to acquire.

We decided to license the software for free to universities for doing digital design. We gave them licenses of Verilog for their scholar work so when they came out of the university they were literate in Verilog. The scholars would go to the companies they went to work for and they would ask for that language. At one point we had two thousand universities graduating people experienced in Verilog. We were the first company to make that kind of decision. It was my decision when I was running marketing.

I had a Director of Marketing, Ronna Alintuck, who came out of Regis McKenna and was an incredible PR expert. What she was great at was spotting opportunities when a reporter was writing an article in a publication and looking for some quotes. She would hunt down speaking opportunities for us. She was connected in the industry and got me into articles in publications such as *Computer Design News*, *EE Times*, and similar journals and papers. We were getting so much press—way out of proportion to our size. We came up with the idea of using our biggest brand-name users and industry icons—such as Gene Amdahl, Gordon Bell, Jerry West, and Forest Baskett—and got their permission to run full-page ads in *EE Times* with their faces. In the ad, they made attention-getting remarks and had strange expressions but said great things about Verilog. These icons endorsed our company, and it was a very successful campaign. These were the people digital design people wanted to emulate. As a chip designer, you cared about what these people said. The idea to do this campaign was mine, but the execution was Ronna's. I think, in the process of running the company, I learned so much about marketing that today I could help almost any company market its product. I know more about marketing today than I do about technology. It was the most incredible experience I had from a marketing standpoint. I was not good in sales. I closed deals and did those activities, but if someone told me to be VP of Sales, I wouldn't have liked it and I didn't know the process. I didn't know how to sell and figured it out myself. I didn't know how to work the politics in a prospective customer's organization and figure out where the obstructions were, who the naysayers were, and who had the budget. But I got it done anyway. Gordon Bell wrote a book on high-tech ventures; he has the story of our company in his book.

BACK TO INDIA AND LAUNCHING A SERVICES COMPANY

In 1992, I was done with Cadence and got involved in a services company with headquarters in the US but based in India. Prior to this, my first company was one of the first companies after Texas Instruments to set up a software development group in India, in Delhi in 1986. We had realized we needed a lot of resources to develop cell libraries for our products. So we had set up the organization in India. Today Cadence in India has a thousand people doing this and software development/maintenance. After Cadence acquired Gateway, Joe Costello decided he wanted to shut down India operations because he heard there was too much overhead. So we acquired those people and started a services company. I funded it, but we had a president who operated the company back in Boston. I started diversifying my assets and started to invest in other start-ups, venture funds, and private equities. I invested in another Verilog company in 1995. It was a Verilog simulator that we sold to Avanti for almost the same amount of money that I got when I sold the first company to Cadence. Avanti did not have a Verilog product of their own, and they were a major company at that time. It was a fortuitous thing that they were there and we had what they wanted.

After I was finished with my first company, and a year or so had passed, I started looking at investing in other companies. That process

Prabhu and Poonam Goel
(photo courtesy of Prabhu Goel)

was slow; I wasn't used to the process of making investments because it was new at the time—1990 to 1991. The first thing I did was to make sure we were also investing our money in public securities, hedge funds, and similar vehicles, rather than just Cadence stock, to ensure more diversification. The sale of the second Verilog company to a competitor of Cadence had a good outcome, and, along the way, I invested in almost forty start-ups. Some did well and some did not, and some were just okay. Those that did extremely well were Exodus Communications and Frontline Design Automation. And there was one spectacular failure, which was a solar panel manufacturing company. I lost a good deal of money. We were going to manufacture in Germany, and we lost a significant amount in that investment. Similarly, there was a networking company. I learned I had made the wrong business decision after the venture capitalists exited. If we'd had a different business model, it would have been a very successful company. Another of my investments was in a company called Synplicity, which went public and then got acquired; we got very good returns. In some cases I would end up getting involved in the operations, but mostly I tried to stay out of it. I also developed a great deal of interest in the solar space as a result of my flopped investment. Now we have a reasonably large amount of capital in solar farms, where we produce electricity and sell electricity to the grid. We have farms in India, Europe, and the US. I feel passionate about this, and it has a steady cash flow and very low operational intensity and risk.

After I exited my first start-up, we were able to spend more time with our children and now with our children's children. We have an incredible time being with them, as all grandparents do. Fortunately, my daughter, who has a son, lives close by, and my son with two daughters lives just ten miles away, so we find it easy to spend time with them and be very active.

HOW TO USE WEALTH TO SIGNIFICANTLY TRANSFORM LIVES

Right after we sold our first company, we knew we were blessed with the wealth that we had and we wanted to see how we could do something meaningful with it other than try to make more money. So my wife, Poonam, and I took a significant portion of our wealth and committed it toward meaningfully transforming the lives of ten thousand children in India. We didn't know how we were going to do it, and we eventually founded what we call the Foundation for Excellence (www. ffe.org). We set it up as a charitable organization in the United States and in India. What we do is find very bright but very poor children, our scholars, who have made it on their own through high school and are accepted at medical or engineering schools but do not have the funds to complete their college education. We assume the funding of those scholars and transform their lives. Their parents might be drivers, maids, or slum workers—that's the economic level of their families. When they become doctors or engineers, they make a transformation not only in their own lives but also in the lives of their families. And they become role models within the communities they come from, so the leverage effect from this investment is very high.

We started this foundation in 1994, so we have over twenty-two years of experience. We have over five hundred volunteers in India who, in the first eighteen years, sourced these scholars from families they knew and verified that they were economically underprivileged. These volunteers would scour their network for prospective scholars for our foundation. Now we are sourcing them through a portal we have set up in India, and the scholar can apply on their own. We now try to do as much verification as possible to make sure they fit our low-income criteria—by low-income we mean an income of less than $3,000 per year. In many cases, the scholars go to government schools or colleges where the tuition is very low. These families are highly motivated to get their children the education the parents didn't get. For example, a maid may work two to three jobs per day to get her children the best education possible. We have almost ten thousand children who have graduated and gone on to become engineers or doctors. I have probably met close to fifteen hundred of them, not one-on-one, but in group meetings. We chose the number ten thousand because we thought it would be a meaningful number as far as social impact.

STARTING A FOUNDATION TO EXPAND AND GROW BECAUSE OF NEED

In 2000, we started to open up the foundation to take outside contributors so that more scholars could get assistance. We have opened the foundation to extensive fund-raising. So whatever we can raise will help us support more scholars. We are working hard to expand and grow because of the need.

We chose engineering and medicine scholars to support because we felt confident that, in India, someone with one of those degrees could make a decent living with a good salary. This also allows the scholars to have a meaningful transformation. Becoming a teacher in India doesn't necessarily assure a meaningful impact. The vast majority of our scholars have stayed in India, but we do know there are probably several hundred who have gone on to the United States to places like Stanford, Purdue, the University of Illinois-Urbana, and others for advanced degrees. One of our scholars got his PhD from Cornell and is a frequent supporter of our fund-raising efforts. In the last three to four years, we have asked our scholars to take a moral pledge, not a contractual pledge, to support two children in their lifetime. Whether they do it from their own funds or from their employer, almost uniformly every scholar has sworn that they will do so. Last year, we got close to $100,000 from our alumni scholars.

We have about 70 percent males and 30 percent females receiving scholarships. I have met some of the parents, and it is quite an emotional experience. They are so grateful for this opportunity, and they respond in such a way it almost makes you cry. The thing that they say to us is, "You don't know us. You don't know our children or our families. Why would you do this?" We don't do it because we think we are doing them a favor; we are doing ourselves a favor—we are doing it because it feels good. At the moment, we are barely scratching the surface of scholars who need money, so we are staying in India, with the significant challenges that our foundation faces in India. In the last few years we have started mentoring those scholars while they are still in the colleges. The characteristic of our scholars that allows them to thrive educationally is that they have a hunger to learn. We have some videos on the website talking about the scholars and their lives, including what their homes look like and how they would study at home. They would sit at home under an oil lamp and read because they didn't have electricity. The desire to learn, whether it was instilled by their parents or developed naturally, is very high. We now teach them the "soft skills"—such as how to do interviews, how to communicate, how to do public speaking—and focus on English language skills. We have set up seminars to teach entrepreneurship. We do this to make them well-rounded individuals rather than just focusing on their textbooks. This requires a great deal of infrastructure and resources on the organizational side, and we are getting a great deal of cooperation in India from companies that are funding the cause and encouraging their employees to be mentors and teachers. We have about thirty full-time people in our office in Bangalore, in addition to more than five hundred volunteers. We are setting up automated systems to track donors, scholars, communications, and how we set up the seminars and help the scholars with the logistics to get there on their own. It is quite a large endeavor, and until we get ourselves into a situation where scaling in India is well managed, it would be pointless to move to another country outside of India. India is like twenty-six countries. We might be spreading ourselves too thin and not be as successful.

IDEAS ABOUT EDUCATION

A lot of parents in the US do not know how to motivate their children as to why education is so important. In the families we are focusing on in India, the parents have a very clear picture of why their children need to be educated. Education is the one thing that can take them out of the poverty cycle. Their motivation is very high—I don't know what method they use to communicate this to their children, but we know they do. In the US, education and poverty don't have the same relationship, because there are lots of entitlements available in the US.

In the US, families that are in a situation like families in India, socially and financially, don't have the same drive or motivation to pull themselves out of it. When a maid takes two or three jobs to get her children educated, the children see that their parents are working very hard to get them an education. It probably doesn't impact every child, but there are enough of them who are aware. There has to be some interest from the parents to make sure the children feel it is important. If the children don't get the feeling that their parents care and value education, the children won't either. If ANY performance is good enough, the children won't be motivated for change. For the Asian community in the US, the children understand that academic performance is important.

IDEAS ON IMMIGRATION

If I were asked to offer advice on immigration, I would say we need to focus on two areas: one is the highly skilled immigrant. If we want this country to progress economically, we have to assure ourselves that the best-skilled people in the world migrate to the US. They will be the engines of economic growth, along with our own domestically cultivated resources. This will allow us to excel and do better than other countries. This immigration program would be similar to what they do in Australia or Canada, where they are open to inviting skilled foreigners to come in and set up base.

The second aspect I would focus on would be to look into job categories where we have a shortage of skilled workers. As an example, if you went into a manufacturing environment today, they would tell you that we don't have enough people who understand the automated manufacturing lines, who understand enough about computer-controlled machines and how to operate them well. In Germany, there is an apprenticeship program with government funding that is a strong part of a public and private partnership. These apprentices spend one to two years of training on the factory line, but they learn in the classroom how to work with machines. They are good at it and can make a difference in manufacturing. In the US, we don't have such a program. We don't teach people how to work on the manufacturing floor. This is an area where I would invite people into the US. If we don't have these skilled workers, we cannot persuade companies and manufacturers to stay in the US rather than move elsewhere.

I am also aware of a problem with agricultural workers. There are very few people who would call themselves "white Americans" who are agricultural workers. It is not seen as a profession they want to be involved in. It is tedious, and the work is very harsh. You are out in the sun twelve hours a day, digging and farming. If people aren't willing to do this, we have to figure out how to get it done. This may not be an immigration program but rather a guest worker program. They would be easily allowed to come here and work and then leave. We wouldn't be permanently burdened with these people, but we do need them because they are hardworking. They would be working in areas where the rest of the population is not willing to work. We have to look at it from the point of view of where the skills are needed in our economy and where they are not available domestically, for whatever reason, and find different programs to get these people here.

THE PATH TO FINANCIAL INDEPENDENCE THROUGH ENTREPRENEURSHIP

With my background as an entrepreneur, if I were asked to be an advisor to people in rural areas who are struggling to earn a living, this is what I would consider discussing with them. My motivation for becoming an entrepreneur was to be economically and financially independent from having a job. People not familiar with entrepreneurship need to know that it can be a path to financial independence. When you have financial independence, you have lots of flexibility to choose activities for your family and yourself. As with education, without motivation, you can't encourage anyone to get involved in entrepreneurship. If they decide entrepreneurship is the path to independence, that gives them incredible insight into all aspects of life. They would then ask, "What else do I need to get there?"

After that, you have to recognize that you have to be willing to work hard—you need to persist and overcome obstacles and not to be cowed by challenges. You should look for areas in which you can do something that other people are not doing. It would be difficult to set up a large manufacturing plant in a rural area or small town, but you could set up a service business, such as a plumbing business, with several people working for you, or a flower delivery company. Lower-skilled people working in a group can garner a larger return on investment. You can approach it from that standpoint and look for simple examples of how people have become entrepreneurs at various levels. You can see how five to ten employees can work together in a company or, with different skills, maybe form a company with twenty to fifty people. Someone needs to create a catalog of entrepreneurs of various company sizes and various company types, from service companies to manufacturing to high tech, and give people a cross-section of what has been done. If they can visualize and relate to a particular company idea that has some connection to the environment they come from, it has a higher chance of success. You can't pitch Google or Facebook to them.

From the website of the Foundation for Excellence (FFE):

> *FFE's mission is to help exceptionally talented but poor scholars in India become doctors, engineers, and computer scientists. FFE awards scholarships to recent high school scholars who have overcome the adversity of their family's circumstances to be among the top rankers in national/state-level common entrance tests.*

ANANT "RAVI" RAVINDRANATH (1947–2013), SILICON VALLEY

BORN IN BANGALORE, INDIA

Posthumously told by Sandhya Ravindranath

EDITOR: *Ravi successfully navigated rapidly shifting technology, from adding machines to networks. He was a pioneer in outsourcing. He died suddenly of pulmonary fibrosis in 2013. Ravi and I had been speaking for months about an appointment for me to interview him. Unfortunately, he traveled often to India and our timing never seemed to align. I called one day to get an appointment, but he said he had a bad cold and lung infection and couldn't meet. His illness proved to be fatal. His widow, Sandhya, agreed to be interviewed to tell Ravi's remarkable story. He is surely remembered for the music they created together.*

I think it was Joseph Campbell who said, "Everything begins with a story." A hero is not only one who goes on an adventure but one who comes back to tell the story. If you don't tell your story, people can't

learn from your experience, and then the job is half done. Ravi's immigration to the States and my life with him was an incredible journey,
a wonderful story. Now I am the storyteller, and the responsibility has
been passed on to me. I need to keep Ravi's story alive for other people,
including our children. Life is so busy they may not have time to go
back and learn about these things. By these words, in a written document, they can perhaps go back and learn about Ravi, once in a while.

In Karnataka in the
1960s and '70s, we didn't
have the concept of last
names as such. Therefore
his father's name was
Ravi's first initial, and his
given name was his name,
and he was known by one
name, and that was what
was used. If there were
two people with iden-
tical names, then they

Ravi and Sandhya
(photo courtesy of Sandhya Ravindranath)

would go with the father's name as the first initial. For Ravi, his father's
name, which was Anant Narayana Rao, became his first initial, and
Ravi was therefore registered as A. Ravindranath in all his schooling.
When the time came to immigrate to the US, in his passport they
listed Ravindranath as his last name and Anantanarayanarao as his
first name. So everyone tried to say the long name and could not. He
told people to shorten his name and to call him Anant Ravindranath.
They started using that name, and Ravi wouldn't respond to it. He
wasn't used to being called Anant, and he would just walk by without
acknowledging them. He was called "Ravi" at home. Ravi means "sun
god" in Sanskrit. He decided to use the nickname of Ravi, so he became
R. A. Ravindranath. He still had the long last name, but it was easier
than Anantanarayanarao!

Ravi was born in Bangalore, India, in 1947, the year that India got
independence. His maternal grandfather was a Gandhi follower. He
had much respect for Rabindranath Tagore, a Nobel Laureate and poet
who wrote the national anthem, and wanted to name his grandson
after him. So Ravi had to spend the rest of his life living up to that

name! The name was a conversation starter for Ravi, and he often said, "My name is the ONLY difficult thing about me!"

Ravi's father was a medical doctor who served in the Indian Army, and after retirement from the army, around the time Ravi was born, he came back to Bangalore and started his own clinical practice there. This was a time of change, a difficult time for his father, who suffered some health issues. Ravi's father, being the first son, also had the burden of taking care of his family after the early death of his father. Ravi was the eldest of four siblings—two boys and two girls—and grew up with many cousins, aunts, and uncles in his home. Ravi was very bright, so his parents' focus was for him to study, get a degree, and find a nice job. He did very well at school and was gifted musically too, but his parents only wanted him to have music as a hobby, not as a way to earn a living. Ravi was very good in mathematics and science—always winning the first place. Ravi's first public exams were in tenth and eleventh grades, and he ranked in the top one hundred students. In engineering, he secured the fifth rank in the entire Bangalore University for his bachelor's degree in mechanical engineering. A bachelor's degree took five years after high school. After that he went for his master's in mechanical engineering at the Indian Institute of Technology (IIT) Madras. Ravi loved cricket. He played it in the field behind his house or in the street with his cousins and neighborhood friends.

Becoming an engineer was a big thing during that time, right after independence. Many things were happening in India, including industrial development, and not only did Ravi have the aptitude but his parents encouraged that path. He was disciplined, but he did well without trying too hard. He was a "law-abiding" type of student. He lived at home while going to the university. He helped others with their work also, such as helping with biology, which wasn't a major focus for him at school. For example, his cousin,

Ravi—husband, father, musician.
(photo courtesy of Sandhya Ravindranath)

who is now a physician, got support from Ravi in the sciences to help her career. He was a natural teacher. His uncle—his mother's brother—was an engineer, and Ravi was very fond of this uncle. The uncle also studied in Bangalore, and even though he didn't live with Ravi's family, he came to visit often and was a great influence on Ravi.

THE MUSICIAN

Ravi could pick up and sing any song playing on the radio. He was mainly interested in semiclassical music. He was able to sing the songs—even though he was not trained, he could sing very well. When he came to Canada, he met other people who liked music and sang. By sheer luck, Ravi got to learn mandolin when he was at IIT Madras. He had a roommate who played mandolin, and when his roommate wasn't using it, he tried playing it and got really good at it. After he finished his two-year degree, his roommate gave the mandolin to Ravi, saying, "You are pretty good on that instrument—why don't you keep it?" That was his first mandolin, which he brought with him when he came to UCLA. He had eight dollars in his pocket when he came to UCLA and the US.

Ravi's engineering friends at Bangalore University were a very smart bunch. There were five of them. They named themselves after the characters in the Mahabharata, which is an epic story with five heroes. Ravi was aptly given the role of Yudhishthira, who is the person who followed the rules and laws, his duties being to check that everything was right and to be an overseer.

Ravi's father did not have time for his children, as he was too busy working. At home he had too many people and demands for attention, so he didn't spend any quality time—not in the way we would spend time with our children now. Ravi's mother was very influential, and Ravi loved and respected her to the nth degree. She finished high school and got married when she was fifteen and a half, and gave birth to Ravi when she was seventeen and a half. Even though she didn't have a broad education, she could influence people. She always knew the right things to say at the right time. She would encourage Ravi to study and be sure to get an A+. He was excited when he came home to tell her he got the fifth rank, and she responded, "Why didn't you get the first rank?" She was very serious about education because she didn't get one. She often stated that she wished that she had more education. Ravi picked up his diplomacy style from his mother and could influence people and mediate between them if there was confusion or misunderstanding. He had the gift of resolving problems. His mother passed away in 2012. Her other son passed away in 2010. So now only the sisters remain and some uncles and aunts.

COMING TO THE US FOR HIS MASTER'S

I met Ravi in 1974. He came to the US in 1970, finished his MS at UCLA, and then decided to move to Canada. Ravi came from India via Hawaii and saw many soldiers sitting around and asked them where they were going. They said they had been drafted and they were flying off to Vietnam. It really made an impression on him that they were sacrificing their time and perhaps their lives for the sake of another country. Before coming to UCLA, he also had a scholarship to go to Ottawa University to do his master's. But a family friend in India convinced him that UCLA was a better school, even though he didn't have a scholarship. It was a very troubling decision because he had to take a loan even to get the airfare to come to California. The government of India was giving out eight US dollars to help students. He was very hungry when he landed in the US—he had a stopover in his journey in Japan—and he had to use the money the government gave him to get something to eat. Even though he was reluctant to part with the money, he bought a hot dog. He couldn't get anything vegetarian. He asked someone what the person was selling, and they said it was a hot dog, so he spent $2.50 on the hot dog and a drink!

Ravi immigrating
(*photo courtesy of Sandhya Ravindranath*)

In 1970, Ravi had taken a loan from a family friend who

was an industrialist in Bangalore. He had come to America before for business and was the one who had encouraged Ravi to go to UCLA. Ravi told him that he had no scholarship, and he gave Ravi the loan for the tuition and flight. The same person who gave him the loan had given Ravi a package to be given to someone he knew, and he wrote that person's address and phone number on the package. The college had told him that a representative from the International Student Union at UCLA was going to meet him at the airport. Maybe he missed them or maybe they never came. He came out of the airport and there was no one to receive him. He was standing there at the curb not knowing what to do. He remembered the package and the name and address on it. With the remaining money, he went to a public telephone to call the person. Fortunately the lady at the address on the package was home that day, and she answered the phone. He told her how they were connected and asked if someone could pick him up at the airport. She called her brother, and he came and picked Ravi up and took him to their house. In those days, America was a strange land, and going to America was like going to the moon! Now in India everyone knows what is going on in America, including our lifestyle.

After Ravi came to America, everything changed for him and eventually for us. Ravi blossomed. So many people were inspired by Ravi's accomplishments here. At UCLA, Ravi lived in a dorm for some time, and then he met a few students who spoke Kannada [the language of the state of Karnataka in southern India], and three or four of them rented an apartment. It took him a little over a year to get his master's, which I believe included a thesis. He had a part-time job with a professor, which was another means of livelihood. His degree was in operations research. He immigrated purely to get an education. He planned to go back to India and get a job. He knew his job chances were better if he had a master's from a US college. It was easier at that time to get a student visa. If Ravi hadn't come to the US, his father probably would have encouraged him to stay in India and get a job as an engineer.

NOT THE TIME FOR A PHD BECAUSE MONEY WAS TIGHT

He wanted to continue his studies. In 1972, immediately after completion at UCLA, he applied to McMaster University in Hamilton,

Ontario, to get his PhD. It wasn't difficult to get a student visa to go to Canada. The country encouraged more people to immigrate. One more time he had to take out a loan to get his PhD. His family was very proud of him going to America to study, and even though they wanted him to come back, they let him do what he wanted. In those days, we wrote letters to communicate. And when he wanted to see his father after his heart attack, he had to take out another loan for the travel back to India. Rather than return to complete his PhD work, he decided he wanted a job very badly. It just wasn't the right time for more school. He needed to earn money. He left Hamilton and went to Toronto to work at Burroughs.

This was about 1972 or 1973, and his first job was in sales support for Burroughs' L Series machines, which had punched paper tape loaders like an adding machine! He even lived in the bone-chilling cold of Sudbury, Ontario, supporting these machines in the area. After a year or so, he got posted to Windsor, but he was working at the world headquarters for Burroughs in downtown Detroit. When he came to meet me in 1974, he told me he crossed the border every single day for his international commute!

CROSSING BETWEEN CANADA AND THE UNITED STATES FOR WORK AND THE SERIOUS HOBBY OF INDIAN MUSIC

Ravi was happy in Canada. He had Indian friends, and they formed a band called Swar Sangam. It was such a coincidence—one day when he was crossing a street in Toronto, he ran into his IIT classmate! The friend, who was a singer, remembered that Ravi played the mandolin. Ravi and his friend got a few other like-minded people together and formed a band. They were performing in Toronto, and that meant that Ravi had to come from Windsor to Toronto and play music into the early morning hours and then come back on Sunday night to Windsor. The band played Indian film music from the '60s and '70s that later came to be known as Bollywood music. They would rent school auditoriums and make flyers and hand them out for promotion, and, surprisingly, people would come. All of the immigrants from India and neighboring countries missed Indian music, and to listen to this band was a treat for them. They charged an entrance fee of one dollar, and the money collected would take care of the hall rental and other expenses. They would have a two- to three-hour program and they were very popular. There were not only people from India, but also people from Trinidad and the West Indies. It was the lifestyle he kept and what I married into.

Later, the group, which was performing on stage, also secured a cable TV show. Canada is big on supporting multiple languages and promoting multicultural information on TV. They had an international channel, and one of Ravi's friends started hosting a show. That was a big thing. On one of those shows, Ravi was singing in Kannada, and Vijaya Malavalli, who was a big fan of the show and watched it on Saturday mornings, heard the Kannada songs and she was thrilled. This wasn't the day of the Internet, where you could just pick up and connect any-where in the world. When one went back to India, one would bring back cassette tapes, which were a new invention at that point. These cassettes were the only means of listening to Kannada music. Vijaya was so thrilled to hear her native language in song, and even today she talks about how pleased she was to hear Ravi singing "Ivalu Yaaru Balleyenu" on that program!

A GOOD MATCH AND MARRIAGE

Friends of our family introduced me to Ravi. My mom's twin sister knew Ravi's mother through some friends. Therefore we knew about their family. I had heard about Ravi in 1970, when he came to visit his father. My aunt and others said to my parents that he would be a suit-able match for me. I was very young, had just finished my bachelor's degree, and, being only eighteen or nineteen years old, I didn't want to get married. Anyway, he wasn't ready to get married on that trip either. He came back in 1974, after he started working for Burroughs. We had about two weeks in the first half of October to get to know each other and got married on October 28. The first meeting was with the family, and after that we met a few times by ourselves. The first meeting was quite embarrassing because we were under scrutiny! However, Ravi made it very easy. He had a way with people. He was genuinely inter-ested in them, and when he spoke to them, he not only made them feel comfortable, but he would make them feel very important! As soon as he came inside, he made everyone feel at ease, cracking jokes and telling stories about Canada. The prescreening helps to get a good match between people. We clicked and got married, and he brought me to Detroit, as he had moved to Detroit by that time. So our married life began in Detroit, and in 1975 we moved to Toronto. Ravi and I are Hindu Brahmins. Family prayers were at home, and we visited the temple on important days.

When he got the posting in Windsor, people started recognizing his capabilities. In the corporate headquarters, he was working on Burroughs B 1700s, developing business software on these platforms. All of this was within one and a half to two years—he climbed the ranks, and he was able to pay back the loans little by little.

SINGING BRINGS FAMILY AND COMMUNITY TOGETHER

Our focus was family and bringing the community together, and singing was the vehicle. We were active members in our club where the Kannada community got together, and that's how we spent our time. Music was my hobby, and I have been trained in classical Indian music. My bachelor's degree was in physics and math, but I also sing. I wrote poetry and Ravi composed music for the poetry, but that came later. Ravi was still part of the music group, and since I shared the same love for music, life in the new country was just beautiful!

Our son Divy was born in 1977 in Toronto, and around that time, Ravi changed his job to the Bank of Nova Scotia. He worked on a project called SWIFT, which was building software for international funds transfer. He got to use his talents well on this project, and he was a project lead—more of a manager and less of a programmer. He would go to New York frequently and cities in other countries too. His understanding of people, and helping and influencing them to do what he wanted them to do, was his big attribute. People followed him because of his interpersonal skills and diplomacy. He was good at assessing people and what they could or could not do. When Ravi walked into a room, he made everyone get close to him—he made the distance between people melt away. He saw the positive in any situation. He spread his enthusiasm wherever he went. He would get his energy from the company of others and, in turn, inspire them. He was kind and generous, and helping others was always top on his list.

We had to make our own friends and family in Canada. We went back to India before our son was born, again when he was six months old, and then we went back every other year. When we went back to India, Ravi would drag me back to all the institutions that he loved so much. He showed me where he sat, and where he had his cup of tea that he shared with five other people. He wanted to help me know about all the years we weren't together.

I would long to get letters from India and write detailed letters about our life in Canada. My parents were in a very remote part of India, so we couldn't talk to them on the phone. When we wanted to talk with Ravi's parents, we would tell them in a letter ahead of time when we were going to call and they would be waiting. The call would go through the operator. We'd maybe get three minutes because it was very expensive. We only had time to say hello and then good-bye to everyone. We wanted to go back to India, but there weren't jobs where Ravi could use his newly acquired talent, and we had loans to pay back. It felt as if India was ten years behind the US at that time. No one in India tried to talk us into returning. Ravi's parents felt we had a better life in North America. We knew Vijaya and Kumar [Malavalli] through the Karnataka group—about 150 to 200 people who got together periodically, four to five times a year, to celebrate festivals such as Diwali. Friends and Kannada groups were big parts of our lives. We were missing India so much, and any little thing we could do to bring back memories of our motherland was very satisfying. From time to time, we would get together. The women would cook Indian dishes and invite all the people over, and after eating we would all sit around and sing.

THE MUSIC OF KANNADA

People ask, "What are the essential elements of a Kannada song that you and Ravi sang?" The songs that we liked are called *bhaava geete* in Kannada. Basically, they're all about feelings and emotions—human nature, falling in love, happiness and sorrow, etc. Some are devotional songs with deep philosophical topics, such as death or God. I wrote a poem about the wind and how it is your companion until your last breath and omnipresent like God. The feelings are expressed through the words, and the mood is enhanced through music. They are not long songs. There are two lines called *pallavi*, like a chorus, and four lines called *charana*, like a stanza. So you keep coming back to the chorus line. The songs are distinct based on the language. I think Maharashtra and Karnataka have a wealth of these *bhaavageethegalu*.

From 1980 onward, our lives were seven days a week with family, high-technology jobs, and music. In Toronto, we had Divy in 1977, and in 1980 in Ottawa, we had our daughter Krithi; both Ravi and I were and are so proud of them, as they turned out to be marvelous people. Both of them are doctors now, living in the Bay Area. Krithi is married and has two children now.

In 1978, we had moved to Ottawa for Bell Northern Research (BNR). Ravi met people along the way and utilized those connections. Working for BNR offered challenging technology and kept him interested. He loved his family and spent a lot of time with the children. But he didn't like the cold weather. So the first opportunity he had, in 1981, he transferred to BNR in Palo Alto, as he made the connection through his BNR work in Canada, and we moved to Silicon Valley as a company transfer. We got the H1 visa with the company transfer, and BNR sponsored us for a green card. We both knew we wanted to live in the US. Frankly, the main reason was the weather, but there were many Indian events going on, including Karnataka activities. We thought it was a better environment to raise a family in Silicon Valley.

FAMILY, WORK, AND EDUCATION

It wasn't easy to do songwriting with two small children, and I was also taking computer language classes in the evening. Ravi would come home and care for the children while I went to school in the evenings. I completed a degree in information systems. Ravi was a big supporter and pushed me by saying I could complete the degree. He said that I needed a break and encouraged me to find a way to grow and blossom. It was actually his idea to get this degree. Money was tight so I couldn't have any help with the house or children. We didn't buy any property in Canada while we were working there, but we did buy our first home in Silicon Valley, and it was tough financially. We still wanted to take our children back to India every two to three years, so we started saving for the next trip the minute we returned! I couldn't work because of raising the children, so once Krithi started going to kindergarten, I got a job and it was with Intel. I was with them for twenty-plus years, until 2008. I held positions in IT support and marketing.

Ravi stayed with BNR, which came to be known as Northern Telecom, from 1981 to almost 2000. At that point, Northern Telecom wasn't doing well, and Ravi had always wanted to try something new, like a start-up. He was now into VoIP networks and telecommunications, and he joined companies like Rapid 5 Networks and ADC Telecommunications. He continued to do program management and started managing offshore development. Actually, he had started this with BNR. He started working with Wipro doing development in India for US companies as an outsource service. He was now "living" on airplanes to India.

THE LOVE OF FLIGHT

Ravi's other passion besides music was airplanes. He loved to fly and knew all the airplanes. He knew all the configurations, and we even had to take a trip to Seattle to see how they manufacture all these planes at Boeing. He was a true plane buff. When we went on walks and we heard an airplane, he would say things like, "That's an MD-80 or a Boeing 737." He knew the interior, the airplane structure, and the engines, including the sounds. He would not only talk about the planes, but in those days you could walk to the cockpit and talk to the pilots and have a conversation. He would report to me about the lives of the pilots. He gave them his business cards, and he would invite them to have lunch when they came back to the US!

His last job for offshore development was with Brocade and HCL in Chennai. Wherever he worked, he would make friends—from the CEO to the last person in the chain—and learn their life stories. They would ask for advice about their career or, sometimes, work-life balancing. Ravi could make community wherever he was. People remembered him not only at the office, but also in the restaurants where he ate. One time I accompanied him on a trip to Chennai, and we went to eat breakfast in a restaurant where the owner remembered him and asked him what happened to him because they hadn't seen him in three months! They even remembered where he sat and what he ate. I don't know how he made such a big impression on everyone he met. He had a kind of radiance—an aura that impressed people and influenced them, so they naturally wanted to be with him. His demeanor didn't have judgment. He disarmed people with his sincerity. It was a natural instinct for him. He had a sense of responsibility and a sincere concern for others.

FOREFRONT OF THE TRANSITION TO OFFSHORE WORK IN INDIA

For US companies, Ravi was at the forefront of the transition to offshore work in India. He felt that he was giving back to India, in appreciation for his life and his education. The people who came in the '60s and '70s paved the way for the next generation of engineers from India. When we came here, we had to prove ourselves and make an impression about what we were doing. Ravi came here as sales support, and worked his way up to the positions he held. It was like plowing the land and preparing for the crop. With the Y2K problems [technology transition to the year 2000] companies needed the talent and found it in India. We always thought about going back to India, but there just were not good jobs for Ravi, and after the children reached ten years old, we decided we couldn't go back. This liaison work was Ravi's chance to give back to India. Now it is different with all the companies going to India and setting up operations there. But in the early 1990s it was different. If you asked why to understand something better, it was a negative reflection on you. People were afraid to speak up. Ravi was an educator and transformer between North American companies and Indian companies. He continued to do this his entire working life. He groomed people to be good, responsible workers and managers, and I continue to get e-mails from these people who tell me how much they learned from Ravi. Or how they got an award or a promotion because Ravi taught them how to speak up or how to address a problem or communicate an issue with everyone. I even get e-mails from female employees because they blossomed under Ravi's guidance. One woman had children and wanted to work, and Ravi advised her properly how to come back to work and still be a good mother. Ravi impacted their lives, and maybe by them telling the story, they will return the good that Ravi did to others around them. Perhaps they will carry his enthusiasm and energy in their own way and spread it around.

Ravi changed jobs several times, from Rapid 5 Networks to ADC to MaXXan to McData, which was acquired by Brocade. He continued to do program management and liaise with Indian operations. His titles and scope of responsibilities included Director of Engineering, Vice President of Engineering, and similar positions.

EXPLORING, EXPERIMENTING, AND CREATING MUSIC

Ravi continued to create music, and he always said that the 1980s and 1990s were the best years of his life. We were young, we had good jobs, we were in California, and we had done everything we hoped to do. That mood continued. I was writing poetry all the time, and in a room in our house we had many musical instruments. Ravi didn't know how to play all of them, like the sitar. Every time he went to India, it seemed, he brought some musical instrument back! We have a sitar, a tamboura, a couple sets of Indian drums, a tabla, a bongo, and other drums. A real music store was his favorite hangout! If he didn't show up on time for dinner, I always knew where he was, which was in a music store in Cupertino! He would explore everything. He experimented with everything. He would take my poetry and set it to a tune for me, and put in all the interludes and whatever it took to support the words. I would be inspired by the tune and moods, and I would add stanzas. I would start two lines, Ravi would put them to music, I would add more, and the song would evolve—my poetry and his music together. With the instruments today, after Ravi created the music, the device could print out the music so someone else could play it if they wanted.

In 1996, we made a collection of our songs, and Ravi took it with him to India. One of his friends asked why he didn't produce an album or a cassette full of songs. The local artists in India sang for him, and it turned out to be an album of my lyrics and his music. We put it on sale in some stores and brought the cassettes back, and after selling them we gave the money to charity. We helped the musicians in

India do their projects with the money from the sale of our cassettes. They could use the money to produce their own albums. We did two of those projects and on the second album Ravi sang. Now my two-year-old granddaughter, who has just learned to play CDs, plays them one after another. So Ravi's music permeates our house all the time. Fortunately, she is gifted with music.

We played music late in the night or on weekends when we didn't have a commitment. Even in the morning, Ravi would sit in the music room, and I would bring him breakfast and coffee so he could keep creating! He was glued to the keyboard and computer for his music. It would take several iterations but not many—maybe some work to get the initial music down and then some more days to enhance it. We would play the music for special occasions such as weddings, a sixtieth birthday, or if someone had a baby—or for any special event, we would make custom songs. I would write the poetry and Ravi would create the music. Our children took music lessons when they were young, but after a bit it got to be too much and they dropped it. Our daughter took years of Indian dance, and before she set off for college, she did a two-hour dance performance called "Rangapravesha," which means "entering the stage."

PRIDE IN JOBS WELL DONE: HOBBIES AND WORK

Our hobbies and interests revolved around friends and family. Ravi had such pride taking our visiting friends to San Francisco. He toured San Francisco so many times. Ravi always encouraged people to take pride in what they do. Sometimes people in India don't take the extra step to do things properly. Sometimes they try to explain things away as to why things had to be like that, if it wasn't right. In America, we know nothing is ever perfect—we keep working on it and making continual improvement. That is how technology came to be the way it is today. Innovation, improving processes and products, and taking pride was Ravi's work philosophy. He wanted to help people. Ravi was very sincere and kind when he helped others. He wanted to help every homeless person that he saw!

This story really happened a few years ago. When Ravi worked in Chennai for HCL, he had a driver. Ravi always struck up a conversation with people he met and wanted to learn about their lives and children and what they were doing. The answer always came back that they wanted their children to have an education because they didn't want their children stuck in a job like the one they were doing. They wanted them to learn, study, and have a proper job. Ravi's driver kept saying that he had to take care of his children, and the cost for clothes and school was too much, and he could not afford it. He was worried about the money because his health was not good. Ravi asked him what was wrong, and he said he had to have bypass surgery, and he didn't have the money to get it done. When this happened, Ravi was on the way to the airport. When Ravi got out he said, "Take care of yourself," and his driver drove off. The driver realized that Ravi had left a bundle of money on the front seat, something like 50,000 rupees. The driver thought Ravi had dropped it, and he got scared that Ravi had left such a big amount of money behind and now he had it. The next morning, the driver took the money to HCL and told them that Ravi had dropped it in his taxi. Then HCL called Ravi and told him that the driver had returned the money that he'd dropped and how would he like it returned to him. Ravi said, "No, I didn't drop it. I wanted him to have it, because he said he needed money. I wanted him to have it." The company people were flabbergasted. "You wanted him to have that kind of money? That isn't right—just give him a proper tip." Ravi told them, "No, give him the money, and whenever I am in India, I want him to be my driver—always." Ravi believed philanthropy was personal. Charity was linked to organizations dealing with issues facing people he knew, such as a heart foundation. He didn't have one favorite charity. He believed in personal, human, face-to-face contact.

Ravi thought about what he would do as a young engineer now. He believed young engineers should go back to India—that India is the new America, the way America was in the '80s and '90s. He felt that if they were in India, they should stay and contribute to society there, not come to America. Education in India is very good and is getting better, and the top schools are equivalent to the top schools in the US or any institution in the world. Ravi's brother has twin boys, who are now in their twenties, and he told them to stay in India where there are more opportunities. One turned out to be an engineer, and the other one is a doctor, and they both live in Bangalore.

THOUGHTS ON EDUCATION

Ravi liked education in the US in one aspect—critical thinking and asking questions. In India, when we were growing up, you could not ask questions in the classroom environment. Here children are encouraged to speak up. Ravi liked that. If you went on the street here and asked someone their opinion about something, they would, without thinking, come back and tell you what they thought about it. Ravi felt positive about the desire for learning, respect for parents—all those good attributes coming from India. He especially valued the Indian philosophy of helping others. That was his motto in life. Because everyone is connected, if you are a good human being and you see someone suffering, that could be you—but through luck or some good fortune, you haven't had those problems. He wanted to experience God in his lifetime. And I believe he did so in so many small ways, like the driver or others whose lives he touched. There are people who say they are where they are because of Ravi's good advice. Those are the ways he touched humanity and touched God.

LOVING AMERICA

He really loved America because it is so free. If he hadn't gotten a chance to come to America, things would be so different—not only for our personal lives, but for the many people we have affected. We have encouraged some and discouraged some from leaving India. It is a big decision. Indian immigrants in this country have a choice to go back, unlike other immigrants who come here because of war or other problems and cannot go back. We had a choice. It was our choice to stay here, and it happened because America let us do that. We have always felt blessed for that. We feel it is free here because you can live as you want, choose where you live and what religion to follow. Ravi was very happy for that. Ravi believed America was built by immigrants and still has great resources, and we should continue to be open to immigration until there is a problem of resources that will run out. May the abundance of resources in America never run out! I hope America will always be the land of opportunities for young people from all over the world, for they are the heroes—the heroes who go on their missions and pave new ways for others to follow!

I was blessed to have Ravi as my best friend, husband, and philosopher, as my life turned out so full with him. It was all a gamble, like all lives are, and with our friends, family, and music, life has been excellent.

SAT PAL MAHAJAN, SILICON VALLEY

BORN IN LAHORE, PAKISTAN (THEN PART OF INDIA)

EDITOR: *Sat's family was personally impacted by the 1947 partition between India and Pakistan. He later received an education at IIT. His immigration to America included drafting blueprints and working at a car wash before landing in the nuclear industry, where he finally used his engineering background and experienced the thrill and the challenges of running companies both pre- and post-IPO.*

I was born in Lahore, which is now part of Pakistan. After the partition in 1947, my family moved to India. In 1947, the Hindus were killing Muslims and the Muslims were killing Hindus. My family was considered rich because they owned quite a bit of land. I came from a large family, and this land was part of a sizable holding. I was only three years old, so I didn't know anything about the partition. I was the only son born to my father's family of three brothers. I was very close to my mother's side of the family and my father's. When the partition happened, we moved with my uncles to Pathankot, in the Indian state of Punjab. My father was to come later. We had to leave everything behind. We had to get out, and we were worried we were all going to be killed. My mother, my uncle who was married, and my uncle who wasn't married—we were all lucky to get a house where we could stay. The government of India gave us the house until we could get settled.

We didn't hear from my father for six months. We didn't even know if he was alive. He knew somehow that we had gone to Pathankot. He was looking for us and asked people everywhere. After looking for us for six months, he eventually found us. The sad story was that he was rich before the partition, and in India this means he had servants and he didn't have to do anything himself—not even cook himself a meal. He knew nothing practical. When he came to Pathankot, he had to make a living. So he started buying chicken eggs to sell in the market to support the family. Unfortunately, I got sick—really sick—with typhoid, and I was the only child in this extended family. You need lots of money for medicine, and we didn't have it. These were terrible times. I don't know where my father and uncles got the money for the medical bills, but they did.

Years later, we did get land from the government of India—maybe 20 percent of the value of the land we used to own. We moved to a place called Fatehgarh, near Amritsar, where our family got some land. Then, because my dad understood farming and he knew how to make money in agriculture, he hired the workers and started over again.

Both my uncles were now married, and we all lived in one house. We cooked and ate together, the entire extended family. There was no separation. It was a big house, given to us by the government. We all had our own living quarters, but everything else was combined. It was a beautiful system. It was amazing to grow up in that environment. There were eight of us in the house. I used to sleep with my uncle rather than sleeping alone. My grandfather was there. My aunties would help take care of me.

I grew up in a village, and in that village there were only two schools. My family provided partial funding to run those schools. My father believed in education; he was educated to the high school level. He never asked anything of me, except to get good grades. From the earliest time I can remember, I only wanted to be number one in the class. In the Indian system, you had to understand all the subjects as you went through the classes because there were comprehensive exams. If you tried to just memorize everything, it wouldn't work. You had to know all the basics. I was inquisitive and wanted to know how everything worked. I went to a public school, and my father hired a tutor. It was like an insurance policy, to make sure that I was studying well. The tutor came to my home to teach me, so I had that advantage, but I really wanted to study, and I knew how to work hard. I enjoyed studying, and I just loved math and science. I had to learn Sanskrit, which was a requirement in our school if I wanted to graduate. I took it for two years and I loved it. I had a special teacher who taught me Sanskrit after hours. I loved how the words were put together, how everything worked together.

My father had no time to read to me. He was busy with his agriculture work. My mother was not educated. I had my own passion and my self-motivation. I knew I would get out of the village. I had no desire to take over my father's business. I wanted to be a mechanical engineer. Right from the beginning, I liked looking at things mechanically. I would open up an engine and want to put it together, because mechanical things were my passion. I knew I was going to be an engineer.

ATTENDING IIT AND THE CHALLENGE TO BE NUMBER ONE

After high school in my village, I went to DAV College for two years and Benares Engineering College for five years. The college, in Benares, now known as Varanasi, is part of IIT (Indian Institutes of Technology). Vish Mishra, who also lives and works in Silicon Valley, went to the same college, but I met him later. In those days there were only five or six good engineering colleges, so you had to be special to get enrolled. I was among the top one hundred students of two villages for the national high school exams. I had a friend in the village I thought was going to do something with his life. He had good grades in high school, but when he went to college somehow he lost it. I don't know what went wrong with so many of the kids. They did well in high school, and they were really good. But when they went to college they lost it. College was fifty miles away, and we stayed in dorms. There weren't problems with drugs or other things. They just didn't study. It sometimes goes back to the same old thing. Lots of people get good grades by spending time memorizing things. But they never really know the basics and fundamentals. A teacher can give you an equation, but you need to know why an equation works. Maybe that was the reason. My education in the village wasn't rigorous, but I think the difference was that I really needed to understand whatever I was studying. I wanted to do something with my life. Maybe the others just didn't have a desire to do something different with their lives.

My father wanted me to be number one. I graduated from high school in 1961, and you can go to the same school today and see my ranking as number one. My father was proud of me, but he didn't know how he could help me. It's not that he didn't want to do something to help me. The only thing he could do was give me money if I needed it. Apart from that, he didn't know how he could help. He had a keen sense of business. He lost everything and started again. My interest was to be educated as an engineer.

When my first two years of college were over, there were frustrating times, because I was so used to be being number one and it was different now. I had to make some compromises with myself. If I wasn't going to be number one in everything, I had to remind myself I wasn't in the village any longer—I was in the big city with three hundred other smart students. I was not number one the first year of college, but the second year I recovered to be in the top twenty students. I had my own competition with myself.

We had some engineering colleges in Punjab that were good and were just opening up. But I didn't want to go to any of them. My dream was to go to the top engineering college, which was in Benares. I applied, took the test, and got accepted. Here I was, seventeen years of age, and had never been away from home. Benares was sixteen to seventeen hours away by train. It's not every day that a kid from a village goes to an engineering college in a big city like Benares.

GROWING UP IN PUNJAB AND STUDYING ENGINEERING

Growing up in Punjab, you are very sheltered. You only see Punjabis. In Punjab, you don't see people who aren't Punjabis. You see the guys with turbans (Sikhs) and Hindus like me. When I was growing up, Hindus and Sikhs were family. It was only later that they started fighting each other. My best friend was Sikh. It was a different time. No one cared what you were. We were all best friends. I went to Benares, and I saw people from the south and the west and from here and there. I knew nobody. I showed up at Benares Engineering College, and it was quite a while until I finally met some other students from Punjab.

When I got there, I didn't speak Hindi very well. The good news is that the classes were in English. The program we went to was a five-year program. I showed up with the other three hundred kids. There were three dorms, and when I got there all the dorms were full. It was first come, first served, and I had no room. They had a run-down lodge, which was about twenty-five minutes away by bicycle. They put me there. There were about forty other students at the lodge. Nobody was supervising us. When you go into that environment, there is a lot of freedom to do anything you want. But we were different. We were more into putting our effort into studies. I started making friends after a few months and found guys with ideas similar to my own.

If you failed in three subjects, they threw you out of college. There were ten thousand students sitting for the exams and waiting to be in your place. There were no options in the engineering college. I had to take a carpentry class to learn how to work with wood. There was a graphics class that we had to take. I had to learn how to hand-draw items, such as a glass. I had no experience in either graphics or carpentry. I was worried all the time because I had no clue what I was doing. I was sure I was going to fail and have to go back home. Luckily I passed. I passed by a small margin. It meant I got just a passing grade, which was something like 35 percent, not like math where I was in the 99th percentile. Other people went back to their dorm, and I had to go back to the carpentry class and keep working. That was quite an experience. In some of my other classes, I had subjects that I had to work on extra hard. But I got lucky and I had good grades in everything else and graduated. When I went to the next level of engineering, I didn't have to take those other classes.

When I got to second-year engineering, I got to study the subjects that were interesting. I started taking a lot of practical classes, which included civil engineers doing surveys and mechanical engineers doing activities like opening an auto engine. There was lots of practical analysis. It was fun. I played badminton and table tennis. I loved those games. I still play badminton once in a while. And now I had made friends—at this point life was feeling better.

MEETING MY FUTURE WIFE: PADMA THE MEDICAL STUDENT

When I was in my first year in engineering, in 1965, I met the girl who ultimately became my wife. She was trying to get into medical school, and Benares had a medical college, a science college, and an engineering college. It was one of the biggest campuses in India. It was so beautiful and everything worked together. I met Padma at a college function. We started to see each other. At that time, in the '60s, you weren't supposed to go out with a girl. It wasn't socially acceptable. We were both without our families in Benares. Her family was in Calcutta and mine was in Punjab. Yet we still went out together, most of the time to a movie house or restaurant. Everyone knew at the campus that we were going together. It was countercultural to do this; even the professors told us not to. I once got so scared when I was going out with Padma and a professor saw me—I thought he was going to fail me. He could fail me just for seeing me with Padma. But things worked out okay.

Padma and I dated for four years, and in 1969, a few months after I graduated from engineering college, we got married. She was still in medical school. It was unusual in our situation for us to get married like this. I was from Punjab. She was from Calcutta and a Sindi. We weren't the same caste, but they were similar. I wasn't sure how my family was going to react. They had never met her. I had only met her sisters one time. In 1968, I met her mother, but I still had to go tell my dad. We both thought we should get married, but I had to go home, without

Sat and Padma Mahajan
(photo courtesy of Sat Pal Mahajan)

Padma, to tell my dad. My parents were unhappy because Padma was from so far away, and if I'd married a nice Punjabi girl, I would come back closer to home. I went home and told my father that he had to agree to us getting married and support me in this decision and bless me. After a while, he was okay, I think because my father always proclaimed "education, education," and, as Padma was in the medical college, this appealed to him. And Padma was and is very pleasant. She will go out of her way to please my parents. So our parents agreed. We were married in Benares in 1969. Both sets of parents came and so did many family members, thirty-five to forty of them. It was unusual to be married outside of either person's home.

MY WORK ON AN IRRIGATION PROJECT

So in 1969 I had a degree, and Padma was still in college. I went to Simla. It is the most beautiful place in India. A hill station at seven thousand feet above sea level. I got a job there in a lift irrigation project. I was one of twenty thousand engineers they hired. Padma would take the train and visit me once a month. There were no planes like there are today.

I imagined I would further my studies in the US. I knew I would come back to India because I wanted to be close to my dad. That was important to me. I planned to get a master's degree in the US and wanted to go to the University of Pennsylvania. My wife's brother used to live in Delaware, so I thought that Pennsylvania would be convenient. I never read books about coming to the US, because in those years of engineering, there was no time for anything else.

The engineering college was like a boot camp. You literally worked every waking hour. You had your classes, and then they gave you tutorials. The next morning you had to reproduce the things you learned in the class. If you couldn't answer the question, your teacher was going to be angry. You had to be careful and you worked hard. There was another serious concern—a teacher can fail you if they don't like you. The teacher gives you 25 percent of your grade, and half of that was for participation and the teacher's attitude about you for the whole year. So you can fail if the teacher doesn't like you. Getting a degree in India required you to work hard.

GOING OR NOT GOING TO AMERICA?

In 1970, one of the guys who was sitting next to me in our office in Simla, where I was working, told me he was going to America. I told him I wanted to go to America. I asked him how he was going to go. He said he was going to the American embassy in Delhi to apply for a visa. I didn't know anything about a visa. We went to Delhi together, which was about a six- to seven-hour train ride, and the man at the American embassy asked me what I wanted to do in America. I told him I was an engineer. He gave me an application and told me to fill it out, and that in six to eight months I would get a visa. I thought that was okay and filled out the application. I didn't apply for Padma yet because I felt I had to get to America, and Padma's brother and mother were already in America. So I knew she would not have an issue. Padma was actually the main force behind going to America.

I got a letter in six or seven months, and I was told that the US consulate had approved my green card and that I should come and get it. I had no contact with anyone up to that point. I was involved in my job and really didn't spend much time worrying or planning how I was going to go to America. That was 1971. I went home to talk to my dad and Padma, and they told me it was too early to go because my sister was getting married. I went to the consulate and told them I had to have an extension for a year, which they approved. They were looking for engineers in America, so they just gave me the green card. At the end of 1972, I still didn't want to go, so I went back to get another extension, and they told me it would be the last time and I would never get a visa again if I didn't go. So in January of 1973, I came to America. Back in India, my son was born in August of 1972, and in January I left everyone, my four-month-old son, and my wife, and flew to New York.

In New York, Padma's brother picked me up. He lived in Parsippany, New Jersey, with his mother and someone else—all in a one-bedroom apartment. There was no room for me, but they gave me a corner for a bed. Now it was time to find a job so I could bring my wife and son here. Padma was still in her medical residency, but I was missing them and everything seemed kind of terrible. I was thinking, *I had such a wonderful job, why did I leave India?* The day I left, my wife said, "Why don't you take six months off and see if you like it?" I told her if I was resigning my job and going to America, I was going to make it. You just can't live between two places, and I didn't want anything making me feel that I had to go back. I wanted to start life in the US.

I lived with my brother-in-law and my mother-in-law, who did the cooking, and I started looking for a job. Before I started my schooling in the US, I wanted to have some money. When I left India, I had $150 after changing rupees to dollars. Since I was a new immigrant, the government of India gave me eight dollars, and I had to figure out where to get the remainder. I got some money from Padma's brother to come up with the $150. I got an airplane ticket, and I knew $150 wouldn't get me far. Living in Parsippany, New Jersey, you can't walk anywhere. I saw my first snowfall. And now I needed money to survive for a while.

I took a bus from Parsippany, with sixty-five cents for a one-way fare, which was a lot of money in those days. I went to New York City and bought the *New York Times* and looked at anywhere they needed engineers. I walked all around New York looking for a job. I had a résumé that my brother-in-law made for me. I looked everywhere for three months and no job. I got to speak to people, but everyone wanted experience. I had no experience. With an Indian accent and no experience, who was going to give me a job? Then one day, I didn't have money so I decided I had to do something. There was a car wash nearby. I went to wash cars to make some money to survive.

BLUEPRINTS AND THE HOPE FOR BETTER WORK

I had been going to employment agencies to see if they could find me some work. I eventually got a call. There was a company that needed someone to make blueprints. The company was thirty-five to forty miles away. It was an early-stage biotech company. The ammonia would bother my eyes, but I took the job and didn't have to work at the car wash. I now needed a ride to get to work. There was a guy named John who was a manager at the company. He knew I needed a ride and he gave me one every day, saying it was on his way. I wish I could find him now—I would fly him over to Hawaii and we could spend some time together. He did so much for me. He got me to work on time. Then my brother-in-law asked me why I didn't have a car. I told him I had no money, but he said he would front me the money. He worked

as a chemical engineer at Allied Chemical. He didn't have any intro-
ductions for me, as he is a laid-back guy. So my life revolved around
blueprints and looking for better work.

PADMA AND MY SON CAME TO VISIT

I saved enough money to send for Padma and my son to come visit. All
seven of us were in a little apartment with one bedroom. They visited
for about one month. Padma had gone to the US consulate and asked
them for a visa. The man at the consulate told her, "Look, your husband
lives there, your mother lives there, so you aren't going to come back."
She said, "I have to come back and finish my medical degree. Just give
me a tourist visa for three weeks. I just want to see my husband and
I'll come back." He said, "Come back in two weeks and I'll give you a
green card." He thought she wasn't going to come back to India, so he
might as well give her a green card and not a tourist visa. She came to
visit for one month, and in the meantime, while she was there, I found
a drafting job in Piscataway, New Jersey. I was glad for the job but realized that I was a horrible drafter. As luck would have it, my young son
had to get a vaccination, which gave him a high fever with convulsions.
We went to the hospital in an ambulance, and they admitted him and
gave me a prescription to buy medicine. I thought, *Where am I going
to get the money to buy medicine?* My new roommate didn't have the
money to give me even twenty dollars, and so Padma's mother loaned
us money to buy the medicine. My son was okay, and Padma later
returned to India to finish her studies.

MY ENTRY INTO THE NUCLEAR INDUSTRY

In the meantime, I saw an advertisement in the Philadelphia paper for
a mechanical engineer who could design pipes for nuclear plants. I
applied and got the job. I just couldn't imagine that now my salary was
$1,300 a month, which was a lot of money. I started the job, and for the
first time in my life I had money. I shared an apartment with someone
I knew from Benares IIT who was single. My employer wanted me
to work as much overtime as I wanted. The money was good. They
liked me because I could design these pipes. Design was done by hand

and given to drafting people to draft. This is how I became a nuclear engineer. I went to school in the evenings and got further education in nuclear engineering at the University of Pennsylvania. The company was so nice, they allowed me to work from four to eleven p.m. so I could go to school and work. They increased my salary from $1,300 to $1,700. They were so good to me. Everything was finally working out. Padma finished up her MD internship, and my daughter was born in Philadelphia. We moved to Lindenwood, New Jersey, which was close to Atlantic City, and had a car to get around. Padma would drive me to the train station and go back to take care of the children.

Bechtel in San Francisco had an advertisement seeking a nuclear process engineer. They hired me and moved me to San Francisco, and that is where I started with a salary of $50,000, which was a lot of money in those days. Then I joined a start-up company called Nuclear Services Corporation (later called Quadrex). In 1977, I had a reputation as a good Bechtel junior executive who got things done, and I had secured good connections, such as employees at GE. I could speak with any utility about hiring our company. So I joined Nuclear Services in Campbell, California.

PRE-IPO AND PUBLIC COMPANY CHALLENGES

Padma was doing her residency at Santa Clara Valley Medical Center, and we had two small children. I was working in a start-up company, not realizing I was never going to be home. After six months, as our financial situation improved, I could afford to send my children to a good school—Harker Academy. Harker was a lifesaver for our family. As Padma was finishing her residency and I was traveling all over the world, Harker had a dorm where the kids could go if we didn't pick them up. They could eat and sleep there and do their homework. Financially, we were okay. Nuclear Services Corporation became Quadrex, and it went public in 1981. We opened up at $15–$16 per share, and it went up to $90. But it was no longer fun. I didn't look forward to going to work. Pre-IPO, I could do anything I wanted to do. Once we were public, I had to seek approval for everything from the board or president. One day I got so angry with the board that I quit. I took a year off.

In the meantime, I got very interested in buying properties in New York and Hawaii. New York because my son went to Princeton, and Hawaii because we went there for vacations. So I started buying residential real estate. The timing was right. I spent lots of time with the children

Sat and Padma's family
(photo by Mark Kopko)

because during my Quadrex days I was never able to spend any time with them. Then I decided to join another company that was started by a friend. It was a niche nuclear engineering idea for fracture mechanics. It is a very boutique field that you had to be an expert to start in. If you look at nuclear power plants, there are two types: boiling water and pressurized water. Pressurized water reactors use steam generators, such as at Diablo Canyon and Fukushima, and that was my area of expertise. We built the company up to 250 people, and, in 2006, we got a good offer from a German company. Since then, I have been investing money with VKRM (Kumar Malavalli's investment group), and that takes time, along with managing our properties. We fortunately sold several properties before the subprime problems, but we have many that we don't want to sell and have a property management company that takes care of them.

THOUGHTS ON IMMIGRATION

If I were asked what to do about the US immigration policy, I would recommend that anyone who gets a master's or PhD in a US university should be given a green card. Attach the green card to his or her degree. Those are the people who are going to make this country move forward. Go to the TiE (www.tie.org) conference and you can see how young people who have only been in this country for a few years are already making a difference.

MY FAMILY IN INDIA AND STAYING IN AMERICA

The day I left India was the biggest setback for my father. He loved me so much. He wanted me to stay in the US for a year and come back. He got very sick, but he gave me his blessings for life. He was the wise elder. So many people were connected to him through working on his land. Before my father passed away, I went back to India often. After he died, I did go back to see my mother, and whatever my mother wanted I gave her. She lived in India with my brother, and if she wanted a new car, she got it. She died in 2008—in her sleep. My mother saw me become financially successful, but my father didn't. He saw me struggling. When my second sister was getting married, I had two children, a wife, and a house. I couldn't tell my father I didn't have the money for the wedding, so I went to the Bechtel Credit Union to borrow the money. I sent $5,000 for the wedding. In those days one dollar was seven rupees. She had a beautiful wedding.

I never desired to go back to India to live after a year or two, because I was in the nuclear business and there was no future for nuclear in India. I didn't have to wait long for citizenship. We had to go into the power plants, which requires US citizenship, so Bechtel got me citizenship after only six months. My family sold the farm in Punjab, as my brother lived in Delhi. I built a religious shelter, in my father's name, where poor people can go and stay overnight. I never had time for hobbies during all those working years. I worked to give my children everything they wanted. My only passion, as such, is the NFL (National Football League). There's lots of strategy involved. It's the only game I really like to see, especially the 49ers.

When I think back to when the government of India gave me eight dollars, they told me that I would always be Indian and that someday I would come back and repay the dues to my country. It was always a symbolic moment. We all have to give back, not only in India but here too. There are lots of kids who are very intelligent, but they can't go to college because they can't afford it. In India it takes $2,500 a year to support a person through engineering or medical school. So I support kids from India through the Foundation for Excellence (FFE) in Sunnyvale, California. We need to help the children here too. They have parents who don't have the money to send them to college.

America is the place that gave us what we have. And now I need to help more in the US.

FRANKLIN GUMMADI, MINNESOTA

BORN IN GUNTUR, ANDHRA PRADESH

EDITOR: *Franklin's story is unique among the others in this book in that he never did receive the eight dollars from the Indian government. Instead he immigrated with his wife Shirley, whom he met in India, where she was visiting. They were married in India and in Minnesota. Franklin's work has had many twists and turns, including time at 3M that was interrupted by an autoimmune illness that left him completely paralyzed. He provided years of leadership to the India Association of Minnesota. Now his and Shirley's life work is with the marginalized people in India through an organization they founded, PUSHPA.*

Mine was a unique journey—I never had to go through the same process as other people. It was easier for me to emigrate from India because in 1965 I met my American future wife, Shirley, from Minnesota, who lived in India at the time. She came to India as a short-term missionary from the Lutheran Church in America, on a three-year assignment to teach English at a mission school in Guntur, India.

I was born in the town of Guntur in Andhra Pradesh, about two hundred miles from Hyderabad or Chennai—five to six hours by train or car to either city. At the time, Guntur was a small town and the main

Franklin Gummadi in India
(photo courtesy of Franklin Gummadi)

industry was agriculture—mainly Virginia tobacco for export. Guntur has since switched from tobacco to academics and has now transformed into a big center with colleges and high schools, most of them being private schools, with people coming from all over to study. There are lots of preparatory schools for the big national exams for engineering and medicine and the like. It's almost like a factory. But it is now also a chili-growing capital, and traders come from all around the world. Only a small portion of chili production is mechanized, with most of the farmers on two- to five-acre plots and rarely more than ten acres. Cotton is also a main crop.

My father worked as a revenue officer for the State of Andhra Pradesh, and before my mother was married, she was a teacher. My father had to move frequently for his work, and as our family grew, I was sent off to live with my mother's parents because I was the oldest. I spent sixth grade in my grandparents' house in a place about eighty miles away from my family. I felt left out being sent away. But that year I learned a great deal from my grandfather, who was a teacher in the same school I attended. My grandfather taught at the high school level, so I was not in his class.

My father was an early graduate of college. He never shared how he got to college. Someone in his village, I guess it was missionaries, saw that he had aptitude and knew how to work hard, and they helped him get to college. He never shared anything. He was a very, very private man.

My father's mother was illiterate, and my father had no memory of his father, who died during World War I. He had been sent overseas and was never seen again, although we do know that he came back as a patient in a military hospital. My father knows they received a bundle of paper after his father's death, which was delivered to the local village clerk, who handled the village affairs. My grandmother never saw the papers or knew what it was all about. My brothers and I thought about going to the military hospital and the big cemetery there. We'd like to find something in their records, but we haven't done this yet.

My father was in the revenue department of the government and traveled to rural areas surveying government land to transfer to people. I don't know how the government qualified land for people to acquire. It was all unclaimed government land that he would survey. I didn't know much about my father's work. He did not share about his background or his birthplace (a remote village near Guntur). He finally shared his story toward his last days of life, and he died at the age of 101. He was the longest-living government pension drawer in that state. The government, I am sure, didn't plan on having to pay retirement that long, as he retired at the age of fifty-five!

SCHOOLING IN REMOTE VILLAGES AND KNOWING YOUR JOB: DO WELL

The first memory I have of school is that it was in such a remote village that you had to get to it by a horse-drawn carriage or bullock cart. Not even a bus would go there. It was a very backward area of the district. We spent three years there, and I went to first, second, and third grade at that remote village school. Mother was at home during this time. I now travel in villages, with a project that Shirley and I started for families of the poorest caste—those that are rat and snake catchers. We try to encourage parents in these tribes to get their children educated. I compare that school of my memories to the government schools in these villages. Every village has a government school up to the fifth grade. Even now, the teachers don't show up until late. They probably spend about two hours at most in the school.

My father and mother were very strict disciplinarians, and the first thing was that you had to be good at school. This was not ambiguous. You knew your job. All the children knew this. It was the message the parents gave. In the sixth grade, when I was sent away (to my grandparents' place), I was a very good student. The class elected me as the class leader even though I was new to the school. Even though I was away from my parents and brothers and sister, I was encouraged by the others. My grandfather was also a very regimented person. He would have his walk, meditate for an hour, eat breakfast, and go to school. This was his routine. We were Christians. My great-grandmother, on my mother's side, was the first to convert to Christianity in our area. On my father's side, the grandparents were the converts. Every Sunday after church, we would come home and go to the big market. There was no market open during the week to buy something. On Sunday everyone would bring in their produce and animals and wares. My grandfather would do the marketing, and my grandmother would not get out for anything. We had no help in the home, as my grandmother did everything.

As I reflect on this phase of life, I see there was both good and bad. I had lots of kids around, and there were teachers' families with children, as we lived in staff quarters. We would go fishing and have fun in any free time I was given. I was good in sciences. The language at home was Telugu, and no English was spoken at home. In sixth grade, you started learning the English alphabet. By the time you completed your school, you had a large language background. We learned all sorts of poetry, from John Milton to Wadsworth—mainly it was memorization in those days. I only felt comfortable with English after completing two years of college in Guntur.

LEAVING HOME FOR BOMBAY

I left home to go to Bombay [now Mumbai] on my own, along with a friend named John Milton, without permission from my parents. I wanted to explore. I didn't tell them exactly where I was until I came back after a year. They didn't say anything. They had found out where I was and that I was safe. I worked as a painter in a large British construction company in a huge office building. We lived and worked in the same building. This was 1956 to 1958, and we didn't know anything like Bollywood or even Bombay, as we do now. The company had a cafeteria where we could eat. We had a good time. There was another Gujarati who was our contact. He told me we wouldn't last long as painters, and he told us to join this other man. After three months of painting, we quit and joined the Gujarati job. We worked for a Gujarati businessman as salespeople. He got dried fruit from the Middle East, and he would package it up for us to sell to restaurants. We would go on bicycles all over the city of Bombay and get orders. We would get the packaged goods and deliver them to the customers.

After one year, I went back to Guntur. There wasn't a great deal of choice. My father and friends convinced me to come back. I was nineteen and started all over again. I trained for one year as a pharmacist in a hospital. I took the training and worked there while I lived at home. After that I applied to a pharmacy school at a big medical center, Christian Medical College in Chennai. I got my bachelor's in pharmacy at that school. Christian Medical College was a hospital and college that had a foundation from an international conglomerate of churches to support its activities.

WORKING IN A HOSPITAL PHARMACY AND SELLING MEDICAL EQUIPMENT

I worked in the hospital pharmacy in the summer while I was in training. While I was in pharmacy school, the Christian Medical College was very cosmopolitan, with doctors and nurses from all over the world. I had an American boss, a Mr. Victor Oesterling. For the pharmacy degree, I did have to take a National Exam and then be registered, which was different from the exam. I was a registered pharmacist in New Delhi in the 1960s. The pharmacy college office manager asked me, "Franklin, would you be interested in going to Qatar?" He gave me the address and told me how to apply. I had an idea that I needed to get away from India for betterment. I knew I would thrive better outside of India. In those days, a few people went to Kuwait and Saudi Arabia. The guys who did immigrate did quite well, and worked for American companies such as Aramco, which had its own hospitals. Today the people that go to the Muslim countries are Muslims from Kerala, although many Kerala Christians migrated also. The Muslims had a better chance. I wrote some correspondence, but nothing happened and I didn't push it. I am sure my parents wanted me to get married, as I was in my early twenties.

I was interviewed by a company in Delhi to sell medical equipment and travel all over South India. They interviewed me in Chennai, and I was selected. I didn't have any idea of how to present myself to this job. My boss told me he would give me his suit but told me that I would swim in it as he was huge. I wore a tie and shirt. They weren't looking for someone in an Indian shirt. They wanted someone to talk with surgeons and the decision makers who bought safety equipment and anesthesia dispensers for hospitals. After I took the job as a salesman, I worked and traveled in Delhi and all over India, except Calcutta. I had an Anglo-Indian chap with me, an ex–Air Force person from the time of the British. He and I traveled together, and we had very good times. Work was work, but we had the freedom to do whatever we wanted and go wherever we wanted.

I quit the sales job after two years, as I was tired of traveling. In those days, you would travel first-class on the trains, and we could stay in the best hotels available, but it was still hectic. I quit the job and told Mr. Oesterling, who was now the chief pharmacist in Vellore, that I wanted a job as a pharmacist. He got requests from all over the country for people. He asked me if I wanted to go to Ambala, Haryana, where there was a vacancy. I didn't need an interview. I was on my way.

MEETING MY FUTURE WIFE, SHIRLEY

I met Shirley in Delhi, where I had been working for just six months. She had come to an all-India student conference. In those days, they had the nice custom of going to the train station to send you off and receive you. My friend from Guntur was going to meet the Guntur people arriving at the station. He just happened to meet me on the way and asked me to come along, and so we met Shirley's group at the station. We caught each other's eye at that meeting. Shirley happened to stay there another week to go to an American dentist. We met a couple of times. It wasn't taboo for a white woman and an Indian man to be together. It was very natural, but then, Delhi was an international city—actually much more so then, with all the hippies coming into the city.

We hit it off almost immediately, knowing we liked each other. I was very fluent in English, which is what Shirley spoke, and had good diction, so that made it easier for us. We didn't really date because that is how it was in those days. We were always in the company of someone else. I did pursue her, though. Shirley went to Madras, and I just

Shirley and Franklin
(photo courtesy of Franklin Gummadi)

"happened" to be walking by the Baptist guesthouse where she was staying. Shirley went to the hospital in Vellore, and she stayed in the home of the chief pharmacist there. I, of course, just happened to show up there. She went to the hills for the summer, and another missionary friend brought me up to see her.

ATTITUDES TOWARD MARRIAGE

My parents met Shirley, but Shirley's parents had not met me. Shirley's parents came from Minneapolis to visit India. They knew about me but didn't want to discuss us. My parents asked Shirley to bring her parents over to meet them. My parents didn't think anything would come of it anyway and thought we couldn't be serious. The experience was that white women marrying an Indian man wasn't like a traditional Indian marriage that would last. Shirley returned to the United States in 1967, and we didn't know how things were going to go. So my parents went ahead and found a girl for me. The issue had not come to the extent of them telling me I was going to marry the girl they selected—at least not yet. I was twenty-four years old. When Shirley and I talked about being serious, our idea was if she came back we would settle in India and I would find a government job. She would be teaching, and we would make a life in India with what meager means we had. We envisioned that life would be simple and things would get better and better. But this wasn't the case for my family. All this was happening when I was in Haryana. I was working in an American Presbyterian hospital. Within three months, I was promoted to be the business manager, to be in charge of all the medical staff, including the office. It was a two-hundred-bed teaching hospital, with several international staff; the guy in charge was a New Zealander. I was a foreigner in my own country. I came from down south with an entirely different culture and practices. I was in the land of Sikhs. Things were going well, but things change fast in situations like this. Often a new administrator comes and brings his own people, and there are different outcomes than what I expected. Church institutions were like this, with a political morass, as they are today.

I wanted a steady job with benefits, so I applied for a job at Indian Railways. I got the job, but I didn't take it. Many of the employees on the railway were Anglo-Indians; they had the jobs of the operational staff as engineers, the frontline people, but were not highly regarded. These were the facts of prejudice within India. In some circumstances, we saw that the Anglo-Indians were almost reduced to begging. I was getting vibes from Shirley about the job because it didn't support upward mobility. So I kept the job in Haryana, and Shirley finished up graduate school back in the United States. Although we corresponded, it was too expensive to call.

Shirley received a Fulbright scholarship to study early childhood education, doing fieldwork for her thesis in India. It was a cliffhanger, as she was enrolled in a school in New York City where one of the professors was on the Fulbright advisement group. He would tell her the status of her application as it was going through the process. He didn't have anything to do with her being accepted, but he kept her informed. All of a sudden, he dropped out of sight the last two to three weeks of the process. Shirley was thirteenth or fourteenth in line, and a week before she went back to Minnesota she learned she received the scholarship. It is amazing that thirteen people had something better to do! So we were back together in India. We hadn't seen each other in a year. We actually didn't see each other much. I was still out in the hinterlands and only had time off over Christmas.

THE DECISION TO IMMIGRATE TO THE UNITED STATES

We decided that I was going to immigrate to the United States. We did this blindly. We had no imagination. I would come to the United States to meet Shirley's family, find some meager job for a couple of years to pay back the expense of this visit, and then return to India. Shirley's family somehow came around to the idea of us being together. They had not even met me until I came to the US. We got married in a civil wedding in Delhi in 1969 in support of my visa. We also got married in a church in Minnesota.

There weren't that many visa applicants those days, and therefore the process was fairly straightforward. They asked me if I wanted to change the order of my name from Gummadi Joseph Franklin. That was the only thing they asked me. I told them it was okay the way it was, although it was not very smart of me to do so. Franklin became our last name, although it was actually my baptized name. When I came to the United States, Gummadi became my first name, although it was my surname. This became awkward when my two brothers came here later. We came back to the United States with a great deal of debt. We borrowed money from friends and family to relocate. We were completely broke. We didn't even have the eight dollars that was given to some Indian immigrants. We ate hot dogs in New York. We were there for two or three weeks as Shirley was finishing up some of her academic work. We stayed with a girlfriend she had met at the Salvation Army dormitory during grad school; by now, she had a radical live-in boyfriend. There was nothing in the refrigerator; the girlfriend came back late from work and didn't bother to cook. It was a miserable experience. I went knocking on many doors.

Shirley had hopes of a teaching job, and I had been encouraged to apply for a job and possible study at the University of Michigan. Neither panned out. You get used to relying on connections, a form of cronyism, as is done in private institutions in India. A missionary nurse who knew the chief pharmacist at the University of Michigan naively promised to help me get into graduate school, although at that time the Indian qualifications were not considered equal to American qualifications. She told me, "Franklin, don't worry—I know the chief pharmacist at the university in Ann Arbor, and you won't have any difficulty getting a job through him." We went there and they said, "Wait a couple of months—right now it's tight." So we had to come back to Minnesota.

EARLY DISAPPOINTMENTS AND STRUGGLES

We faced the disappointment in Michigan and the struggle in New York. We didn't know what we would do. And also we knew Shirley's dad had been totally against her marrying someone from another color and culture. We had already been married in India, but I can't remember if they knew this. Her parents came to pick us up at the airport. We dropped off the suitcases, and Shirley's dad and I went on some errands. He was a smoker and offered me one; we both lit up, and we instantly became friends. That lasted to his death. We became so close and had lots of bonding experiences. Fortunately, I quit smoking a while later.

Shirley's dad was very affable, and his earlier fears of her marrying an outsider changed. We stayed with Shirley's folks in North Minneapolis. I took Shirley's dad's broken-down three-speed bike and went everywhere knocking on doors. I went to Honeywell and General Mills and pharmacy agencies. I bicycled all over Minneapolis, St. Paul, and the suburbs. We both worked in an hourly wage job, doing inventory in a store for a couple of days. We bought an old chair from a hotel that was closing, and Shirley reupholstered it. Shirley applied for a job as a teacher and got one right away. We got married in May, and she found out she got the job in June but had to wait until September to start. I was still going around and inquiring and applying.

JOINING 3M IN MINNESOTA

I was called for an interview at a 3M facility in Arden Hills in the Twin Cities. It was during the Vietnam War. Shirley's mother dropped me off, as it was a rainy morning. I got dropped off at the entrance but had to walk a few blocks to get inside. My suit was totally wet. I interviewed all day to work in developing radioactive diagnostics that were going to be used in urology and other specialties. My pharmacy experience was back in activation. The hiring manager told me that he would let me know soon and that everything looked good. I told him I had no ride back home. He dropped me off in North Minneapolis and in doing so said they were talking about making me an offer. The next week the offer came. I was expecting some ordinary job, but it was a nice position with good money. On July 7, 1969, I became a 3M employee. Probation was about six months. I stayed at 3M until 2000.

My parents came to the United States when everything was good in 1974, just before we adopted our daughter Priya from India. When my parents came here, they had a wonderful visit. Their visit was documented in several of the newspapers. My parents weren't encouraging of our adoption, thinking we were only trying to do some great social service. But a year later, our daughter came to join us. She was seventeen months old when she came from India.

THE CHALLENGE OF A PARALYZED BODY

I worked for eleven years and took a trip to India for my brother's wedding in 1981. I came back severely ill. I had caught something in India. A week later, on Valentine's Day, I couldn't get up from my bed—I was totally paralyzed. I had Guillain-Barré syndrome. It is an autoimmune response, and they still don't know where it comes from. I was like a cadaver and on a respirator for three months and in the hospital for nine months (from Valentine's Day to Halloween). Thankfully, I was fit because I had played soccer on a local team. The people at the hospital were terrific and told me that eventually I would get better. I came home in a wheelchair. My recovery was one day at a time.

We adopted our second child, Prashant, in 1981. He and his sister are about six years apart in age. We got the court guardianship papers for Prashant two weeks after I came home from India, but by that time I was already hospitalized. He was ready to come, at six months old, and we had court guardianship ready in Bombay, but we couldn't go get him to bring him home since I was sick. My mother went to Bombay to pick up Prashant and brought him to the United States. She didn't speak English, but she went and picked up her grandchild and came here by herself.

THE INDIAN COMMUNITY IN MINNESOTA

I was active in the Indian student community activities that were based at the University of Minnesota. We had fifty to sixty Indian students who were involved. We organized activities such as picnics, and we watched movies and talked. We also formed a group of Telugu-speaking students and others living in the community. We had a friend who spoke Telugu who worked for the army as an engineer and had done his PhD at the University of Minnesota. Irrespective of our backgrounds or which languages of India we spoke, we enjoyed our time together. There are now about thirty thousand Indians (people of Indian origin, or PIOs) in the metropolitan area of Minneapolis and St. Paul, but most of them came in the last ten to twenty years. Now Chicago has the largest community of Indians in the central United States. In the 1960s and '70s, I believe, there were fewer than one hundred PIOs there.

We came here just to get to know my wife's family for a couple of years and go back to India. Every once in a while, Shirley asked when we were going back to India. I kept saying, "Next year, next year." Our dream of going back to India was there continuously. We made plans and took steps by corresponding with the Indian government. I was going to start a small company in the pharmaceutical industry making generics. The government wrote beautiful, encouraging letters. I became a member of a share-purchasing consortium. This was something the government of India cooked up, but the result was always the bureaucracy with nothing but nice letters. Things are different now. We tried to go back but it was "one foot here and one foot there." We formed a Telugu community that was going well, but when I got sick I was disconnected from everything. All our friends, our church, and these groups were very supportive and voluntarily came to help our family and offered money and support. They always said that they were here to help us.

THEY REMEMBERED MY PREVIOUS WORK: RETURNING TO 3M

After coming home, it took me two years, until 1984, to come back to work. I started [back to] work one hour a day. A taxi would come to pick me up along with my wheelchair. They don't hold jobs that long for anyone, so I had to be the new kid on the block, starting all over again. Who would hire a guy who is coming back with half a life and who has lost touch with all the aspects of the job? I did some clerical things just to get a routine going. Work increased to three, four, and five hours, but then I needed to get a substantial job. Fortunately, I had some good people that I worked with, and they were in higher positions by that time. They were familiar with my work and agreed to hire me as an advanced engineer in the microbiology group. Luckily they had great projects for me to apply myself to. They had acquired a company in the Netherlands. I was supposed to be the liaison with this company. They asked me to travel internationally when I was back on my feet. I would work in microbiology until I retired in 2000.

I was not a citizen of the United States at this time because we were always preparing to go back to India. I am now. I recently applied for a PIO card, and they wanted a stack of information that had to be submitted to the consulate. It is a special visa with the Indian government, and my frequent trips to India helped me.

After I started working again, the community asked me to become a board member of the India Association. I told them I wasn't ready to do that quite yet. I participated as a member instead. In the early '90s, I started to be part of the board leadership of the India Association of Minnesota. I was the president in 1998, before that a board member, and after the chair of the Advisory Committee. What I learned from this volunteer board work, in spite of the diversity of the people and communities of India, and in spite of all the bickering for the rights of the people from each state [in India], is that we could do in the United States what we couldn't do in India. The India Association of Minnesota was truly a cross-section of India. They asked me to form an advisory group to the association, and I eventually became an advisory board chair to the India Association. They continue to do a phenomenal job.

COMMITMENT TO THE MARGINALIZED
COMMUNITIES OF INDIA: PUSHPA

Shirley and I started an organization called PUSHPA (meaning flower in Sanskrit), which works with a tribe in India called Yanadi—an indigenous people who are the rat and snake catchers in marginalized communities. They live off the land and go around during harvest times to do this work. There are at least a *lakh* [one hundred thousand] of them. We are in twelve hamlets in Andhra Pradesh. In every hamlet, they

Franklin with sewing machine for PUSHPA
(photo courtesy of Franklin Gummadi)

are still catching rats. It is not a full-time job any longer, but they are still doing it. They find other jobs during the rest of the year. They are in the caste with the untouchables, and most of them are not educated. They are migrant workers and not quite as nomadic as they used to be. During harvest time, they pack up their belongings for two to three months to do this work. Only the men do the work, but women do the supporting work.

We periodically return to India to visit family in Guntur, and we started PUSHPA right after retirement, as we had plans to go back to India that did not materialize. In some ways, you feel guilty for not accomplishing what you planned. The alternative is to go back to paid work and maybe encourage a few young people. Or maybe work as a consultant for a company and do our own thing. We debated the ideas, and my brother-in-law, who has been in development/NGO work, was involved. We discussed starting a pharmacy or other clinics. We did trial-and-error programs for three to four years. We learned a great deal and came to the conclusion that to help these people was the right thing to do. First we looked at donating a buffalo through Heifer International in honor of Shirley's birthday. Then we decided that we could do this directly. We spoke with many people; we looked at the statistics, and there are one hundred subtribes in India. In Andhra there are four major tribes. The people of the tribe we work with are the least empowered to claim their right as citizens of India, including [their right to] government grants and programs. They are not integrated into society and don't know how to get resources. Most resources are consumed by the gypsy tribe, and they secure about 97 percent of what the government allocates. They are go-getters and know how to work the system.

We had never met these people before we started. When we started working, I had second thoughts to our approach. They didn't seem motivated nor did they seem to care. Even today it isn't that easy. After all these years, we have found leaders, and they have accepted our message. They were suspicious of us even though we speak the same language (Telugu). They think we want something from them. They don't speak out, they nod their heads, and they go back to the same routine. Recently we have seen some results. Some villages do want their children educated, which is our main focus—as education should be number one for all parents. We helped them use their assets, their health and wealth, as best we could. They had to have a stake in the improvements.

ORGANIZING, MONITORING, AND ADVISING

We started by giving grants and told them that this was their money and they had to manage and rotate the money. They could open a small store, get a bicycle, or implement other ideas based on micro-finance. I met with the community group and suggested that they organize, get a name, register themselves as an entity, and open a bank account.

Franklin addresses the village
(photo courtesy of Franklin Gummadi)

This way the community got the grant. They did form a group, but they didn't meet as a group to discuss the issues of the community. It was like someone had to ask them, "Did you meet last month?" and "What were the issues of the community?" We didn't want to monitor them too closely. They need the freedom to organize and to move ahead. This was not a good approach. In retrospect, they weren't ready. We probably should have done better organizing, monitoring, advising, and keeping track of what was going on. The

motto is "Helping peo-
ple help themselves," but
how would they know to
come up with the idea to
ask, "Please help us"? How
can they keep track of
finances? They don't keep
track of anything. They
just live day to day. This
still has to be addressed.

We have group meet-
ings twice a year. I go to
them, and Shirley has
been once, this year. I
make two trips of two to

Franklin and Shirley with the PUSHPA team
(photo courtesy of Franklin Gummadi)

three months at a time. After these ten years, I believe we will see a
person coming out of the community ready to really take charge. We
would like to have that person come from this community. We are sub-
contracting another NGO to help us. We have some people we hire
for projects, but the overall organization will come from this NGO.
Now we have high school graduates and college dropouts. We need
to work with these young people, who are not well guided, to at least
finish some college education. They don't need to graduate, but they
need to demonstrate that they have initiative. Our board members ask
us why we think they will come to work for PUSHPA when they can
go work for the government or some IT organization. For PUSHPA,
they don't need to have finished college, and we have people who have
opened some small businesses and shops, and a seamstress. We are
learning how we can best help them. Until they get a voice themselves,
we have to continually ask where we are going and where we can take
this organization. We have a board in India and a board here. Half of
the India board consists of members from the tribes from different
villages within India so they have a voice.

The organization is our pleasure. Our children may or may not
become involved. We want this to be an autonomous transfer of leadership. The first thing is that the people in India have to become a
fully functional board. The board was just started a year ago, and they

became the spokespeople. They have to identify who will be the leaders from the tribes and encourage the locals to take over. The India board will eventually function as the owners of the organization. It will take time. They have to realize what they need to do themselves. The government has started to give them small strips of land to build houses, as now they live in mud huts. The government has a scheme to subsidize toilets. We have hired a nearby literate person to do evening tutoring to help the students.

THOUGHTS ON EDUCATION

When I think about educating children in our area, and as much as I know about secondary education, I feel we distract from true education with lots of extracurricular activities. There is too much freedom in the school district. This is how it has been, with budgets allotted to art supplies, sports, and music. Very little attention is given to the education of the person. Yes, you need these other things, but the focus must be on the person's learning. Shirley has been a teacher. She notes how little classroom time is spent in the process of learning required subjects. Yes, it is a diverse community. Minneapolis schools have fifty-seven different first languages. But the main issue is that no matter where or when you go to school, your focus has to be on education. Even both of my grandchildren have focused their lives around sports. This is their priority. In India they would be going to a tutor before and after school.

Everyone I know in India—mother, father, and children—does their morning wash-up and the children go to tutors before school, and they do the same after school. This is the other extreme. They don't have time to be kids. There has to be a balance between the two methods. Here in the United States, they need to concentrate on education. Education is the job of the child, and after they finish this they can do other things. Parents have to go to the parent-teacher conferences, and they have to supervise the work of the child and get a tutor if needed. But a child must own their education and have a serious fundamental knowledge.

ABOUT PUSHPA: PEOPLE USING SELF-HELP TO PUSH AHEAD

PUSHPA is the result of our commitment to India, which we've had ever since we were married. We had hoped to go back to India earlier in our lives to help people but were not able to do so. When we began PUSHPA after retirement, we chose to help the "poorest of the poor." Our premise is that everyone has an innate, God-given capacity to learn and grow. We understand that people benefit most from development projects based on their own choices and active participation.

Currently we work with nine villages. We have a teacher and an evening school [tutoring] facility in each. The facility is a place for the community to meet, as well as [to come for] the evening school. Approximately 250 kids attend these schools, combined, in the evenings for two to three hours. We have a sewing school that teaches tailoring to young women. Periodically we conduct community meetings as a form of leadership development. Health camps are conducted occasionally in collaboration with local resources and doctors from town. Small groups of American volunteers have helped our villagers build latrines in one village, community centers in others, and they encourage the villagers by working alongside them. We welcome volunteers who share PUSHPA's vision and willingness to work alongside villagers on projects of the villagers' own choosing.

As for results, we do not have systematic, solid data collection yet. Reasons include irregular attendance and mobility of villagers and undisclosed social pressures from some people in other groups with whom the PUSHPA villagers' children attend public schools, and as the PUSHPA villagers themselves assert their right to use public space. Health care and community building have been emphasized with each village group from the time PUSHPA began working with them. Each village was initially challenged to identify elders to form a working leadership and create a group identity, registering with local authorities as a prerequisite for working together with PUSHPA to identify and address their needs—one of which is a community center at which to meet. If you don't have [a community center], you can't have an evening school.

We have learned that it is not easy to work with people who come from nomadic backgrounds or for them to come together as a community. Even now, people live here for some time, migrate, and come back. In a sense, it is a very hopeless situation. Most parents in our communities don't have high expectations for their children. Only a small percentage do, and they don't have a clear idea of how to realize these expectations. Practically speaking, it's not their priority. What they are mainly concentrating on is the battle for their day-to-day survival: work and wages. Strong leadership and role models are lacking in most of the villages.

So far, since PUSHPA began working with villagers these last ten years, there is increased interest in children's education in all the villages. Parents are sending their children for the classes PUSHPA evening schools offer, and the children attend enthusiastically. Villages that didn't have any students going on to high school in the past now have children who've finished elementary school and entered high school. But the government school curriculum has been changed to English, and students at every level are floundering. Until now, only five or six have attempted college, all of whom have failed and/or dropped out, except one boy who has gone on to study engineering with a college of engineering. One girl has finished two years of college and is studying to prepare for the competitive exams for a government job. We've graduated around one hundred women and girls at our sewing center since 2005. Records were kept by the teacher, and certificates were awarded for the six-month course.

In the future, we hope to help the communities envision and find their own solutions to the needs that arise while growing healthy families and communities. We will continue to encourage development of leadership and support and supplement children's education within the community and beyond. We want to see the youth succeed at every level of education and become contributing members of the workforce and their communities. We hope that they will eventually take the initiative and become the leaders and role models that their communities, and PUSHPA, need. In the last two years we have hired additional teachers to teach English, math, and science to high school students in villages where there is a need, and where local teachers are available. We need to continue to draw educated persons from nearby communities and neighborhoods to teach in our evening schools, align expectations with government schoolteachers, improve the quality of instruction and skills in the sewing school, and convene community leaders to share ideas and common goals. Our original goal still stands: to help people help themselves to build healthy families and communities.

VISH MISHRA, SILICON VALLEY

BORN IN AGARAWA, UTTAR PRADESH, INDIA

EDITOR: *Vish's family life started in very rural India, and he knew that he had to own his own education no matter where he went to school. He immigrated to the United States for the purpose of securing a master's degree in engineering, but he was brought into the burgeoning world of mainframe computers (CDC and Burroughs) before joining the start-up networking company Excelan. Vish has been one of the backbone supporters of TiE and as a venture capitalist continues to identify and mentor entrepreneurs. Vish has developed a talent as an extraordinary networker.*

I first thought of emigrating from India when I was in high school, around 1962. I always enjoyed reading about America because it was a great country. The brother of one of my friends in high school had come to the US to go to school, and I learned about America from him. I was inspired to listen to the American story. I learned from things such as *Time* magazine, which was very widely read in India. When John F. Kennedy became president, *Time* had a big story on him. He inspired me because he was young and became president of

Vish Mishra
(photo courtesy of Vish Mishra)

this country. I vividly remember seeing Kennedy's photo in the magazine, and I kept it for a long time.

I grew up in a rural area in a small village in northern India in the state of Uttar Pradesh (UP). UP is the largest state within India. We come from the Brahmin caste—father was the local priest, and he would perform all the ceremonies right from birth until the final time of life. He didn't get paid a regular salary. When he went to perform the rituals, the people would pay him with a sack of rice or clothes or something else. We owned land so we had access to agriculture. Farming was all contract farming for rice and wheat; we owned the land, but someone else farmed it. I presume the land was inherited and some was purchased, I am not sure. My mother did not work outside the home. My father was a learned man, and everyone came to him for advice. He didn't go to college, but the learning was passed on from generation to generation. He learned from his father and local mentors. He learned in Sanskrit and they spoke a dialect of Hindi. Many languages are spoken in the "Hindi belt"—I think there is a new dialect every ten to fifteen miles.

I had a brother and sister, so that made three of us. I was the middle child, with my brother being seven years older and my sister three years younger. Everyone just relied on their own family, and we ate whatever was grown, including all the milk from the goats and cows. We were vegetarian and had many fruit trees, such as mangoes. We even purchased our clothes locally.

I attended the local elementary school that was in a small town of probably not more than five hundred people. We had no way to judge whether the elementary teachers were qualified or not. We had two teachers, and whatever they said, that is what we did. All the kids were in one room. We started the class with a prayer, which was a devotional song about God. Then you sit down and you have your morning classes.

The teaching was oral. You learned your numbers and math tables that way. You never had to have tools because you relied on memorization. I enjoyed learning. Because my brother was older, he had gone to the same elementary school. When he went to middle school, he started learning English, and I learned from him. We spoke Hindi at home, and I only spoke English with my brother.

I finished my fourth or fifth grade in the elementary school, and I had to go to another village for middle school. One day my brother took me to his middle school, and while I was waiting for him, the principal came over to ask me what I was studying and if I could do the math tables. After the query he spoke up and said I was too advanced for the work in that school, so I was brought into seventh grade and skipped three complete grades. One moment I was waiting for my brother, and the next thing I know, I was moving ahead rapidly! I was excited for the middle school curriculum, and I could figure out geometry and other mathematical concepts very easily. My father knew I was good in math, and his vision was that I would go study the science of astrology because I had the capacity to know in my head the positions of the sun, the planets, and the moon.

I finished middle school at that small school, and in 1959 I was admitted to the high school in another town. The high school encompassed grades nine, ten, eleven, and twelve. When it was time for high school, we moved to the other town as my brother was also in that school along with another boy from our town. We made our own dormitory. We rented a place and had a cook to help us and someone to do our clothes and maintain our place. The cook was another young boy.

When we wanted to go to the village, we biked and walked to get there. When we had monsoons, the roads would be washed out from the floods. In the morning we'd go on the roads, and by the evening everything would be flooded. Under these circumstances, when you crossed the field, you just carried your bike through the water.

We had excellent teachers in our school and they were very collegial. Being a good student, and with the help of the teachers and my other interests, I had a solid basis for science, math, and other languages. The science and math teachers were really very good and they inspired and challenged me. One of my teachers in high school taught me to play chess; he was good, and I was glad when I beat him. He

was teaching me and I was playing with the teachers. That was exciting. I have to admit I was a teacher's favorite, and when it was time
for projects, they gave me special assignments to lead and tutor other
students. I tried to be inspiring to my fellow students and teachers.
The principal was fantastic. He took a liking to me, and because I had
learned English, I could choose between the Hindi medium or the
English medium. In the ninth grade, I chose the English medium. I
already had a background in Hindi and Sanskrit. At this point, I took
all my tenth and twelfth grade state exams in English, including the
exams in math, chemistry, and biology. I wasn't alone in this area as
there were others that were comfortable in English too. State exams
were the same throughout all of India, in contrast to the local exams.

THE FOUNDATION FOR ATTENDING
BENARES HINDU UNIVERSITY

While I was in high school, the one university in North India that was
well regarded was in the holy city of Benares (now known as Varanasi)—
Benares Hindu University (BHU). In 2016, the university was one hundred years old. It was built as a central university, because they would
admit students from all over India as well as foreign students. BHU had
a very strong reputation, along with being in the holy city for Hindus.
It is ironic because my full name is Vishwanath (lord/master of the universe). When my mother was pregnant with me, my parents went on
a pilgrimage to this holy city, including the Vishwanath Temple dedicated to Lord Shiva, one part of the Hindu trinity. There was a great
deal of knowledge around the university and I thought that this would
be a good school for me to attend. The principal and teachers in the
high school all supported this idea. They were learned people, and the
father of one of my other friends in high school had attended BHU, so
they all knew about this university. Because it was a highly regarded
university, to get accepted you had to have high marks and take exams.

The college exams were not held locally. There was only one exam
for the entire state, and it was administrated by the state. There was
only one place for anyone in UP to take the final exam, and everyone
had to appear. The state wanted to make sure that no one could see the
exams in advance—not the teachers or anyone—so the exams were

sealed. We had proctors or monitors, called invigilators. The exam was in a residential area, and you had to stay about a week until all the exams were done. After the exams were complete, you still didn't know how well you did. All the students who took the exams would see the result in the newspapers, at the same time as the public. The newspapers were published somewhere else, and when the time came for the newspapers to arrive, we all knew what time the train was coming to our town and that the newspaper listing would be posted outside of the train. We even knew which car held the posters.

SECURING A NATIONAL MERIT SCHOLARSHIP

I finished in what they call the First Class. I was top in my class and ranked very high for the entire state. As a result, I was given a National Merit Scholarship in both tenth and twelfth grades. The second scholarship lasted for four years, as long as I maintained good grades. At that time, in that high school, no one had yet won a National Merit Scholarship, which is based on the grades you receive. The principal saw this as a real honor. He even had to go to the district office in another town to find out how to deal with this award. My brother told me that if our father were alive he would be very proud of me. My father had passed long before this time. Mothers are always happy with your accomplishments and pray for their children every day—in India there is a prayer for everything.

I finished ninth and tenth grade, which was called high school, and I had two more years to go in the eleventh and twelfth grades, which was called intermediate college. With this scholarship, I got 50 rupees a month, with the exchange rate at the time of five rupees for a dollar. Even when I later came to the US, the exchange rate did not change much until recent years. When I finished twelfth grade, the scholarship doubled since I ranked first in my class, having taken the exam one more time with others in the state. The scholarship was very significant and increased up to 120 rupees a month. Being the recipient of this National Merit Scholarship financially supplemented my attendance at school through twelfth grade and into BHU, but there was the requirement to maintain my level in both the school and exams. In college you had to pass all the exams or you were held back an entire year and had to repeat all the classes for just failing one class.

WANTING TO BE AN ENGINEER

At this point I knew I wanted to be an engineer. I was good in biology, botany, and all the sciences and had thought about going to medical school. Still, I felt the field of engineering was much broader. I was inspired to go into engineering because one friend's father was the chief engineer at a local sugar mill. This was a huge influence because I knew what engineers did. He had to know all the machinery and all the processes: building, creating, and operating. I also read and studied at this time, trying to understand what is involved in engineering. Additionally, my teachers thought I would be a good engineer, and they knew me from our four years together.

We had all the advanced textbooks in my school. I didn't have all the knowledge and awareness at that time that I have now, but looking back on it, I see the value that the British created in the educational infrastructure in India. The foundation was laid by the British to create a solid educational system in a big way. With this background, I could go to BHU, which was the best university and number-one ranked engineering college in India. If you went to any factory or organization, all the chief engineers in the major industries were BHU graduates. Pune had an engineering college, and there was one other in North India. This meant that no matter where you went in the world, chief engineers who were educated in India would come from these schools. These schools were known to produce good engineers because we had all the labs and materials that were needed to study mechanical, civil, or electrical engineering. We had mining, metallurgical, and chemical engineering also. The vice chancellor of Sarvepalli Radhakrishnan University later became the president of India. The staff enjoyed the most coveted positions you could get, and you knew you were among the most learned people. Until the time I went to college, all the principals (heads of each college) were British people. Even after independence, the British remained at this university. The staff at the engineering college were amazing. They studied abroad and had PhDs from within and outside of India. It was a very tough school, and I felt very fortunate to spend four years and get my degree at BHU.

All four years I lived in a dormitory, which was the normal thing to do. We could either eat in the canteen or we could hire our own cook after planning the menu. We had no complaints about eating. We had better food at the engineering college than other colleges did. We planned the menu and told the chef what we wanted and he made it. My friend from back home was in the physics department and he ate with us. Everyone wanted to eat with us, and I was busy "adopting" others so they could eat with us too. I was eighteen or nineteen, but was the guardian (mentor/big brother) for kids who were sixteen and seventeen.

After we all had the final exam, I ranked in the First Class (in India, rankings are described as First Class, Second Class, Third Class, and so forth). I was now an electrical engineer. College was a five-year program, but I was able to enter in the second year, which was like an advanced placement, due to the area I had already studied in high school and intermediate college. While I was in my fourth year of college, I had figured out that I needed to go to the US embassy in Delhi to get information on the processes necessary to study in America. We knew lots of people who were going to America, and the professors understood all about studying in the colleges. A year before I graduated, in 1966, I went to the US embassy and told them I wanted to go to the US, and they gave me a list of schools to apply to. There was another agency within the embassy called US Information Services (USIS). Through the helpful organizations in the Embassy and USIS, I got the information I needed. Of course there was still filling out applications and forms, getting transcripts, securing recommendations— and all that had to be done early. I vividly remember writing what I considered a solid cover letter telling the college that I would need financial aid because without it I could not come. I graduated from BHU in June and by September of 1967 I was in America.

ACCEPTANCE AT NORTH DAKOTA STATE UNIVERSITY

I got my first response from North Dakota State University (NDSU) in Fargo, with an admission letter, congratulations and welcome, and the offer of a half-time teaching assistantship, which started right away, as a partial scholarship. It covered the college costs, which were about $200 to $240 per month, and my fixed expenses of about $75 for room and board in the dorm. I probably got more than eight dollars when I left India, as they saw that I had a scholarship from NDSU and therefore had a need. I didn't have to look for a job because I had the scholarship and teaching assistantship. Many people who came from India had to find jobs. They went to school for a while and had no stipend or scholarship, and realized they couldn't make it without a job or had to borrow money. I probably had it easier because I had structure and I knew what I was doing.

I did not know anyone at NDSU. I had developed a good friend at BHU who had a cousin who graduated from the Illinois Institute of Technology in Chicago in 1964. He was from Bombay [now Mumbai] and was working for IBM in Poughkeepsie. This friend's cousin invited me to fly from India into New York and from there back to Minneapolis and then to take a small plane to Fargo. The friends in New York not only greeted me but also took me to all the sights, such as Radio City Music Hall and other New York landmarks. With whatever money I had, we shopped for a corduroy-lined coat and a cap. I was able to land in North Dakota in September with something warm to wear.

I started my EE master's [electrical and electronics engineering] in Fargo. The head of the college, Professor Edwin Anderson (who I would be sharing the teaching with), personally came to meet me at the airport. Not only did he receive me, but he invited me to stay with his family, because the dorm wasn't ready. They were so welcoming, and I stayed with them in their house for three days. They had asked me what I ate for breakfast and I said, "Eggs." They cooked eggs and bacon. I had never even smelled bacon before. I woke wondering what the smell was. My room was in the attic, and the smells went up. I didn't like the smell at all. Even after moving to Minneapolis after I was married, when we were living in an apartment, neighbors would be making bacon for breakfast and the smell would be all over our apartment. It still stays with me. I was now in America, but I could only eat the eggs and not the bacon. They explained to me that this was something I had to tell people I wouldn't be eating. In college in India,

I learned to eat chicken and fish because we were with people from all over India who ate them.

Later, two of my BHU classmates, including the one whose cousin received me in New York, joined me at NDSU, and a third BHU classmate went to USC in Los Angeles to study. We took a summer break from NDSU for three months, took a Greyhound bus to Los Angeles, and stayed with our friend in his apartment. We did things just for fun, and two of us had saved enough money so we could buy a car. I think we bought a Corvair for $200. We learned to drive, got our driver's licenses, and put ten thousand miles on the car in three months. At the end of the summer, we sold the car for $100 and took the Greyhound back to North Dakota.

EXPECTING TO RETURN TO INDIA

I expected to go back to India after my master's. We developed this theory we called X+1 for the time of our return to India. X is of course the variable, and that is when we would go back. We all had these aspirations of coming to the US to get an education, maybe earn a bit of money, and go back to Mother India and help the country. I didn't have any notions of what I would do in India; we were already working in industry so I didn't want to go back to teaching. Those of us who came early on in the '60s and '70s found that things got better the longer we stayed, and we realized we weren't going back. America was now our country. A US visa wasn't difficult to obtain. The timing was right because US immigration had a big explosion in 1965 with a new immigration act. It allowed people from South Asian countries to come. At that time both the Mexican and European immigrants took a backseat to Asians. You could come with a student visa, but the US space program was getting launched and there was a shortage of technical people. Admissions were tough to get into the colleges in the US, and the immigration department knew where to get the best students from the best universities, so they made it easier for us. I am sure many were applying who didn't get their visas.

It was very interesting that there weren't that many Americans in the graduate school programs—it was more foreign students. I remember in North Dakota we had people from Korea, Japan, and India, as

the school easily took foreign students. America is the land of opportunity. It really did not matter what you studied. You could still have a
career and do well in America. Part of the enculturation that was going
on among the American students was that even with just a high school
diploma you could do well in America. So the students who graduated
from college with a bachelor's degree went on to get a job. They figured
that graduate school was for those people who wanted to teach or do
research. Americans opted out of graduate school because they figured
they could be set in their career and there was no compelling need to
go. The foreign students were always an attraction to the universities
because they were good students and had a good basis of knowledge
for coming to America and seeking advanced knowledge. The graduate programs in the US system even today probably wouldn't survive
without foreign students. You visit any university and look at where the
students are from, and many are from abroad. This has been a trend for
the last fifty years.

AN ENGINEERING JOB AT CDC

I liked all my classes at NDSU, and even though I was teaching half-
time with Ed Anderson, I had to design the class, teach the lessons, and
grade the students. I was teaching the junior- and senior-level classes.
Because of the foundation of my college education in India, I found
that graduate school was very easy. I decided to get a PhD in electrical engineering, but first I decided to take a break and get a job for a
while. I was hired by Control Data Corporation (CDC) in Plymouth,
Minnesota. That is what took me to Minneapolis after finishing my
master's in four quarters and doing my thesis. I took thirty-six credits
in my major, but I took a minor in physics since I had a keen interest in
quantum mechanics, which excited me a great deal. My thesis was on
systems engineering because it was broader than just learning about
the narrower systems design or something similar. My inspiration for
systems engineering came from all the space programs that were happening at the time. There was a phenomenal level of engineering just
for that. I wrote about the reentry of space vehicles, which was unique,
and was able to cite the more advanced research going on in Russia
at the time. I was a holistic thinker and tried to think of a problem in

a broader context. Systems engineering also required more math to understand the systems, along with the physics.

CDC had a communications systems division that was different from the mainframe group. My first job was in communications because CDC thought it was a good match for my education. Later I went to the terminal systems division in Roseville, and following that into Arden Hills to the mainframe group. In 1971, after two years at CDC, I was promoted to management rank and moved to Bloomington, Minnesota, which was the headquarters. I was working as the head of all the computer systems, from the CPU to the communication and core systems. Storage and peripherals were a separate division. I enjoyed what I was doing, and rather than doing hands-on design engineering, I got to work on products that were already in the field. I did more redesign based on feedback from customers. As a result, I was interfacing more with people outside the department—such as in sales, marketing, and field support—and I liked this. In this role we could determine which products needed improvements, and by talking with people you could learn about what the priorities should be. We can't change everything, but I looked at what can we do and what the engineering limitations were.

WORKING WITH PEOPLE AND SORTING OUT ISSUES

Working with people and sorting out issues became second nature to me. Lots of times I became the peacemaker between groups. I worked on the redesign and release of the product as a product manager. Interfacing with people, from the original designer to the salespeople, was very interesting. This is one thing I loved and still love about America. If you have the talent, work hard, and work well with other people, you will find that others will give you a chance. I hold this concept very dearly. People complain about this and that, but I have found that, in America, if you give it your best, you can excel. America is the best place for people to get a shot at success. There is no other society that does this like America. At this time, the Midwest was the only place I had experienced, so maybe midwestern values are different. People work hard in the Midwest and are very sincere. Because I was a foreigner, there was much I had to understand and absorb from the culture and other sources of knowledge. I had to produce a lot more.

For both Control Data and my next job at Burroughs, I traveled a great deal, both in the US and Europe. I recently did an analysis and discovered that I have been to forty-four of the fifty states in the US. I still have to get to Alaska and some of the states in the South, such as Mississippi. Traveling with the field people, I really came to understand how diverse and different America is. I remember the first time I went to Texas—I couldn't understand what they were saying. Were they speaking English? I remember once when I was in Montgomery with one of my colleagues, he said he would meet me in the hotel lobby. I went to the receptionist and asked if she knew where this gentleman was. She told me he was already "gown." I asked her where "gown" was and discovered she was trying to tell me he was already GONE. I remember many times not being able to figure out what people were saying.

WORKING IN THE STRONG VALUE SYSTEM OF THE MIDWEST

I worked in the strong value system of the Midwest and also brought my work ethic from India. I knew I had to do more than was asked of me. I was always available and always ready, and therefore got promotions and raises. After five years at Control Data, they did a joint project with NCR and formed a joint systems lab that would design a new architecture for a complete new line of computers, from the low end (for NCR) to the high end (for CDC). They organized an integrated product line. They chose the best of both companies, about one hundred people total. I was picked from CDC to be part of that group. My very smart boss, Dwight Thompson, was in Minneapolis, and NCR's advanced group was in Rancho Bernardo, California; they brought people from the corporate headquarters in Ohio too. My last of six years at CDC, I joined the group called the Advanced Systems Lab, which combined the talents of the two companies. They wanted a really new team with supersmart people to battle the competition, as some of the business was sliding for both companies. IBM was dominant. The computer industry had only seven players, and IBM had the majority of the market. The remainder of the market went to what was described as the BUNCH: Burroughs, Univac, NCR, Control Data, and Honeywell. [Digital Equipment Corporation (DEC) was in the microprocessor business from 1969 to 1970.] These were my formative years, and I had an amazing career—from junior engineer to the Advanced Systems Lab by the time I was twenty-eight, which could only happen in America.

MEETING MY WIFE, COOMIE, IN MINNEAPOLIS

I met my wife, Coomie, in Minneapolis. She came from India with a green card to work for First National Bank of Minneapolis. My boss at CDC, Bob Bonner, belonged to an international club at the University of Minnesota in Minneapolis because of his interest in other cultures. He and his wife, Beverly, were especially nice people and he told me about the club. He suggested that I come and meet the one Indian girl who also attended. He invited me as his guest. Coomie and I met in 1969 and were married in 1971. Before meeting Coomie, I thought about whether I would go back to India and someone would be found for me, but I also thought it would be better if I found someone myself. I had numerous thoughts of what to do about getting married, knowing the culture I came from. It was very early in my life, and I was focused on my job. But I met Coomie and it stuck. We got married in February of 1971, and we were a novelty—two Indians getting married. People found out and asked if they could come to the wedding. We suddenly had 175 people coming to the wedding and had to rent the Knights of Columbus hall. We made a trifold brochure so the attendees could follow the service. Coomie was Zoroastrian and I was Hindu, but we got married in a Hindu ceremony. We found a professor at the University of Minnesota, Dr. Padmakar K. Dixit, who taught in the medical school but was also licensed to perform weddings other

Vish and Coomie's wedding party
(photo courtesy of Vish Mishra)

than Muslim and Christian. He could do Hindu, Buddhist, Jain—whatever. I dressed in a wedding tuxedo and so did my groomsmen, Bob Bonhardt, Jack Wiehe, and Amarjit Singh. Coomie had one girl she met at the bank, Susan Wright, along with other friends who all wore saris. Our two daughters were born in Minneapolis, Usha in 1972 and Reena in 1975.

By the end of 1974, I got a job offer from Burroughs, in Plymouth, Michigan. They were looking for new blood in the company, as they were a very traditional company. The recession was coming, and I thought it was a good opportunity since I would be coming in as a manager in the engineering department for a brand-new line of computers that Burroughs was producing called the Small Systems Division. It gave me the opportunity to do something very cutting-edge. Burroughs had groups in Belgium, Scotland, and France. For the first time, they said they were going to have the products designed in the European countries, mainly Scotland. The design was done in Europe, and, as the product engineering manager, I had to transfer the design from the US to them. It turned out to be a billion-dollar product line, so that was very good experience for me. There were three of us who managed portions of engineering, including customer support.

We didn't know a single soul when we arrived in Ann Arbor. Dwight Thompson, one of my bosses from Minneapolis, had a cousin who was the dean of the medical school at the University of Michigan. Dwight wrote to him and told him to meet me. His hospitality was awesome.

We lived in Ann Arbor, which was a college town, but worked fifteen minutes away in Plymouth, Michigan. Eventually we knew we needed a change, and we wanted to move someplace warm. The inspiration to move came from another colleague at Burroughs, Joe Bauer, who was from Westlake Village, California (where Burroughs also had an operation), and who was transferred to Michigan as part of his job. Every day he told me how much he disliked living in Michigan, and he eventually got a chance to work for Amdahl in Sunnyvale, California. He told me to come and check out Amdahl because they were expanding big-time. They had done some amazing work with Fujitsu as their partner. I interviewed all day long, and before I left in the evening I had a job offer. This was 1977.

ENGINEERING MANAGEMENT AND OPERATIONS

I started as an engineering manager in the area of new mainframes. I managed equipment engineering for very sophisticated equipment that allowed the manufacturing of the product. I stayed for two years and then was recruited by National Semiconductor. Every semiconductor company wanted to be in the computer business. National had an advanced systems division, which I joined as an engineering manager and later moved to director of operations, but seven weeks after I started, they decided to get out of the computer business I was in. Most people left, but I stayed in the microcomputer division. In 1983, I came in as the founding VP of Operations of a start-up company called Excelan doing TCP/IP. When I came to Silicon Valley, I met some people who had just left Zilog, which was a chip company. They wanted to start a new company and needed someone with maturity and experience, so I joined them after being introduced by a mutual friend who was at National. The core design was by Kanwal Rekhi, Dr. Naveen Jain was doing software, and Inder Singh was the president. They needed a broad-based businessman with operations background, and that is what I did, including QA and manufacturing, test engineering, production, delivery, and customer service. I had to organize everything as a product, get it delivered, and secure satisfied customers. As vice president, I also functioned as the chief operating officer. We took the company public and two years later sold it to Novell; I left Novell in 1992. I then cofounded a low-end Windows database software company called Ace Software and after that was involved in several turnarounds and venture-backed companies and served on many company boards.

JOINING THE TiE LEADERSHIP TEAM: THE ENTREPRENEURS

In the early '90s, an amazing development took place in our lives, and that was working for the creation of the organization TiE (The Indus Entrepreneurs). In December 1992, the TiE organization was founded. I joined in March of 1993 at the third meeting of TiE. I was now able to work with Kanwal Rekhi, Kailash Joshi, Suhas Patil, and many other talented people in an entirely new way. Most of us were good students in India, and wherever we settled we did well. And the motivation for TiE was to get people together and do well. We understood the American dream and applied it to this organization. The immigrants made America, and America made the immigrants. If you have skills, have a good attitude, and really work hard, you can absolutely succeed in America, even in tough times.

The core fundamentals of TiE have not changed over the years because we worked hard to stick to them. When TiE was being launched, it was heavily Southeast Asians. We started with the intent that we wanted it to be an organization focused on business and did not want it to be cultural. Even today, in Silicon Valley, there are at least one hundred cultural organizations here. Every region and subregion has their cultural organizations, and that is the immigrants' story. When they came to this country, what kept them together was their culture, their own people. They brought mini-Israel, mini-Italy, and mini-Germany with them. There is comfort when you are able to meet with people who do things the same way you do, eat the same food, and talk in the same manner. As an immigrant you feel safe. This is how society has evolved. All over the US, there are organizations for Indian people to be together. When India's prime minister Modi first came to the US, there were four hundred–plus organizations, from Alaska to Mississippi, who were sponsors, and they joined the twenty thousand people at Madison Square Garden who came to hear him speak.

GETTING SUCCESSFUL PEOPLE TOGETHER TO HELP OTHERS SUCCEED: TiE

I doubt we could have started TiE anywhere else but Silicon Valley. Not even in India. The whole notion of getting successful people together to genuinely help others succeed seems strange to people. In other cultures, they ask, "Why are you helping others when there is nothing in it for yourself?" "You have nothing to gain and you are trying to help somebody. What gives?" This is a real problem in society. This whole notion of volunteering to help someone become an entrepreneur, give someone honest and frank advice, and help them succeed is something that is accepted in Silicon Valley. TiE has not deviated from that focus. This has withstood the test of time. We are promoting entrepreneurship and giving back, and we never had to drive it from the top down.

Only 2 percent of people have an entrepreneurial bent. Six million people start a new business every year, from boutique stores employing five people to a person who starts an auto repair shop because he used to work for a car dealer and found an opening against the higher prices of the dealers. This is in contrast to the people who start the Googles and Facebooks and Intels and HPs. We are the most enterprising country on the face of the earth, but there are only 2 percent of us that are really out there. The thesis we maintain is that if you are an entrepreneur, you don't need a lot of help. If you need a lot of help, you aren't an entrepreneur. If you need help in every direction, you aren't ready. This goes to my five points of a business plan. A lot of Indian entrepreneurs are not ready. I ask them a simple question: "Why do you want to be an entrepreneur?" You would be surprised at the wrong answers I get. The answer is that it isn't about you—it is about other people and the pressing need you want to address in society. I get answers like "I want to take on the competition," "I want to make money," and all sorts of responses. They have not holistically figured it out. Once you know, you always keep the customer in mind. The woman who opens the boutique store may have a goal of dressing a thousand women a year and making them feel wonderful. This is a good business. Google wanted to organize the world's information and uplift a billion people. It all comes down to uplifting other people's lives. People have to consume your product or service and feel good about it.

LEARNING THE COST OF BUSINESS

When I came to Excelan, I had broader experience in operating a company than the other people I worked with. Having worked in various companies, including National Semiconductor, where I was one of the fifty top execs, I had the experience of having a large budget, and with my background as an engineer, it was natural for me to be the operations person. And in the project where we took on IBM (CDC, Burroughs, and NCR), it was very entrepreneurial in that new division and like a brand-new company. Even at Burroughs, they wanted to bring in "new blood from outside." When I joined CDC, it had been a company for twenty-nine years, and when I joined Burroughs, it had already been around for fifty-eight years. In those days, all the computer companies were vertically integrated—they made everything. The plant was a million square feet in Plymouth, Michigan. It wasn't the headquarters, but it was this vast operation and one of the largest factories that they had. They had a machine shop, they made their own tools for metal and plastic, they had had their own electronic chips operations like the other companies had. As a result, I had broader business experience. It wasn't that I had design experience, like many people do, but I knew the production operations, sales, support, and marketing. I came with a holistic approach coupled with my own nature. I made myself available and learned other disciplines as well. I really learned the cost of business. I was thirty-eight years old when we started Excelan.

BEING A VENTURE CAPITALIST: INVESTOR AND MENTOR

I am a venture capitalist (VC), and therefore I look through the lens of my own experience now as an investor and mentor. When the dot-com bust occurred, people were just clueless, even guys from brand-name companies. They were in their late twenties and early thirties and directors of this and that. After the crash occurred, these guys found themselves on the street and found they had no real skills. They hadn't developed the breadth of skills they needed because their companies were growing so fast. Rising tides lift all boats, which happens a lot. At Excelan, we had guys working for us that we didn't think had much potential, and they surprised us. We had people that we identified as having potential, and they disappointed us. Part of it is their own nature. The drive has to come from the individual; it has to be within you. When an opportunity comes, an individual can be oblivious or can rise to take advantage. We just don't know what will happen in advance. A person can find the people with expertise and learn from them or not. Some people have ambition to learn, and others don't have the desire, and that's why they don't accomplish what they could.

LOGICAL CONVERSATIONS

One thing I realized a long time ago, and I still believe this—it is all about people. When I mentor people, I ask them to come to grips with themselves and get to know themselves better. When people first come to me saying they are entrepreneurs, I tell them that I don't want to learn their business, I just want to have a conversation. I ask the person to let us have a logical conversation, and there are five steps to this logical conversation.

First and foremost, if you want to start a new business, explain to me clearly what pressing need you have discovered that you want to address. This brings us to customers. I ask them not to tell me that it is "pressing" because they just thought of it. If there is a pressing need out there today, there are many people trying to meet that need. They might not have a good idea, but they are working on it.

Second, who is working to solve those needs, and how good of a job are they doing? You could call this "market," but I don't call it that. I want to know who needs a pressing need met and want to hear them clearly tell me so.

Third, what is your approach to address that problem? Not just the technology but your approach.

Fourth, what does it take? It certainly takes a team and starts with you. Are you honest enough with yourself to say, "I know some things, but I am clueless about other things"? You need to have other people who complement your skills. Most engineers have this problem. They think they can read about accounting, law, finance, or whatever. You can't. It takes a team. You can't just read up on some expertise you need. It is not a school where you are going to be educated. You are going to build a company. You have to go deep in whatever you do. You have to maximize on the strength that you have.

Fifth, what does solving this pressing need bring in? Where do you get the profits? You have to have some sense of this profit. If you have no profit motive, you can't succeed.

No plan is complete. You have to figure it out. We want to bet on a real honest person, a person with integrity. If you want to bring in a cofounder, employer, or investor, they will need to buy the company strategy and say, "I can help here or there." Investors all have cash. They want to know how they can help. This is where the partnership occurs. Everyone has to come together in a system. Ultimately it is you. You have to be enthusiastic, tell the story, accept the feedback, and figure out how to build your business. No one knows the future. People don't change. We are biological creatures, and most of our habits are learned in our teenage years. Over time we just have better coping mechanisms in our society. Let's say a five-year-old doesn't like something. He will be super direct and say, "I don't like this." When you mature, you can say, "It just doesn't quite suit me" or "I am allergic to it." You don't want to leave someone with a bad feeling. Society teaches us to live within that society. But people's personalities don't change, and if you don't like something, it is hard to change.

We are in the time of specialization, just as in the medical field. How many general practitioners are there? Everyone wants to be specialized—heart, GI, diabetes. There aren't that many general practitioners in medicine, and the computer business is the same, with many specialists. Fundamentally, the computer architecture hasn't changed since the beginning. Innovation occurs at specialized levels. There have always been central processors, input and output, applications, and a method to communicate in computers. If innovation occurs on the processor side, it creates a bottleneck in another area. We just experience innovation shifting around. We can talk about artificial intelligence and different realities, and science-fiction writers start telling new stories, but basically everything is the same as it has always been but with advancement in technology. Conceptually, there is no difference between what computers did originally and what they do today. We have made enough innovations that ordinary people can use computers. In the past, who could use computers? Only the specialists behind glass walls. The point is that you definitely need specialization.

I sometimes see a kind of arrogance developing, which I don't think is wise. People live in their own world. That happened two thousand years ago too. People will continue to be self-centered and live in their own world. It is always about biological evolution, which isn't as fast as technological evolution. I have faith in the human race and that computers won't take over. There will still be wise people in every society, and, even in the age of specialization, there will be people who can weave this all together. Specialists will exist because so much is happening and so much new is going on.

PERSPECTIVES FROM RURAL INDIA TO
THE MIDWEST TO SILICON VALLEY

I appreciate the unique perspective about living I have come to after growing up in rural India, followed by the US Midwest (Minnesota and North Dakota), and finally the urban areas (Silicon Valley). People can be involved wherever they live—rural or urban. Forty years ago, you had to be in a "place," a place where innovation happened, because information traveled at a snail's pace. Someone did the research, and the report had to be published and the book or magazine printed and shipped out. This whole notion that information is available anywhere means that people no longer have to congregate in big cities. Creature comforts are available in many areas. The problem for the rural people is the social infrastructure. Take the example of doctors in the US. They don't want to be an old country doctor any longer. The mind-set has changed. It used to be when you grew up in a small town, you had the church, you had the doctor, you had the fireman. The minister was the psychiatrist in small towns, and now there are fewer ministers, and the specialty of psychiatry has just mushroomed. Doctors don't want to go to rural areas because they don't make enough money and there isn't the social connection. This is the challenge of what people in rural areas have to contend with.

In the US, urbanization isn't such a problem because we have few cities of over a million people. But China, for example, is much more urbanized than one imagines. They even have an internally organized visa system to go from rural villages to urban centers or other districts. They have a big problem. In India there is the problem of urbanization also, but they are trying to figure out how to take the city amenities into the rural areas. Mexico and Venezuela are heavily urbanized. You can hollow out the land, and everyone congregates and puts many pressures on the systems and communities. It has social ramifications. Our friends are no longer the people who live next to us. We live in high-rises, and we don't know the people next to us. You know who your friends are, but they may have no connection to where you live.

This is a big change from how people used to live. Proximity determined who our friends were. In this big, interconnected world, it can be different. We have lived in the same house for thirty-seven years, and we make an effort to know our neighbors. But many people don't. Conversations with neighbors are frequently just superficial because your friends live somewhere else.

THOUGHTS ON EDUCATION

I always wanted to be the best I could be, and I tried to do this through mastering the subjects I studied. I have a curious mind, and even today I read a great amount. I continue to consume knowledge. If I have the opportunity to speak to parents today, I tell them, "Please take an interest in your child's education." We complain about how the educational system has gone bad, but the parents have to take some blame. Sure, many parents are stressed and don't have a lot of time, and they are poor and have two jobs or are overextended and are trying to build a big career—being CEO, being this or that. On both ends of the spectrum, the parents are not taking care of the children. It doesn't matter whether it is a public or private school, you can't leave it to the teachers. The parents have to take an interest, and this is essential at the formative stages. It is too late in high school. I think it is especially hard for women. The first place children learn is in the family, and as women do spend more time with the children, it is important that the women are educated. I want to do anything I can to help women be more educated. They will pass it on to the children. In the US and Canada, the family system is so broken. This is causing a problem. Improving the education of a child is the parents' responsibility. The child is an innocent person, and parents must make that child a better person. Spend more time with their children and less time fighting the teachers and the schools. Some children are born with a natural curiosity, and that is a gift. It probably doesn't matter with a curious and gifted child whether they go to public or private schools. But for children who aren't naturally curious, the environment can make a difference for them.

The way we are trying to put bureaucracy in the educational system is not useful. The typical high school principal has very little control over the school. Principals should be allowed their "principaling" job and the teachers the teaching. All these rules and reports drive principals and teachers to focus on the rules. This can even cause teachers to fudge the results. This bureaucracy takes advantage of society, and the system is dysfunctional and is perpetuated. The schools need major reform. The parents can't control everything, but they can effect a change with their children.

RAM AND NAYANA KRISHNAN, MINNESOTA

RAM BORN IN TRIVANDRUM, INDIA; NAYANA BORN IN BOMBAY (NOW MUMBAI), INDIA

EDITOR: *It's easy to forget what it meant and means to rural America to be able to purchase food that is fresh and inviting. The logistics of getting vegetables picked in California or Florida, transported for days, and unloaded into individual grocery stores, including ensuring that the frozen food stays frozen, was difficult. Ram's life work led to the creation of software for the management and design of food warehousing and distribution in the north-central United States. Nayana emigrated as a child from India with her family because her father's expertise was needed at the University of Minnesota's medical school. Ram and Nayana have committed their family's talents and resources to rainwater harvesting and proper water usage, a present and future gift to a water-hungry world.*

RAM: I came to the United States in March of 1969, on St. Patrick's Day. I found many of my colleagues and friends who studied with me in India; they also came to America, and a lot of them came here before I did. I studied mechanical engineering in IIT Madras (Chennai), received my bachelor's degree, and did another one-year postgraduate course in industrial engineering. I had only worked for a short time as an engineer in India, as a type of trainee in an electrical shop in a suburb of Chennai. My father was an engineer and worked for a service in India called MES (Military Engineering Service), but he was a civilian. He would go wherever there was a need, such as helping to build an airport runway or housing quarters. At that time in India, there were always problems with China, and there were roads known as "border roads." I remember my father telling me that one day they would build a road, and the next day it would be filled with ice and snow, and they wouldn't know where the road was located. These were difficult circumstances. My father had to move every four or five years, so for most of my studies I stayed in one place. When my father was in Delhi and Bombay, I went with him, but all the other time I stayed with my grandfather and grandmother in Madras. My mother was with my father, and I was the eldest of four children. My grandfather's profession was in the temples as an administrator, managing the money and the festivals. He worked directly for the king in Kerala. My grandmother was not educated.

I attended a public school in Madras. At that time in India, you had to look at the rank in your school testing, and if you weren't in the top three, there were many other people who wanted those seats. My father did tell me I would be a good engineer. At the end of an exam, my father would go through the exams at home, and I knew how I did before the teacher even posted the results. When I lived with him in Delhi and Bombay, he would help me with my studies. He was, of course, nervous about me doing well. He went to an engineering college in Kerala, and in his time, the IIT system didn't exist. The IIT colleges were set up post–British rule (post-partition). Right after the British rule, as part of the five- and ten-year plans, Nehru made sure India had enough well-trained engineers and doctors. Engineering was pushed in India, and the IITs were set up for engineering education. They knew they couldn't build just one IIT, so they established several with various collaborations with the Germans, Americans, and Russians.

IITS: A CONTRIBUTION FROM THE WORLD COMMUNITY

Initially, much of the faculty from IIT Madras came from the Indian Institute of Science in Bangalore. My father was still getting transferred, and my grandfather was still in Chennai. I decided I wanted to stay in one place for a while, so I went back to Chennai and stayed in the hostel at the university, which was compulsory for anyone going to IIT. There is a specific IIT entrance exam that thousands of people take, and only 1 to 2 percent gets into IIT after that exam. That is how rigorous it is. I had to borrow money to pay for the entrance exam, which I believe was 40 to 50 rupees. My father was on a fixed income, and he accounted for every rupee, so 40 rupees was a lot of money. I was in Ruia College studying in Bombay, where there was an art track and a science track for engineering and science. At that time, being a physician wasn't so prestigious, but being an engineer was much more rigorous. It was said that if you couldn't do well, you would choose the path to be a doctor. Engineering was very rigorous, and there were only two students from Ruia College in 1961 and 1962 who wrote that exam that got into IIT. My ranking was high enough that I could choose whatever IIT I wanted, rather than being assigned. Being able to visit my family on weekends was very attractive after staying in hostels for the week.

Fortunately, all the IITs were of the highest quality. In every IIT you had people from all over India, and you could count on all the students being excellent. We all had to speak Hindi right away, although my mother tongue was Tamil. We all knew English, which was the medium of instruction, but Hindi was the language of life in the hostels. We went to English movies and, of course, in my friendship circle, if they spoke Tamil, I would too. But northern students had excellent Hindi, and I didn't; we still spoke it together unless we were with other English speakers.

IIT had a ranking system after the exams; we would know the results, and we would keep track of everyone's results. It was important to know because if you did well in one or two subjects but not in others, it would pull your rank down. We had some time for games, but mostly we took our studies seriously. We knew how much time we had to spend studying in order to stay in this prestigious place, where there were many people who wanted our position.

COMING TO THE UNITED STATES TO GET A PhD

In my final year of college, which was a five-year program, we all knew who was going where for advanced degrees. The postman delivered letters, and the entire hostel would know where someone was going for their next level of school. There were some immigration rules in the US that only allowed us coming for masters or PhDs. We had to have a bachelor's already, so, in India, finishing a bachelor's is what we did. I got an F1 student visa in India, and I originally came to the US to get a PhD in industrial engineering. I had already earned my master's in India. I took a few classes in industrial engineering in the US and already knew the curriculum because IIT Madras was very rigorous. Ironically, over half the engineering students at the University of Minnesota were Indians, and I wanted a broader group of students to learn from. My family's economic background was middle or lower-middle class, but in terms of education and values, we were very upper class. I knew I couldn't afford to do five years of a PhD and had to get a job, so though I started on that path, I switched to a master's in business administration (MBA).

When I came to the US, my grandfather mortgaged his house, which he never had to do, to pay for my airplane ticket to America. When I came from India, I didn't know whether I would get a stipend, and I took the risk that I might have to go into debt. The government of India gave me seven dollars when I left. When I came, I flew from Madras to Calcutta and caught an international flight to New York and then to Minneapolis. There was a problem on the plane trying to get something to eat, as I was a vegetarian. They provided these boiled vegetarian things, but I didn't want to eat them. However, they did have apples, and I kept as many as I could. When I went through customs and immigration, they asked me why I was smuggling all these apples to America. They told me I had to throw them out or sit in the corner and eat them, and that after I was done they would let me in to the country. Apples were a delicacy in India—when we had one, it was cut into many slices and you were lucky if you got one or two slices.

Even with the apples, I was very hungry when I came to New York, and I could eat french fries, so I used $1.25 of my seven dollars to buy french fries.

A SNOWY ARRIVAL IN MINNESOTA

Arriving in Minneapolis, I knew one person who lived near the University of Minnesota. He came to the airport, took me to the university, and helped me get oriented for several months. The cold weather was a big switch from Madras. I remember all the snow and ice and remember slipping because I didn't have the right shoes or even the right overcoat for March. It took a long time to reach the apartment with this snow and ice situation. We would loan clothes to each other, as we were all in similar circumstances—no one had much money. I was pleased when I paid back my grandfather for the mortgage he took out for my travels. Getting a mortgage was not common at that time. If you needed to buy something in India, you saved up for what you wanted.

My family was happy that I was going to America for higher education. Going to America for school was good on anyone's résumé, and it almost assured that if you were a good student, you would get a good job in India. Many students would say that they would work a year or two and then go back to India. I didn't know when I was going to return to India, but my parents always wrote letters wondering when I was coming back to India. Letters were the way that I communicated with my family. Of course, there was no e-mail. My family expected me to come home, and they had been seeing candidates for my future wife. Everyone knows everything in India, and the fathers with daughters would visit my family in hopes of being associated with someone with a degree and good prospects. They knew I had been to America and got an advanced degree and done very well. My parents had many people coming by to talk. But I was seeing Nayana, and we were speaking about being engaged.

MENIAL BUT NECESSARY JOBS

Since I came in the spring, I worked through the summer at local companies, trying to earn the money I needed. I bought an old car so I could keep two jobs. In the morning, I worked at Graco, which made paintbrushes, and in the afternoon I worked at another company as a janitor sweeping floors. At the University of Minnesota, I got a job washing out tubes that had horse blood in them from veterinary research. The trick was not to break the tubes, as they were very expensive. I never told my Hindu father that I was a horse-blood test-tube cleaner or a janitor because they were all menial jobs. I hid the truth from him and told him I was working for an industrial company. You didn't come to America to do menial jobs, and he didn't send me to America to do this type of work. I saved enough money and got a scholarship as a teaching assistant (TA) in September when I started school, so I didn't have to go into debt. A TA could pay lower tuition and still get a stipend for the TA work. I was willing to do whatever it took.

I shared a single-room apartment with four or five other Indians I met there to keep the cost of living down. The apartment was so small that we had a rule that one of us had to be in the library at all times! There were some senior students who had been at the university for several years and had learned how to cook, so they made the traditional South Indian dishes, such as sambar, curry, and rice. After one quarter of the PhD program, I switched to the MBA program and was able to finish in less than two years because they gave me some credit for my studies in India. I felt there were already too many engineers and that businesses needed people with a broader base of expertise on how to work in companies. MBAs weren't as popular then as they are today, where it seems that everyone, no matter what they are doing, has to have one. Being employable was my objective, and as soon as I finished my program, I had some employment opportunities that I might not have otherwise had.

RECESSION AND JOB SOURCING

The industrial sector was growing in India at this time, from Tata to Cummins to English Electric and others. Just before I started looking for a job, companies like Honeywell would come to the Department of Electrical Engineering at the University of Minnesota, and they would hire the entire class of engineering students. But when I started looking for work, it was a time of recession and the Vietnam War, so it wasn't easy to get a job.

My first job was at Gambles—even after all those years of studying engineering and business, they gave me a large pile of invoices and I had to count the actual invoices on the old-style

Ram at work
(photo courtesy of Ram and Nayana Krishnan)

adding machine, prepare a slip, make sure everything was correct, and give the result back to them. During a lunch break, I went into a conference room, and on the blackboard there was an organizational flowchart on the board. I started to correct the diagram, and someone came in and asked me, "Who are you, making these corrections?" He had a higher position and knew what he was doing. He immediately called my boss, for whom I was doing the invoices, and told him I was not going to be on another team any longer but would, in fact, be working for him. He took me with him on business trips as an industrial engineer, flying to the various parts of the business, from California to Michigan. I first went to Coldwater, Michigan. I tried to apply whatever I knew at the time—plus I had to learn a great deal more—and I brought to the table my interest in talking to other employees. I suggested they knew more than I did about what they were doing, and I invited them to share what could be improved. It worked. I had a lovely office with a not-so-impressive salary with my new position. With this better office, I started to become attractive to my future wife, Nayana, and so it became important that I could have my own apartment. Nayana and I became engaged, and my life was changing. I worked for Gambles for several years and was laid off. Luckily, someone I knew said there was a company in Hopkins, Minnesota, called Red Owl that was looking for people. I spent a great deal of my career at Red Owl. Basically I told them I was looking for a job in the industrial engineering department under Alan Green. I eventually became the head of that department, where I looked at all the layouts and how to improve the efficiency of the process in the warehouse—from pallets, forklifts, and warehousing to the staffing structure. I spent time in retail in the stores, which were all union stores. Because of union rules, I couldn't touch the cases, so I had to do things in the back of the store, and before the crew came, I had to put everything back so they didn't notice any change. I was charged with improving efficiency, so I spoke with the union members and understood that they had to make a living. I spoke to them and the company, and they all made improvements.

DESIGNING COMPUTER SOFTWARE FOR
RETAIL WAREHOUSING

Red Owl had a large population of stores in the upper Midwest—Minnesota, Wisconsin, Michigan, and the two Dakotas. I really learned warehousing from this job and built a career on this knowledge. I was an analytical person and wasn't afraid to use even time-sharing computers in the early days for analysis. I worked at Target for a few years, and I eventually went into my own business at age forty. I learned the bulk of what I needed to learn and applied it at Target and my own company, with little income but with the strength of my understanding of computer programs that had nothing to do with warehousing and my skill as a programmer. I wrote programs for $1,000 a month and knew that I had a family with a wife and small child I had to support. So I continued to write code to help companies improve efficiencies in their warehouses. These were the days of BASIC coding. I used computer cards for FORTRAN and BASIC. I was one of the first to purchase an IBM PCjr personal computer. To get computer time on the big machines, I had to go to downtown Minneapolis in the middle of the night when they would allow you to use the machines. I was paid on a consulting basis and didn't know anything about software licensing that is used today. There were business problems to be solved, and I solved them. Coding was crude compared to what it is today. I remember one time we were not ready to license the software for fear it didn't work. We created a program that generated random numbers to test our software. It required us to keep the computer running all night long, and in the morning if we discovered a problem, we had to start the test all over again until it was right. I eventually got a few employees, so I had to keep everyone going in earning a living. If business was good, we shared the outcome, and if business was slow, we all had to take a salary cut.

In America, efficiency achieved in food selling could be applied to other areas because the margins were so small in food that if it was applied in other areas, it was more productive. A mistake in food warehousing was very costly. There were difficulties in having my own business, but any mistake was my mistake—so I had a keen desire to do it well. I needed the testimonials from my client base to get the next job. I never worked as an employee of another company again.

BUILDING A CONSULTING BUSINESS

To build my consulting business, I used to send out flyers to various companies that might want my services. It was a home industry, printing and mailing the flyers out ourselves. Our entire family was involved because we had to separate by zip code for the bulk permits. We would mail out three thousand flyers, and we would get 1 percent return; of course, there were fewer than that who would initiate a contract. I had to absorb every expense, even for visiting them to set up the contract. It was almost a time-and-materials type of business. If I got one pilot project, from companies such as Campbell's Soup, Kimberly-Clark, or Georgia-Pacific, then I could keep going on additional projects within the company. I learned about changes in my occupation by attending national conferences. Higher-level executives usually attended them at that time, and this allowed me to talk with them and find out what was going on in various companies. My focus was warehousing and distribution, which was much easier than food. The staff I hired were good learners—people with a wide background of computer experience and those that got laid off from other companies and called me. I had to worry about the entire big picture and what the outcome had to be. This required me to check on their practices, because we couldn't cause any problems for the client.

NAYANA: I was born in Bombay. From 1952 to 1954, my father was sent to the United States by the Indian government. I was born in 1953, so my father didn't see me until I was over a year old. This was just after India secured its independence from Britain. The government wanted to send people out for training. He was a researcher with a PhD in biochemistry and was sent to Cleveland. He did such excellent work and was highly recognized, especially by a Dr. Arnold Lazaro, who was involved with the government programs working with these students. My father returned to India, working on nutrition. He received a letter one day from Dr. Lazaro, who said he was going to start a department at the University of Minnesota in anatomy, with facilities for research, and needed people. He remembered my father as a good worker who was very smart. None of us realized how difficult it would be to get someone from India to the US. But Dr. Lazaro did all the paperwork necessary to get him to the US in 1959. I still have the letter, which said he would be paid $7,000 per year and benefits. Not all of my family could come to the United States—my older sister and mother and I had to stay in Pune with our grandmother. My father worked very hard to get us there, but it was very difficult. In January of 1961, when I was seven, we were able to come to the US, after needing to leave the country quickly because they would rescind the visa at the end

Dixit family with Nayana
(photo courtesy of Ram and Nayana Krishnan)

of six months. If you didn't read the fine print, or didn't show up for an interview at the appointed time, you had to start the cycle all over again. We had to hurry also because my sister was eleven and a half, and when she reached the age of twelve, we would have to buy a full-price adult airplane ticket. My father was not only a good man, but he helped the community. We were the early settlers of Indian people in Minnesota. We became the "welcome wagon" for many new students. They came here to go to school and not to go to work, as it is today. My mother was educated with a bachelor's in the Marathi language, not English, and she was very smart and wrote well, just not in English. We still cherish Dr. Lazaro in our family.

MINNESOTANS' BLANKET AND CLOTHING AID TO BANGLADESH

During the war between East and West Pakistan, with India right in the middle and a thousand miles between the two Pakistans, many people from Bengal were suffering and fleeing into India. My family in Minneapolis organized a blanket and clothes drive for these refugees. We were one of the only families that had a house, and it was right on campus because my father was a professor. Everything was coming into our basement, and Ram, being the vice president of the Indo-American Student Association, got involved with this project. His job was determining how to get the clothes and blankets over to these people. This was actually the difficult part of the project. They had to be shipped to East Bengal, now Bangladesh, via Calcutta, and we had to negotiate a deal with Northwest Airlines and manage the logistics. You can get the articles to India, but would it go to the right party or be sold in the black market?

Ram came to the house for this project, and we also met on campus. I was very young, only eighteen, and a freshman in college after graduating high school one year early. I was put ahead two school grades because of my education in India, which wasn't in sync with American levels and enabled me to test at a higher level. Because of my age, they wouldn't put me up two grades, but they did put me up one, so I graduated at sixteen and was ready to go to college at seventeen. This made me a very young student at the University of Minnesota. I also joined the Indo-American Student Association, and Ram and I went to many meetings together, although we were both shy. We had mutual friends, and I was a rare creature—a female student. Most of the students were men in their early twenties looking for dates.

HINDUISM AS A RECOGNIZED RELIGION IN MINNESOTA

My father, Dr. Padmakar K. Dixit, was a professor of anatomy and taught in both the dental and medical schools. He was a Brahmin, which is the priestly class, and served as a Hindu priest because he knew the scriptures and could say the prayers. He was licensed to marry people, and in 1961 he married the first students who couldn't go back to India, so the girl had to come from India and stay with my family until the wedding. We not only served as her parents but did the ceremony. It was a Vedic Hindu–style wedding, and everything had to be proper. The most important thing in any Hindu wedding, whether it be simple or extravagant, is to have fire and a priest. Sometimes you could get by without the priest, but you needed the fire, which was considered a "witness." This didn't hold up well with the authorities, to get the legal papers with only fire as a witness. My father had to go to the Minnesota legislature to get them to acknowledge Hinduism as a religion, along with Presbyterians, Catholics, and Jews. So a special law was passed to recognize Hindu marriages. This was not as contentious as it would be today.

My parents liked Ram. They liked his credentials, and that he had the good South Indian values of modesty and politeness. In order to date, we had to be engaged. I couldn't just go and date this person and that person. It was difficult to tell his family. Ram had to write his family and tell them that he

Ram and Nayana
(photo courtesy of Ram and Nayana Krishnan)

had met someone in Minnesota. His father would write about sending him to America to be educated and that he had responsibility to his family. They had found some good educated girls in India who were rich and ready to get married. I couldn't compete in that area because I was young and going to school as a freshman or sophomore. My family was settled in America. We were both Brahmin, of the same caste, but South Indian Brahmin and Maharashtrian Brahmin, which are two different worlds. They were not compatible, and this wasn't approved. Ram and his father had lots of letters back and forth over this. Ram told him about my family, that my father was highly regarded, that he was the elder statesman of his community. His father would send letters with such comments as "the president of India's granddaughter is available." Ram had to be clear with his father in his letters that he was marrying me. Resistance was finally broken, and he realized that Ram was going to get married anyway. Ram's father gave us his blessing, even though he was reluctant.

THE WEDDING AND THE CHALLENGE OF THE DATE

His father came for the wedding; we sent him a ticket. His mother couldn't come because she was not in good health. South Indians are much more orthodox than we are. We had written out the invitations, and the wedding was for December 28. When his father came here, he looked at the dates and told us we couldn't marry. From December 15 to January 15 is the Margazhi season in South India, which is a bad omen. But in Maharashtra there are a large number of weddings at that time because it is lovely weather. So we had to call everyone and change the wedding to December 14 to accommodate his father's concerns. His father worked and this was his holiday, and in January he would not be here. Financially no one was able to go back and forth to India. December 14 was a Thursday and catering wasn't available, so my mother and her friends cooked our food. My mother was a great cook, and others came to help and were enthusiastic. My older sister had already been married to a local mathematician who was Indian, who had come to the United States to do his PhD. My mother didn't want to teach me domestic skills because she wanted my sister and me to study and not worry about cooking and cleaning. I knew I could learn how to cook when I needed to. My father couldn't marry us because he had the responsibility of giving away the bride. We have the practice of Kanyadaan, which means to "give the daughter away." (*Kanya* means "daughter"; *daan* means "offering.") This is a major part of a Vedic wedding ceremony. He had to participate in that ritual, and he had to have someone else serve as priest for the day.

FROM LOS ANGELES BACK TO MINNESOTA
AND RETAIL FOOD LOGISTICS

RAM: I continued my involvement with the Indian community and programs at the University of Minnesota, even after I was no longer a student. We had an office for foreign students on East River Road, and together we identified what we could do as a community. We eventually had two children, both born in Minnesota. Unfortunately they never got to see my parents or my grandparents. My mother passed away from medical problems, and my father only came for the wedding.

In between various corporate jobs, I joined a consulting company in Los Angeles. Then my former boss at Red Owl called me to return to Minnesota, and I came back to a promotion. I was pleased to get out of the massive traffic jams and hours in transit. While in Los Angeles, I worked as a consultant to Ralphs, the grocery store chain, and it offered me insight into more diversity and a larger grocery volume market. Farmers' produce would come in the morning, and by the afternoon it would be gone. There wasn't the same need for warehousing. In Minnesota it takes us two to four days to get the produce from California to the warehouse and then to the stores. When you deliver a product, how you lay out products within the trailer helps you to unload properly. Frozen food put at nonfrozen temperatures requires you to move rapidly to get it back to a frozen state. These are serious logistical issues, especially when you have a business with small margins.

BECOMING US CITIZENS

During the time that the recession was on, it was difficult to get a green card, and I had planned to go back to India. But when I married Nayana, she had a green card, as she had lived in the US for many years, and I was able to get my card based on hers. After you complete your studies in the US, the law said you could work for up to eighteen months, under a training visa, and then you had to return to your country. If you didn't get sponsorship from a company, you also had to go back. That is still true today. I became a citizen in 1982, and Nayana received her citizenship in 1992, as she didn't focus on it due to her activities as a young married woman.

THE CRISIS OF WATER LIMITATIONS AND PHILANTHROPY

My life expanded when I learned that IIT in Chennai had run out of water and that students had to leave the dorm. When I was in the hostel, we would be given a bucket of water, and we could do anything we wanted with that water, but that was all you were going to get. We had this idea that we had to be very careful with water from that one bucket. There are two types of monsoons—one from the southeast and one from the southwest. Mumbai gets vastly more monsoon rain than Chennai. Western monsoons come in June/July, whereas Chennai (on the east coast) gets less ferocious monsoons in October and November, so we could get more water in those months.

My philanthropy was stimulated by this water limitation. When I was a child, we had to get up at two or three in the morning and go down to the city fountains, with a number of vessels, and get water that they turned on at that time. If you didn't get there in time, you didn't get water. We had bilge pumps, and you had to pump it up, and if there was air in the pump you had to prime it with water. We stored the water in the house in various vessels. No one was allowed to hook up an electric motor to the water system because it meant that others on the street would not get water. I got involved in the issue of groundwater restoration because I remembered back in Madras about the hard times we had getting water. I knew it was time to give something back, and in 1998 I became involved in rainwater harvesting.

Drinking water is always a difficult problem, and I am not talking about gray water. As long as the water comes from the sky, it is fine, but the minute it touches the ground it is spoiled. So you need to capture it, and conditions differ. If we do this in Minneapolis, it has to relate to the conditions in Minneapolis. And in Chennai, it had to be based on conditions in Chennai. It will be different for different places. California has a serious problem that has gone on for years. In India if you say something, they tell you they know everything about it, but if you ask them how to do something, they can't tell you. I had a friend in Germany, who was from IIT, and he said he had a place in Chennai that

he was no longer living in, and that I could use it as long as I was working for rainwater harvesting. We put together two or three working
models of a rainwater harvesting system so people could come in and
learn how to do it. If we got one house in a million it didn't amount to
anything. We needed to communicate the models to the broadest variety of magazines and newspapers to get the idea to the broadest number of people. India has print communications in so many languages
that it was important to get the word out in various languages, from
English to Tamil to Hindu and all the others. Chennai had a chief minister named Jayalalitha, and we invited her through the Rotary Club to
participate. She said she wouldn't come, and instead wanted to do it in
her own house first and come for the formal inauguration after she was
assured it worked. She was pleased and passed an ordinance requiring
other homeowners to follow this program. This was the best outcome
that could happen.

RAINWATER HARVESTING

A man named Sekar Raghavan was doing a lot of rainwater harvesting himself in his own street and area—in Chennai—and started the
program of the Rain Centre (http://www.rainwaterharvesting.org/
network/raincentre.htm).

He was doing this before I became interested, and I learned a great
deal from him. My contribution was to take the same concept to a
bigger area. My background in organizational logistics really helped.
Maybe because I was looking at this as an American coming back to
help in India, I was thinking about how to apply this to a broader area.

We rely on cisterns (large tanks) for capturing the largest amount
of rain during that season. You need to capture the water off the roof,
and in India houses are frequently two and three levels because of lack
of space. You have to take water from cisterns at the top and, through
a series of pipes, get it to the bore well (cistern). Unlike other parts
of India, all the houses in Chennai have bore wells, and this practice
continues to date. At one time, you had to go three hundred feet, then
eight hundred feet, and keep going farther to get water. Because the
city was water starved, and because it is close to the ocean, the saline
water could seep in. You couldn't be sure of getting good water just by

digging a hole. Other places now may not just have the problem of salt water, but certainly contamination is also an issue.

Because of the ordinance, years later they did an analysis in Chennai, and since this project has been implemented, the water table for the entire city has gone up by nine feet. We brought the idea and thankfully the chief minister implemented the ordinance. She was living not too far from these places and might have gone through similar circumstances to get water. The moment she took an interest, it caught on. Every homeowner had to put in his or her own cistern. In Chennai, and in all of India, this is not a lower-class problem, since if someone has a house, that means they have money. She told homeowners if they didn't do this water-saving practice, the government would do it for them and send them the bill. The model house came in handy, and we set up the models that helped many people learn what to do; we had demonstrations, training, and pamphlets in multiple languages. Since all the people who wanted to learn couldn't come to the model house, we had to publish this information in several magazines and newspapers. School classes would come on class field trips to learn. It was very easy to do because it just required PVC pipe from the roof, channeling it, recharging the bore well, preventing the water from going out your gate, and capturing it in a gutter. It was not only simple to do but only cost 5,000 to 10,000 rupees. In contrast, I understand in California where they have severe drought problems they are not interested in capturing the water going over the road.

After the Madras demonstration house, I was motivated to work with the rural areas and realized that the villages and rural areas were even more water starved than the cities. So our family started a program of community wells. We took the help of the DHAN (Development of Humane Action) Foundation, whose mission is to go to villages and make percolation pits and rainwater harvesting systems, including check dams. That was their focus so we aligned with them. They had the methodology with big earth-moving machines to make large community wells—one for the animals and one with filtered water for human consumption. If you don't have a separate well for the animals with their secretions, they will come to where the humans take water. So this is very important. When we dug up the ponds, we had to make sure that we were digging the ponds in two to three separate areas.

When the water from one tank runs over, it doesn't go away, so you have to have enough storage. What we discovered was that during the rainy season, there is so much water they fill up in a hurry. When it rains, all your calculations are wrong because it just pours, and when it is dry, it is dry.

I started doing this work after I retired and sold my company to a Canadian company, although I continued to work as a consultant with them for many years. The sale of the company allowed my family to put a chunk of the money into a charitable fund, the Ramkrishnan Family Trust. A good portion of this money was used to develop this project and fund the wells. Each well costs about $2,000. We would finance our own expenses. Fortunately, our family all supported this effort as something worthy of our time and money. I used to go to India two times per year. Traveling to rural villages takes time and stamina. There is so much to do related to water. Women really carry the burden of access to water. Even city women carry water, but you compound it at least ten times for rural women. They have to walk for miles and carry the water back with them. They can only carry so much, and if it is a two- to four-mile walk, it is even more of a burden. Having the water in the local villages allows women time to do other things, including educating their children, or time to focus more on food preparation for the family. We don't have signs telling everyone that this was funded by our family foundation, as we like it to be a way we could give to many without fanfare. Looking back, water has always been a passion for me. Years ago, in my local city of New Brighton, they had a flat-rate fee for water. Several of us worked with the city for water fees to be based on consumption. It is the only thing that can regulate behavior about water. It took work to create and to develop an accounting system to manage this change of fees.

THOUGHTS ON IMMIGRATION

RAM: Immigration is part of everyone's personal story. Now it seems we say we don't want anyone to come. When people come to America, they should be engaged with the local community. America may be a very rich country, but we still have lots of issues. We want people from every sector. Countries that have intellectual talent and entrepreneurs

Ram and Nayana with daughters
(photo courtesy of Ram and Nayana Krishnan)

can help America. When Indians work here for companies, the same companies go to India to develop their companies' products. If they were shut out of the system and not allowed to stay here, except on a three-year basis, this would harm America. You can't open up immigration for everyone, but we can't let people educated in America be forced to return to their countries. People need to be welcomed to come. Having quality people arriving in America means that America will benefit. You have to be selective but have liberal immigration policies for educated people. I came to America and cast my lot, becoming a fully contributing citizen.

THOUGHTS ON EDUCATION

NAYANA: We were studious children and did well in India. I was a bookworm. Schools in India get into math and science and the fundamentals at a really early age. I started school at the age of four. When I came to this country, my writing was very good and my foundation learning was very good. My speech wasn't good, but my other subjects were good. My parents didn't supervise my homework. My mother was busy with my younger sister and the housework and cooking. She didn't drive initially, so my father took her to get groceries for the week, and she was always cooking, as we had many social events at our house. I asked for my father's help with biology, but the remainder I did on my own.

Every Indian family makes sure children do their homework and gives them the necessary resources. They know they have to invest in education. The new groups of second-generation Indian children are high achievers and excellent performers, and this comes from the parents. They are well adjusted. You can't teach something you don't practice. But they have to have fun, too. The immigrants who came here were highly educated, motivated, and very serious about the education of their children. Parents made sure their children always did their best. The moment the grade sheet came, my father expected to see it. He didn't help with the day-to-day studying, but he had expectations.

RAM: We all had accountability to our families to be well educated. In India we had absolute marks for our standing, so the idea of getting a grade that was measured on a curve was new to us. Testing in America is testing the group and not individuals for what they know. You can be in a class with smart kids and get a C, and with dumb kids and get an A. We prefer stack ranking, since you can know who understands the most. In India, if we didn't do well in school, we knew what was waiting for us. My father would say, "If you don't do well, you will be driving an auto-rickshaw." It was more than a scare tactic. Your whole life depends on how well you do in school. You learned that you had an overall accountability, and if you didn't do well, you knew you had to find out why and correct it so you weren't lagging behind.

SUHAS PATIL, SILICON VALLEY

BORN IN JAMSHEDPUR, INDIA

EDITOR: *Suhas is a lifelong inventor, an innovator, and one of the founders of the global entrepreneurial organization TiE. He was educated at IIT and MIT. Suhas started Cirrus Logic, which significantly contributed to the United States' dominance in computer technology. He provides inspirational and organizational leadership to the Computer History Museum and the Tech Museum in Silicon Valley along with TiE.*

I am very aware of the role education and a love for learning have played in the success of our family, starting from my grandfather. My grandfather started out as a farmer, became a teacher, studied law on his own, passed the law exam, and became a lawyer in a small town. My father was the first one to leave town to go to a university and graduated as an engineer. I was the first in my family to go abroad for graduate studies, to earn a doctorate of science degree from MIT and become a professor. My son earned a PhD in mathematics and served as the first chief data scientist of the US Office of Science and Technology Policy.

I was born in Jamshedpur, the town where Tata Iron & Steel Co. (TISCO) is located. My father worked at TISCO. I do not know why I was not sent to a regular elementary school; instead I was schooled

Suhas with his parents, sisters, and brother
(photo courtesy of Suhas Patil)

at home by a private teacher. When I went to middle school, I had some catching up to do. Fortunately, I survived the transition. I was fascinated by inventors and the things they invented, and I was very interested in finding out how the machines they invented worked. I learned how telephones, sewing machines, and steam locomotives worked. Science subjects were taught well, and in my middle school, I developed an interest in becoming a scientist. My interest in science led me to choose a science major in high school. My high school was run by TISCO and had a very good science lab, and I felt I had a very good high school education.

Along with my formal education in school, I had rich educational experiences at home that most students did not have. First with guidance from my father and later entirely on my own, I built things. I did projects using cardboard, wood, metal, leather, electrical parts, and electronic parts. I learned to sew my own clothes. I learned to fix radios. When I was in high school, I learned to conceptualize interesting things that could be built, and so I designed them and built them. One such project was to design and build a blinking turning light system for my bike. I built wooden fixtures to attach the lightbulbs to the handle of the bike. Electricity was provided by the generator that was already on the bike to power the headlamp. The intermittent connection to create the blinking of the turn lights was created using rotation of the wheel of the bike. The system worked like a charm, and I had something to brag about. I had the only bike with blinking turn lights in my community. Another innovative project I did was to build a submarine for the science fair. The objective of the project was to show principles of physics in the operation of a submarine. It was a working model of a submarine that was propelled by a water jet and went up and down by pumping air into it using a flexible rubber tube to displace water inside the submarine to give it buoyancy. These innovative projects gave me the ability to visualize objects and solve unstructured problems, which was a very important part of my learning as a child.

In addition to his regular job at the steel plant, my father had a radio repair business to earn extra money that was needed to send my uncles and aunts to college. After they completed college, my father shut down the radio business. When the business was shut down, I received all the tools, the broken radios, and World War II junk electronic gear that was used as a source of electronic components. Even before I became a teenager, I had a hacksaw and a drill. They were typical hand tools. I first did things with wood and then metal. My father was there to guide me. Summers were great for projects, and as I had no school during the summer months, that was when I did them. Very quickly, I found the leftover electronic items from the radio business at home. As I became a teenager, I had all of these things to tinker with and had my father as a patient teacher. My uncle who had been in the signal core in the army gave me a book called the *ARRL (American Radio Relay League) Manual*. I also had *Popular Science* magazines that my father had collected. I learned to read English by reading *Popular Science* and the *ARRL Manual*. English was taught in my school, but it wasn't adequate. I wanted to read because I wanted to understand what was being said. I learned the elements of electronics, how valves operate, how the radio works. When my father shut down the radio repair business, the neighbors still had a need to have their radios repaired. They would bring the nonfunctioning radios to me for repair. I would make the repairs pro bono, as I was curious and wanted to fix them; I was learning so much from doing those repairs. When I went to college, I would return home on my breaks to find radios from neighbors waiting for me to service them. I found electronics fascinating, although electronics was not a popular subject in those days with students. Students wanted to learn mechanical and civil engineering because there were jobs in those fields.

I was good in chemistry, physics, and math, but I was below average in languages. This affected my total marks in high school examinations. It nearly prevented me from getting admission into a good college. St. Xavier's college in Ranchi, which was nearest to my town, turned me down. Fortunately St. Xavier's college in Calcutta recognized my excellent scores in chemistry, physics, and math and admitted me. St. Xavier's Calcutta was an outstanding college. Once I got into St. Xavier's Calcutta, there was no stopping me. I successfully made the transition to classes taught in English.

Until I went to St. Xavier's college, I did not participate in any team sports. Fr. Lemming was responsible for me participating in sports. Fr. Lemming himself was a sportsman, and he wanted me to play on the soccer and cricket teams. He taught me how to play tennis, and I even learned to play billiards. Xavier had the facilities, and Fr. Lemming was an outstanding coach and cheerleader.

To get into IIT, I had to take a nationwide entrance examination. I did well enough in the entrance exam to get my choice of a major in electronics and electrical communications engineering. My class of electronics had only twelve students. The department was fully staffed and had all the needed labs. It was like having private tutoring. It was also like being in a start-up company. IIT was funded by the central government of India with help from UNESCO. It was modeled after the Massachusetts Institute of Technology (MIT). It was started in a facility that had once been a jail for locking up freedom fighters during British rule. By the time I got to IIT Kharagpur, seven classes had graduated from the institute, and they had built an impressive building for the library and the departments. The electronics and electrical engineering department had everything we needed for our studies even though it was a small department. I got a very good education there. My peers were good

Suhas with friends at IIT
(photo courtesy of Suhas Patil)

and everyone has done well. My professors had done their doctorates abroad and had come back with great enthusiasm to teach us.

FROM IIT TO MIT AND PREPARING TO IMMIGRATE

I was constantly inventing. At IIT, invention was part of projects I did for class and for exhibitions I participated in. It was a formal learning process that was intense and rigorous. This is where I was exposed to rigorous academic work. The library was phenomenal and labs were very good. I was becoming very aware of what was going on in the world of science at other universities, including at UC Berkeley, MIT, and the University of Illinois. Professor Don Bitzer from the University of Illinois was spending a sabbatical year at our IIT, and I had a chance to work closely with him. He was waiting for funding for his PLATO project (Project for Learning Abroad, Training and Outreach) to come though. As soon as funding was received for the project, he returned to the US. Through him I was exposed to serious research. I also learned how researchers were funded in the US. Professor Bitzer encouraged me to come to America to get my doctorate, and I knew that scientists required a doctorate degree. I applied for admission and got accepted to graduate school at the University of Illinois and at MIT. My father did not have enough money to pay for my graduate education. Besides the problem of not having enough money, there was the additional problem of getting foreign exchange in India. The government of India controlled the allocation of foreign exchange very tightly. The rupee was not freely convertible to dollars, even if one got into a top university in the United States. This is the origin of the eight-dollar limit for travel from India those days. I needed a teaching or a research assistantship to attend a university in the US. Both MIT and the University of Illinois were very aware of this need. I was granted a teaching assistantship at MIT. Colonel Fairchild was the admissions dean at MIT who wrote to me about MIT admitting me to the graduate school and giving me a teaching assistantship as well. That letter both changed my life and started a new phase of my life.

I have asked myself, "How is it that MIT gave me both admission into the graduate school and a full teaching assistantship?" IIT required students to do a project in their final year. My project was developing a high-performance electronic counter. An electronic counter can count electrical pulses at great speed. Events can be turned into electrical pulses, and that is how events can be counted. A counter is able to count the rate of pulses as well. It could be used to count cars crossing a street or the frequency of a radio signal, if the counter is fast enough. All counters at that time were built with vacuum tubes and were not portable. I wanted to build a transistor-based counter that was portable and operated using torchlight batteries.

When Professor Bitzer was going back to the US, he gave me his bundle of transistors and told me, "Suhas, make good use of these." This was the gift that made my project possible. I designed and built the entire counter. I used the transistors he gave me to build the electronics of the counter. I built the counter as a complete product. The basis of my undergraduate thesis was that I designed and built the circuit board, the display to read out the count, and the aluminum chassis, and optimized the performance of the counter. I sent a copy of my undergraduate thesis to MIT with my application to graduate school. I think this made me stand out among other applicants, and I received both admission and an assistantship.

Besides doing the electronics project, I had learned to program a computer at IIT Kharagpur. IBM donated a 1620 computer to IIT in my final year. It was the same model of computer that Bill Gates learned programming on. Two professors, myself, and my buddy got to set up the computer and learned how to program it. I had four months of access to the computer, as if it were my own personal computer. I learned machine language, the FORTRAN language, and the real guts of the computer and how it operated. This was a phenomenal exposure to computing, and I had it before I went to MIT.

THE MOTIVATION TO UNDERSTAND
AND NOT JUST MEMORIZE

I didn't start out at IIT as the top student in my class. When I finished, I was number one simply because I outperformed not only in projects but also in all academic subjects. I had a great memory, but I wasn't motivated just to memorize things. I was motivated to understand and therefore didn't need to memorize. This motivation to really understand a subject went back to my high school when trigonometry was being taught. All my fellow students were instructed by the teachers to memorize proofs. My friends used to recall proofs from memory. But when something changed in the problem, they didn't know what to do. I found it hard to go through the memorizing process. It was very boring. I wanted to learn what trigonometry was all about. I learned the art of how to write a proof. A proof uses a mathematical language to restate a problem from one step to the next or to derive conclusions by combining more than one fact. I learned how trigonometry is supposed to be done. Always I was focused on developing an understanding of any subject. This approach to learning did not matter as much in high school, but as I progressed further in my studies, it made a world of difference. I also gained from my personal style of studying. I had the discipline to read the material ahead of time. I took notes while the teacher was talking. I did problems in the chapter before the next day, and I had good retention as a result. We had exams at the end of the year covering all the subjects we learned during the year. Everyone was frantically trying to memorize, but all I had to do was to go over the materials, refreshing what I already understood. I accidentally adopted this style. Maybe someone suggested it to me. My efficiency of learning improved as I went further in my studies. I stood first in my class, and I was able to do graduate studies at MIT. My parents and teachers were happy about this.

I was a bit anxious about how I would stand up against other smart US students at MIT. MIT helped calm my anxiety by introducing me to Mr. and Mrs. Hawkins. Mr. Hawkins was an alumnus of MIT. Mr. and Mrs. Hawkins' family became my host family, and I became a part of their extended family. This lasting relationship has continued till today, even though Mr. and Mrs. Hawkins have passed away. Their three children are like siblings to me. I was also helped by a program called BASIS, sponsored by the Ford Foundation, which was designed to help foreign students coming to Boston-area schools to adjust to Boston and the United States. The students came from all over the world, and we had a wonderful time going through orientation together. We were well prepared to begin our studies in our respective universities, starting from the fall semester.

Because MIT gave me a teaching assistantship (TA), I didn't have to take out a loan or do jobs such as washing dishes to pay for my education. I did get my eight dollars as a conversion of 40 rupees. I knew that it was impossible to safely travel with only eight dollars in my pocket. I hung on to the eight dollars, but to reduce risk and to have money until I got paid as a TA, I converted $150 worth of rupees to dollars, with a promise to the government of India that I would send back $150 to my father within one year. The government in effect was giving me a loan of $150 worth of foreign exchange for one year. I used up one dollar during my travel to the US. Thus I had $157 in my possession when I came to the US. This was a whole lot better than coming to the US with just eight dollars.

COMING TO THE UNITED STATES

I want to share the story of my travel from India to the United States. I was to come from Bombay [now Mumbai] to Boston, with a flight change in Frankfurt for the final leg of the journey to Boston on Lufthansa flight 420. The flight had been booked by a travel agent in Calcutta and my father had paid for the ticket. A week before my departure, I discovered that CBI (Central Bureau of Investigation) agents were doing a background check on me. When my father called the ticket agency to find out what was going on, he found out that the prime minister of India, Lal Bahadur Shastri, was traveling on the same flight as I was scheduled to travel on. I was elated at the possibility of traveling with the prime minister and being able to see him so close. I was dreaming that he might even come by and chat with me! That was the good news. The bad news was that the prime minister was planning to hold the plane at each stop for longer than the scheduled time. As a result, the plane would not reach Frankfurt in time for me to catch my planned Lufthansa flight. I could not afford to take the risk of not reaching Boston on that Lufthansa flight, as someone from the International Student Association was going to pick me up and take me to Boston University, where I was to stay. I could send a telegram about the change in flight to Boston, but there was a risk that I would not get a reply in time confirming that the information about the changed flight had been received and they could indeed pick me up at the airport. I didn't know anything about Boston. And if I had to go to Boston University on my own by taking a cab, I would use up all of my precious eight dollars and some of my $150. I decided not to travel with the prime minister and asked the travel agent to find me another flight from Bombay [now Mumbai] to get me to Frankfurt on time to catch my scheduled flight to Boston.

The flight was changed to an Alitalia flight to Rome. From Rome, I had to go to Milan to get on another flight to reach Frankfurt. The travel agent didn't check that the flight from Rome to Milan was a domestic flight. He didn't know that I had to go from the international section of the airport in Rome to the domestic side and get back to the international section in Milan to board the flight to Frankfurt. I had to have an Italian visa to board the flight to Milan. I discovered all of this only after arriving in Rome. I didn't speak Italian, and most government people did not speak English. I could easily have been stuck in Rome. Finally a young officer from Alitalia who spoke English and understood my problem came to my rescue. He got me a forty-eight-hour travel visa and rushed me to the plane that was waiting for me to board the flight. The door of the plane closed as I stepped onto it. I did get on the plane to Frankfurt from Milan. Getting an Italian visa and paying the entry fee at the international airport in Milan used up some of my precious dollars. I finally got onto Lufthansa flight 420 to Boston. I still remember this travel and arrival so vividly.

Mrs. Smith from the International Student Association met me at the Boston airport. I reached Boston, but my baggage did not arrive at the baggage claim. I was really troubled because all my possessions were in that bag. The prospect of having to replace my clothes seemed very daunting to me. I would also have lost all my family photographs in that bag. Mrs. Smith was very experienced in these matters. She immediately grabbed one of the air hostesses and asked her to go and check in the cargo hold of the plane for my bag. A miracle happened, as she found the bag. By mistake my bag was tagged to go to Philadelphia, which was the last stop of the plane. Mrs. Smith took me to the Boston University dorm where I was to stay during the BASIS orientation program.

For the orientation, BASIS had made arrangements for our stay at Sheldon Hall at Boston University. Sheldon Hall was a girls' dormitory that had been partly converted to a dormitory for international students. Whenever I mentioned that I was staying in Sheldon Hall, people would give me strange looks, as they knew that it was a girls' dorm. I had Japanese, Korean, and American roommates. We had a good time going through the orientation program. Besides learning about Boston and US culture, I gained many international friends and got used to English as it is spoken in the United States.

AT MIT

When I started work at MIT as a TA, I found that one of the best professors in the electrical engineering department, Professor Amar Bose, taught the electrical circuits class to which I was assigned as a TA. There were 250 students in the class, and the class was supported by seven TAs and seven professors who taught the recitation section classes. After each main lecture, the recitation class met where the instructor solved problems and made sure students understood what had been taught in the main lecture. This was followed by weekly homework that was graded by the TAs. As a TA, I met each student in my recitation section on a one-on-one basis for fifty minutes to go over the answers to the homework questions. I made sure there were no gaps in the understanding of the subject covered that week. Because so much was invested in making sure the undergrad students learned the core subjects thoroughly, all the students performed very well on the tests, which were very tough tests, in my opinion. This was my introduction to teaching at MIT. MIT does a great job of undergraduate education—better than any other American university I know.

Suhas at his graduation
(photo courtesy of Suhas Patil)

Because I was interested in computers, I found a way to meet professors who were studying computer science. Professor Jack Dennis agreed to be my master's thesis adviser. He gave me a research assistantship so I could work in his group at the start my second year at MIT. These were the early days of computer science. A tremendous amount of work was being done at MIT in advancing computer science. I was very lucky to work with the top guys in the field, who also taught me how to teach. They were my role models, and I learned a lot from them.

The summer of 1966 was the first summer break for me in the US. I was looking for a summer job. My inquiry led me to the EE department for the job of building a real-time online information system for their use. The department had difficulty keeping track of who was teaching what, and from what account they were being paid for what activity. They had a hundred professors, a hundred TAs, and a hundred research associates in the department. They had to compile reports to manage the department, the sponsored projects, and the budget. The information was in a constant state of change, so it was getting difficult to manage manually. They wanted it online, with the capability to print reports at the last minute when needed.

THE FIRST ONLINE INFORMATION MANAGEMENT SYSTEM

I looked at the requirement and said, "Sure, I'll do this." I knew how to program even though I hadn't taken any programming classes at MIT. I just needed to know what computer would be available for this project. They gave me one undergrad as my assistant, an office in the basement with one terminal, and an account on the time-sharing machine, which had been built two years before at MIT. There were no time-sharing machines anywhere else. I figured out the statement of the problem and how to do it and build it, and it went live before the fall term. I believe this was the first online information management system built anywhere in the world. I was lucky enough to be in the right spot at the right time, and I did it. The department kept using the system for many years. I am told that the Sloan School of Management also used the system. I built it well enough that I wasn't called for a bug repair. Another research assistant was given the project as his work to keep enhancing it.

I was made an instructor in the EE department after two years at MIT. An instructor is like a junior faculty position. You don't apply for instructor positions at MIT; you get recommended by your students and faculty. My doctoral work got done while I was an instructor. I had courses to teach instead of being a TA. All professors teach and do research; instructors do exactly the same thing. In the very last semester, the MIT administration was very nice to me, and they gave me no teaching assignment and asked me to finish writing my thesis.

My thesis was on parallel computers. It was about how to build computers without the use of clocks. I felt well-designed hardware should work correctly and you shouldn't need to debug it using test equipment. I thought we were going to be building bigger and bigger computers, and we had to design hardware that was correct by construction. My thesis related to how to build hardware correctly by construction.

MIT offered me a faculty position as soon as I completed my ScD [Doctor of Science] degree in 1970. For my research at MIT, I got my own research grants from the National Science Foundation (NSF). For a short period of time, I was made assistant director of Project MAC (Multiple Access Computer) at the computer lab at MIT. Professor Fredkin, who was the director of Project MAC, was going to be away for one month that summer. He appointed me as assistant director and asked me to keep the place together, to pay the bills, and to handle any issues that came up. When he came back, he found that the place had not fallen apart. I had skillfully handled a few issues that had come up during his absence, and I was made permanent assistant director of the lab. This was an administrative responsibility in addition to my duties as assistant professor. I was only twenty-eight at that time. I learned a great deal about managing people through this assignment. The biggest thing I learned was to listen more and talk less.

STARTING COMPANIES: ENTREPRENEURSHIP

My first chance to get involved in starting a company was one I did not take. My office-mate Larry Seligman said to me one day, "We are about to start a computer company, and we would like you to be part of the team." They had worked at Digital Equipment Corporation (DEC) and had new ideas on building a minicomputer. I thought about it and decided to finish my education instead. They went on to start Data General (DG).

I did enjoy being a faculty member at MIT, and the work I did at MIT became the basis of Cirrus Logic ten years later. I was focused on how to build hardware—bigger and bigger hardware that would work correctly from the time of construction. I was doing module-based systems. A system built this way worked correctly without clocks through a self-timing mechanism. It became clear very quickly that unless the methodology that I was developing could be applied to the design of the semiconductor chips, it would not have any bearing on how computers were made. Computers weren't going to be made by discrete parts but on the surface of the silicon where everything is flat. The method had to have a solution in a flat domain. You had to flatten it so connections worked and transistors could be used in a certain way. That was how the shift was made, and this was my work as a professor. Through my work, I contemplated that this would be the foundation of how computers (chips) with large circuits could be designed. I went from being a computer architect to the problem of the decade, which was design automation of digital chips. I was one of the early people in the field of design automation of semiconductor chips, and I became known worldwide. This was all while I was at MIT. By 1974, I completed my theoretical work and showed how it would work by using discrete components. I did the emulation of how it would work on silicon. People said it was good for prototypes, but would it work on silicon in the real world? The next step for me was to build my solution on real silicon.

TRANSITION FROM MIT TO UTAH
AND GENERAL INSTRUMENTS

I once went to Utah to give a talk, and a few of the people there saw what I was proposing and asked me to come to the University of Utah and use the semiconductor lab that General Instrument Corporation had donated to the university. I needed a lab, and the staff needed important things to do with the fabrication facility in Salt Lake City. So I said to myself, "Suhas, go west!" I joined the University of Utah as associate professor of computer science in January of 1976. I wrote up my vision and a proposal and submitted it to the National Science Foundation for the University of Utah. It was one of the largest grants given at that time by the NSF to the university to prove this concept from theory to practice. General Instrument had a very forward-looking and visionary senior VP, Larry Hill. Larry Hill offered me support not only through the Utah lab but also through another lab they had in Arizona. General Instrument said, "Okay, we will process chips for you at our expense—just show us that your idea works." I had to prove that you could design an entire system on a single chip. This was the 1970s, when no one in the industry was able to do this. General Instrument wanted the entire set-top box, other than the RF part, to be on a single chip. This was a way to dramatically reduce the cost of making a set-top box. When I actually designed such a chip, they looked at it and said, "Well, let's go make it." This was the part General Instrument used to test-market their set-top box in the market in 1981.

After coming to the United States, I was always interested in starting a company, and I was inspired by Professor Bose, who started the Bose Corporation. At MIT, you had to have a minor to get a doctorate, and management was just as good a minor as anything else. Besides, I thought it would be helpful to me if I ever started a company. If I could find the right opportunity, I was ready to take the risk. I had proven the technology with the help of General Instrument Corporation. Now it was a question of what to do next.

At the university, we had done whatever one could do at a university. One option was to go to General Instrument and begin a new program. I was well settled in Salt Lake City with a house, two kids, a dog, and a cat. I did not want to move out of Salt Lake City if it was at all possible. Larry Hill of General Instrument was very friendly with me, so I said, "Larry, would you entertain [the idea of] me starting a company and working for you from Research Park in Utah?" And he said, "That's not a problem. I'll set up a meeting with Mr. Frank Hickey, the CEO, and if he takes a liking to you, we can move forward." So a meeting was arranged, and I had lunch with the CEO of this billion-dollar company. He had already been prepped for the meeting. He wanted to find out how serious I was and concluded that I was worth taking a risk with. So he said, "Go ahead," and asked Larry Hill to work out all the details. I asked Mr. Hickey if General Instrument wanted ownership in the company. He said there was no need. They would have a contract with the company, and if I did well, they would buy the company. He asked me what my personal financial goal was. I said, after all of this effort, if I made five million dollars at the exit that would be good. Companies need to make money to be successful. He liked that answer. I wasn't going to just tinker around; I was going to try to make money and be successful. Clearly, I was successful in making a transition from being a professor to being a responsible businessman.

General Instrument was ready to sign a contract and fund the company, but the university wouldn't give me a leave of absence. I was left with no choice but to resign and set up a shop in Research Park at the University of Utah. The company was started in 1981 and named Patil Systems, Inc. In the first two years of the company, my technical team was made entirely of five students from the University of Utah and one from MIT.

STARTING CIRRUS LOGIC

After spending almost three years developing Patil Systems in Utah, it became clear that we had to move to Silicon Valley to raise money and have a management team for the next stage in development of

Suhas at Cirrus Logic
(photo courtesy of Suhas Patil)

the company. In preparation to raise money for the company, I came up with a business plan for the company to become a new kind of semiconductor company without a semiconductor fabrication plant. We would design application-specific chips using our superior design tools and use another company's fabrication facility to build the chips. General Instrument's semiconductor division agreed to sell processed wafers at a fixed price. The concept of a fabless semiconductor company was born. Now I could be in the semiconductor business without owning an expensive fabrication facility. Today almost all semiconductor companies in the US use the fabless model, which was pioneered by me. In December of 1983, we downsized Patil Systems to just four people and moved to our sales office in Silicon Valley. Dr. H. Ravindra and Bill Knapp came with me to Silicon Valley. Mark Singer, the fourth person on the team, was already located in Silicon Valley and was doing our sales and marketing.

Suhas and Mike Hackworth at Cirrus Logic
(photo courtesy of Suhas Patil)

After moving to Silicon Valley, I sought help from Kamran Elahian, who was my former student at the University of Utah. Through him I met Fred Nazem of New York, who had investments in Elahian's company in Silicon Valley. Fred Nazem became our lead VC (venture capitalist). He had gone to Caltech and was a nuclear scientist. He could relate to what I was doing and was ready to take the risk with me. He helped us prepare the company for a regular round of financing. Nazem and company led the first round of 1.5-million-dollar financing that included participation by top VCs in Silicon Valley, including NEA (New Enterprise Associates) and Robertson Stephens. Fred Nazem introduced me to Mike Hackworth, a highly recognized executive in Silicon Valley, and helped me persuade him to join Patil Systems as our CEO in January of 1985.

Mike Hackworth was able to quickly recruit the best people from other Silicon Valley companies to assemble one of the finest executive teams for our company. He persuaded Dr. Kenyon Mei to lead engineering and Dr. Mike Canning to lead manufacturing. Before coming to Silicon Valley, I had figured out that the start-up with the best team would have the highest chance of succeeding, just as the football team with best lineup of players has the highest odds of success. Mike

Hackworth made the goal of assembling such a team a reality. At the recommendation of marketing guru Regis McKenna, we changed our company name to Cirrus Logic, Inc.

Mike became my partner in building Cirrus Logic into one of the finest semiconductor companies in the world. Mike was a world-class CEO and one of the best executives I have come across. At Cirrus Logic, he was the CEO and I was Senior VP of Research and Development and chairman of the board. This was an unusual arrangement that worked because we were true partners in building Cirrus Logic.

The first million-dollars-per-quarter revenue for Cirrus Logic came from an upgraded version of the set-top chip Patil Systems had designed for General Instrument Corporation in Salt Lake City. In the late '80s and '90s, Cirrus Logic supported the PC [personal computer] revolution that was taking place. We provided application-specific chips to reduce the cost and increase the performance of PC and laptop computers. We provided graphics, disk drive, communications, and multimedia chips.

KEEPING THE DISK DRIVE INDUSTRY IN THE UNITED STATES

It is fair to say that Cirrus Logic helped the disk drive industry stay in the US and ward off competition from Japan. In the late '80s and early '90s, the US disk drive industry faced stiff competition from Japanese companies. Because disk drives are manufactured in very high volume, there was a danger that Japanese companies would outperform US companies. US companies, which were the originators of disk drive technology, decided to fight back by coming up with performance and capacity improvement on a crazy and aggressive schedule. To do this, they needed application-specific chips to be developed on a similarly crazy schedule. Because of its internally developed superior chip design, automation software, and resulting design that could be manufactured at multiple fabrication facilities of other companies, Cirrus Logic was able to support the disk drive industry in maintaining their dominant position in the market.

After going public in 1989, Cirrus Logic became the fastest-growing semiconductor company in the early '90s. As of September 2016,

Suhas Patil
(photo courtesy of Suhas Patil)

Cirrus Logic was earning almost two billion dollars in annual revenue. My father and mother saw Cirrus Logic go public in 1989. They were very proud of me. I was chairman of Cirrus Logic as a public company for nineteen years.

I had mentors, starting from my IIT days. Professor Don Bitzer from University of Illinois was my mentor. Professor Bose of MIT, who started Bose Corporation, was my mentor. My most important business mentor was Gene Ritvo. Mr. and Mrs. Ritvo were my host family in Weston, Massachusetts. They became my host family when I visited them for a United Nations Day celebration. He was a businessman and taught me a lot about business and finance, starting from my student days at MIT. Professor Fredkin from MIT was my mentor. He had built a company. Professors Bob Fano and Jack Dennis were my mentors. Larry Hill of General Instrument Corporation was my mentor. Fred Nazem, who funded Cirrus Logic, also became my mentor. I was able to build mentoring relationships with people easily.

ORGANIZING TiE

As a result of all the support given to me, my motivation to organize TiE (The Indus Entrepreneurs) was very personal. I wanted to find a meaningful way to give back to society. I had already succeeded as an entrepreneur, and I was in my midlife. It was time for me to think about how to best give back to society. TiE came out of purposeful deliberation. TiE happened when a group of entrepreneurs came together and said, "We want to give back." In the first meeting, we decided to meet every month until we figured out what we should do.

After a few months of deliberation, the group chose me to lead it and organize TiE as a formal entity. This is how I became the founding president of TiE. I introduced many key concepts in TiE, including creating a subgroup of charter members who have additional commitments to TiE. Charter members are the successful entrepreneurs and businesspeople who come to TiE to give back to society by mentoring and helping members who aspire to become the next generation of entrepreneurs. We decided that TiE would be an inclusive organization. We would begin by giving back to Silicon Valley, where we lived and worked. Then we would build bridges to other parts of the US and then to countries in the Indian subcontinent. From the beginning, TiE has been an inclusive organization and is open to anyone who wants to join it, without regard to which community they belong to. TiE has been very successful in its mission to help create a large number of the next generation of entrepreneurs. TiE now has sixty-one chapters all over the world.

THINKING ABOUT AN IMMIGRATION POLICY

Policy with respect to legal immigration continues to be debated in the United States. My personal view is that immigration is very important to US vitality in this globally competitive world. The US has a unique advantage over other countries in that the best and the brightest in the world choose to come to the United States, settle down here, and work to advance the cause of the nation. US businesses should have the best individuals on their side, and they should not be forced to join the competition in another country. Immigrants start a disproportionate number of businesses and companies in the US. They create jobs in large numbers. The founder of Tesla is an immigrant. He created many companies and jobs in the US. I was born in India, came to the US for studies, became a professor at MIT, settled down in the US as an immigrant, and started Cirrus Logic. My story is not unique; it repeats over and over again. Illegal immigration is a troublesome problem. I have no thoughts on how to best solve this problem.

The United States is a nation of immigrants. It is the only country I know where immigrants become an integral part of society, regardless of where they came from. Once they become citizens of the US, they are as passionate and patriotic as anyone born here. Those who give up citizenship of the country where they were born and become US citizens are very passionate about the US, as they became citizens by choice and not by accident of birth. I am no different in this regard. I did not come to the US to settle down here, but I discovered that my thoughts had broadened and I related more to the ideals and values of the United States. My circle of friends was here. I accepted the reality and said to myself, "Home is where your friends are," and I became a citizen of the US.

The United States of America was built by people who deeply care for this nation. They made sacrifices and took actions that built this nation. We have to continue this tradition. Technological advances are shrinking the world. Globalization will continue to increase. To be competitive and be ahead of other countries, we will need to keep investing in our people and institutions.

GIVING BACK: PHILANTHROPY AND RECOGNITIONS

I've been involved with the Computer History Museum from the early days of the museum. We're living in a very unique time in history, when computers, for the first time, are profoundly changing our lives and having an impact on what we do and how we will do things for a long time to come. Change has been taking place very fast. Today, we're so close to the development of computers that we often fail to appreciate the historical significance of these developments. Computer hardware and software and important artifacts of this period need to be preserved before they are lost, so that people in the future will be able to study the development that happened so rapidly in our time.

Gordon Bell and his wife, Gwen, started the Computer History Museum in 1979, when Gordon worked at DEC. The museum was started in the facilities of DEC, and as its collection grew in size, the museum was moved to Boston Harbor. This is when Gordon approached me to get involved, and I joined the board of the Computer History Museum. The Computer History Museum had more supporters in Silicon Valley than on the East Coast. Supporters of the museum in Silicon Valley put together funds to move the museum from Boston to Silicon Valley. Supporters helped the museum purchase a beautiful building in Mountain View that once housed the marketing department of Silicon Graphics. My wife and I are happy to have been early supporters of the Computer History Museum.

Mike Hackworth, CEO of Cirrus Logic, was deeply involved in building The Tech Museum. Because of him I also participated in building the Tech Museum. If you go to the Tech Museum, you will see my handprints on the wall, as I was one of the founding donors of the museum.

My larger financial contributions have gone to educational institutions. Besides giving gifts to IIT Kharagpur and MIT, we have given to UC Berkeley and Stanford University. Our family gave a major gift to Harker Academy, a high school in Silicon Valley, to build their fine arts theater. My gift to IIT Kharagpur was unique in that, instead of giving money to build a building, I donated money to IIT Kharagpur to build a campus-wide high-speed network to connect every student's room to high-speed Internet. IIT Kharagpur was the first educational institution in India to be fully connected to the Internet highway.

At Stanford University, together with our friends, we donated money to support Stanford's study of India's telecom policy and help India deregulate telecom. Without timely deregulation of the telecom sector in India, the country would have missed out on the development of its IT industry, and the digitization of India that is taking place would not have been possible.

I received an honorary doctor of science degree from IIT Kharagpur in 1995, along with Dr. Abdul Kalam, who later became president of India. I was the first alumnus to receive an honorary doctorate at any IIT. In 2009, I received the first Entrepreneurial Achievement award from PanIIT USA (an alumni group of all IIT). As 2017 is the twenty-fifth anniversary of the founding of TiE, I have been elected to the newly formed TiE Global Board of Trustees for a two-year term.

You can see that in giving back, it isn't about just writing a check—I like to be engaged in a meaningful way, generally early on, in order to make a difference. I take the risks with people. When you look at what you do, it's who you are. Are you Indian? Are you American? What are you? I was born in India, raised in India, I have Indian parents, so that's a heritage. But then you come here and you assimilate, you become part of it, you're an American. So am I a product of India? Or am I a product of America? I got my start in India, but I am, in fact, a product of America. And if you look at the institutes, I went to MIT and I'm a product of MIT, and I'm a product of Silicon Valley. That's how I think in terms of who I am. I cannot change the whole world, but I can make some contribution. I would like people who are in America to realize that America was built by people who cared about the whole community.

T. K. SOMANATH, RICHMOND, VIRGINIA

BORN IN MYSORE, INDIA

EDITOR: *Sometimes called T. K., sometimes Som, he is a flexible man who chose a path that was very different from a high percentage of Indians in agriculture, medicine, and engineering. Maybe losing his luggage on a bus from New York City to Florida that stopped in Richmond, Virginia, sealed his future as the leader of community housing programs for the city of Richmond. Inspired by local community volunteers, he spent his career Gandhi-style between whites and blacks as they considered the seemingly intractable question of whether to integrate or remain segregated. He has taken community housing beyond just building structures—he understood that you had to deal with the individual, the family, and the community as a whole. His story inspires us to do better and raise the entire community, not just provide a house.*

In the '60s, the Kennedys were really the magnets to the whole world. The Kennedy idealism, especially Robert Kennedy's speeches, made people think about freedom, democracy, and social justice. For people who were interested in science, there was this space war between the Soviets and the US. John Kennedy made it a priority to get on the moon. As a result, we were all hovering around the US Information

T. K. and Muktha
(photo courtesy of T. K. Somanath)

Agency libraries in many of the big cities [in India]. Since both Kumar [Malavalli] and I were in technical schools and interested in reading *Time* and *Post* magazines, it all had a big impact on us in those days. Of course there was the Peace Corps in the '60s—that had a great impact too. We had lots of influence from President Kennedy and his brother. If you followed those articles in *Time* magazine, you never knew about the social inequities until you heard Martin Luther King. His speeches were not known to the world, nor were the social injustices in the US. American history was not taught in Indian schools. I was not exposed to the civil rights movement here, especially about slavery issues. We always heard about the wonderful quality of life and other aspects of life in the US. If you were inspired as an engineer, you wanted to build the tallest skyscraper, or, [if you were] a doctor, to rise to the top of your profession, and we felt that could be done in America. We always saw these things in magazines, but we didn't have an opportunity to work in the consulting firms or companies where you could help build beautiful structures. There was always fascination toward technology or medical fields. Those were the two big areas—and the colleges for them—that were attractive to young people in India. Along with the Beatles, the world was going through enormous changes in the '60s.

When Kennedy was assassinated, all of India really focused on the US. How was it that a madman could kill such an important leader? [President] Johnson wasn't very well known, at least in India, but he lifted immigration quotas from South Asia, the Far East, and the African countries. Johnson's Immigration and Nationality Act was approved by Congress in 1965, and it increased the immigration quotas for technically qualified South Asians who wanted to come to America.

ON OUR WAY TO THE US

Muktha and I married in July of 1971 and immediately applied for (US) green cards. We wanted to go and explore the Western world. We went to the embassy in Chennai (formerly Madras), and in very little time—about a month—we had our work visas. Once we got the visas, we had to figure out what that meant, because we didn't really have a plan except that we wanted to come and see the West. The US was in a serious recession. We didn't really understand what a recession was or meant. Our friends in New York said, "Why don't you try to come—there are probably always jobs in an engineering firm." Muktha wanted to try her luck in the medical field, as she is a trained physician. We packed our suitcases and applied to the Reserve Bank to get some money exchanged. In those days, the Reserve Bank of India was pretty tight in terms of giving foreign exchange. The rupee wasn't convertible, and they didn't have a big foreign exchange surplus.

There we were with two green cards in hand and some savings between us. We bought two one-way tickets on Air France. That's all we could afford. It didn't matter whether we could return or not. On the way, we stopped in London to visit Muktha's classmates. Between us we had maybe a couple hundred dollars. It was getting to be autumn in England, and Muktha said she needed a jacket to fend off the cold. We bought about a hundred-dollar camel hair coat. We had the remaining hundred dollars and two airplane tickets to JFK [in New York City]. We were received by our friends in New York and stayed in their house while we were looking for jobs. We got some of our money converted on the black market. The rates were several rupees to the dollar, but we got a higher rate. But a big hunk of our money was gone with the camel hair coat.

The second day in Manhattan, I started pounding the pavement. I was going to large engineering firms and didn't know the protocols for getting a job. I just knocked on the door with my résumé and drawings under my arm. The people looked at me strangely and with pity that a person would show up with his engineering certificate and a bundle of drawings. Every morning, I would get up, get ready, look at the Yellow Pages, and call people to find a job. It was quite a challenge. There were no jobs due to the recession. Just like now, the US was in the middle of a war and there was no money for jobs. I thought, *How could this be? How could such a wealthy country not be able to give me a job, with all my skills?* They told Muktha that she would have to pass an entrance exam and do some of her training and residency over again, and until she passed the exams she could not work in a hospital, so she had that challenge. At this point it looked easier for me to get a job.

TRAVELING SOUTH AND THE STOP IN RICHMOND

Some friends suggested I take the Greyhound bus, at the Forty-Second Street terminal, and stop in Philadelphia, Baltimore, and head down south on the Interstate 95 corridor. Muktha was tired of not seeing the sky and felt trapped in the high-rise district. We were staying in Midtown Manhattan, at Seventy-Third and Third Avenue in a one-bed-room apartment, and she felt she was suffocating. We were looking for a way to get out of the city.

I knew it was my job to find some work. I would get up and take the Greyhound bus down the New Jersey Turnpike and visit engineering firms and city halls. No jobs. I would return and borrow some money from friends. It was a routine. I would get lost in trying to find my way around—east side, west side, East Broadway, West Broadway. I didn't understand the differentiation. It was hard not to get lost. I had an interview around Seventy-Fifth and Broadway and didn't know that I needed to be on West Broadway. I missed the entire interview. The worst part was that there were those elevators where one set went to certain numbered floors and the others to others. I got on the eleva-tor that went to even-numbered floors, but I was supposed to be on the twenty-third floor instead of the twenty-second floor that I was on. I felt it was no problem—I could just use the staircase. One day I started on the twenty-fourth floor and went down the stairs, but then the stairway doors were locked. I had to wait until eight or nine o'clock when the janitor came to open the door. I never made the mistake of walking the stairs again. There were some good lessons.

My friends told me the South was kind of rough—they had all these riots, and there was a lot of confusion—so be careful, but Florida would be a good place, with weather like Bangalore/Mysore with a lot of sunshine. And it might be a good place to get a job. I just headed south. Greyhound was the method of transportation in those days. I was impressed with the roads and highways and bridges. Somewhere between Washington and Alexandria [Virginia], the bus lost my luggage when I changed buses heading toward Florida.

I had my three-piece suit that Muktha's parents had given me when we got married. On my way to the South, I was wearing this suit and a nearly new pair of shoes that were so badly stitched that they were wearing out. They couldn't stand the pounding on the pavements of New York City. It was getting late, and the bus driver told me to stay in Richmond, Virginia, and they would find the luggage. I told him that I didn't have a whole lot of money and asked where he thought I could stay in Richmond. I asked him how long I might need to stay until my luggage arrived. If I had to lose my clothes, that would be fine, but I had my drawings and credentials. He said, "We'll find it for you—it must have just been put on another bus. There is a YMCA right across Broad Street from the bus station, about three blocks. They have reasonable room rates." Muktha was not there because I needed to work on interviews and she was working on getting a job in a New York hospital. I could stay at the Y for about three dollars per night, and I eventually stayed about a month. For three dollars we had good sheets, common bathrooms—the typical YMCA. It was located on a bus line right in the heart of downtown.

The front desk at the Y had a big switchboard with buttons. If you had a call on the switchboard, it would turn a button blinking red in your room, and you could go down and pick up your message or call. The lady at the front desk was obviously a volunteer, but I didn't realize it in those days. She was in her late seventies and running this big switchboard. She told me, "I can't really pronounce Somanath, so why don't I call you Mr. Brown?"

T. K. Somanath, Richmond Redevelopment and Housing Authority CEO
(photo courtesy of T. K. Somanath)

I told her she could call me Mr. Brown, but that I needed my messages as I was looking for a job.

I made friends with a Mrs. Morton. She had a little restaurant called Mrs. Morton's Tea Room right across from the YMCA. Everything there had some meat; even the "vegetarian" dishes had something like bacon. I was not fond of any of that so I asked her if I could have some vegetarian meals without any meat. She would bring me homemade buns, which I believe were her specialty. I still remember her pink lemonade and buns. She made a special effort to boil some beans and corn without any bacon. That was the standard fare.

In a few days' time, I got a job with an engineering firm. The job was surveying party chief—that meant I had to take responsibility for surveying construction sites. This was a private engineering firm, a consulting firm. They asked me to do surveying work with a bunch of high school dropouts. I didn't know how to drive and had to get someone to drive me. But they took a chance on me. I had to learn the tricks to handle the dropouts to get the job done. I was also looking for a better job than just doing field measurements and staking out construction sites.

JOINING THE HOUSING AUTHORITY IN RICHMOND

Every state has an employment commission, and that is where I would go to find jobs. A lady in the employment commission told me to give her my résumé and she would see what she could do for me. In a couple of weeks, she called me about a job with the housing authority. There was an entry-level job that she thought might work out for me because I liked housing. I went and saw the director of the housing authority, a gentleman by the name of Fred Fay. He took a fancy to me, probably because he had never had an Indian guy in his office. I suppose I was a curiosity, and he wanted to see what I was up to. He gave me a job and a tour of Richmond. I just couldn't believe the divide between the rich and the poor. There were unpaved streets right in the middle of the city that looked like a third-world country, like in India. How could a country with so much wealth have cities that looked like this? Most of the families and children were African American. They were in ghettos, all packed. The houses had some structure. They were brick. They were built originally as indestructible houses with even concrete floors. I really didn't understand the significance of the [housing] projects in those days. I said that there must be some kind of way to help improve the quality of life for these people.

It was a job, and I started learning on a fast track. The second week I was there, there was a city council meeting with all the white people on one side of city hall and black people on the other. The housing authority was trying to develop some properties in what looked like a predominantly white area. All hell broke loose. People were yelling at each other—just a chaotic scene. I remember thinking what a blood-bath it was. I went to the archives at the housing authority to under-stand why there were such divisions in this country. I read about the civil rights laws and what Kennedy and Johnson were trying to do and reasons why Kennedy was assassinated and about Martin Luther King Jr.'s marches in the South. It was very interesting to see what had hap-pened in the last ten years. I thought it was worth it to stay and see how I could make difference.

It was both a technical and government job. One of the projects I was working on was housing development for seniors. The project was eight stories high, and there were lots of challenges with engineering construction and getting money from the government. At the same time, I kept wondering why. Why were all these social inequities there? I didn't realize there was such a divide in America. I wasn't white and I wasn't black. They were probably curious about who I was. Back in the '70s in Virginia, there weren't many Indians. The first Diwali festi-val had about ten or twelve people. We formed an Indian association, and I was treasurer, secretary, and president. One of things we used to do was try to get the films that families wanted to see—the Hindi Bollywood movies. I would go pick them up at the Greyhound bus depot, where they were sent by some distributor in New York.

THE INTERMEDIARY BETWEEN WHITES AND BLACKS

I had access to both the white and black camps. They knew I was competent, and both sides just wanted the job done. I started to help build bridges and find solutions that made for good choices of how families could live in better neighborhoods. In the '40s, '50s, and '60s,

T. K. at an East End community meeting, 2016
(photo courtesy of T. K. Somanath)

they were building these large public housing projects for hundreds of people, and with it came the problems of such mass density of people in poverty. I read what the 1964 Civil Rights Act meant, and we started executing that in a way that was right—small units that matched the historic fabric. Instead of six hundred units, we would build thirty- to forty-unit housing. We wanted to provide choices in access to families that didn't really have any choices for finding those kinds of houses. I was looking at the deeds of trust for houses where there were clearly prohibitions against selling houses to blacks, and the banks redlined neighborhoods and wouldn't help them with their financial ability to buy. Fortunately, I was curious about the situation and how we could change this for people. People not only did not read the laws, but people said, "It just can't be done." I was challenged. I wanted to provide leadership and choices.

There were developments being planned that would put highways through historic neighborhoods. They wanted the land for the roads, not housing. The constituents had no voice in living in well-planned neighborhoods. I wanted to make sure that they had a proper voice in the process. We started to speak with some of the leaders of the communities. We got them organized and engaged in a bottom-up planning process. Some of the developers would bring the money from Washington through their political connections. I'd work with the local citizen leaders to tell them their options and how to prevent creating another ghetto. Adding more huge developments just didn't make any sense. They needed to get into neighborhoods that would help support the families with educational opportunities for the kids. As a neighborhood activist working as a government advocate, I was really advocating for the poor people. I tried to get an early childhood education center and community centers built. I did that for about fifteen years. I realized more and more of my time was spent in fighting with the federal government for resources and managing the politics, as opposed to doing really good work.

THE BETTER HOUSING COALITION

A lady by the name of Mary Tyler McClenahan, along with her friend Carter McDowell, wanted to provide some alternate local solutions and raise resources to address homelessness and the lack of affordable housing. She managed to organize some well-meaning, good-hearted persons together to address issues of poverty and social inequity. She would hold retreats and sessions and started a nonprofit organization called the Better Housing Coalition. The idea was to empower local citizens to do community development work as a bottom-up process, with a stake in the neighborhood by the people and families who were living in it, so that they would take care of it. It was a great model. We found a national partner to help. There is an organization called LISC (Local Initiatives Support Corporation) that had a similar sort of goal to help local communities address neighborhood and afford- able housing development. This group was initially funded by the Ford Foundation, back in the '70s, to help in big cities such as Chicago, New York, and Detroit—cities that had similar issues on a large scale. We wanted someone as a partner to work with us. So we brought LISC to Richmond by raising funds from local corporations and wealthy donors to fund some of the local fledgling nonprofit housing groups, with matching funds from LISC. We started a million-dollar loan fund to support the Richmond community development industry, and Mrs. McClenahan hired me as the director of the Better Housing Coalition, with a small operating budget of about $125,000. The first few years, we did a lot of advocacy and organizing neighborhoods. Then LISC started its work, providing grants and technical support for local non- profits. But there were areas that LISC would not cover, so we thought it was time for the Better Housing Coalition to jump-start this work where there were no activities. We were careful not to compete with the other local nonprofits. We started organizing people block by block and getting nationally known architects to work with us. Our target was to build or remodel the thirty- to forty-family units, single family units, and rental homes. We were looking after the needs of both the families and the communities in a holistic manner.

There were lots of folks living in deplorable housing conditions. With careful planning, we took a vacant property in the block, fixed it up, moved a family into the remodeled home, and brought services to those families. We even helped them get their GEDs and made sure the kids had after-school programs. Once you really touch housing, you get into people's lives. You find out why there was persistent poverty. We had families—third-, fourth-, and fifth-generation kids and families—caught in cycles of poverty. Historically, these families came as sharecroppers from the South, and they'd moved up to broken families, teen pregnancies, and boyfriends living in the house, up to no good and taking advantage of the single women. The only way to get them out of these conditions was with programs with a good wage. But they needed job training, job preparedness, and they needed to learn the strengths to break old habits. It was important for us to have the third leg of the stool, and that was to have a community social-work program that provided housing with enriched services.

We not only wanted good-quality housing, we wanted them to be successful with their families in their way of living and raising their children, so we brought social workers to them. I followed that model and was fortunate that I could find some local funding organizations that wanted to fund the social work model. It was free of cost to the residents so that they could talk to the social worker about issues and problems. We brought services to the site so the people didn't have to figure out what to do and how to manage between the mishmash of services available. As a result of doing this work for the past twenty years, we have seen some really great outcomes, not only for the neighborhoods but also for the families.

SUPPORTING THE GRASSROOTS COMMUNITY LEADERS

In 1997, the HUD (Housing and Urban Development) developer had a property foreclosed on and had to "give the keys back." There were some two hundred low-income families with an average annual income of $6,500 in HUD properties throughout Richmond. In the middle of all this, there were wonderful families who heard about all these programs.

One lady, Judy Cox, who was a truck driver and who chose to live in the neighborhood, made sure that HUD did not [get foreclosed on]. (What happens in foreclosure is that the highest bidder gets the property. The new owner could be a slumlord to all these low-income families and the cycle would begin again.) A group of ten or twelve determined women who lived there wanted to bring transformation to the neighborhood, so they contacted us. We used to have a lot of community meetings to talk about organizing for various causes. Community activists heard about what we had done [in the past]. There were twenty-seven acres with housing outside of the Richmond city limits, and the county didn't want anything to do with the development. They wanted it to go away so they didn't have to do anything about it. We entered into negotiations with HUD and blocked the sale for almost a year. In the meantime, we organized the residents and came up with a plan. We went to HUD and bought the twenty-seven acres and 424 apartments, which were half-empty, for $100. We assembled public/private financing with foundations and Wall Street, acquired various properties around it, and made it into a planned mixed-use development of sixty acres. It had affordable senior and family housing, childcare, a medical clinic, and a retail center offering jobs. It was going back to being like a little town. For the families that made $6,500 in 1997, their income today has tripled. There used to be three hundred police calls every quarter. Now police calls are almost nonexistent. If they get a call, it is about some stranger walking the streets.

We learned how to rebuild some of these family-friendly neighborhoods, and we've made a significant impact on people's lives. Of the kids that were in this development in 1997, now almost ten of them are going to college every year. The model of the children going through the childcare center designed for 150 kids, with wraparound services under the Head Start program, has created pathways to colleges and careers. The result is that the Better Housing Coalition is the leader in this type of holistic community development work in the Richmond metro area. This really is a way to break the cycle of poverty.

MY EARLY YEARS

I was born in the city of Mysore in the state of Karnataka, India. My father was a successful lawyer in Mysore. My grandfather had passed away due to illness before my father was born, so he never knew his dad. My father was raised by my great-grandfather. They were Brahmins—priestly families who had migrated to the Hindu kingdom of Mysore to escape harassment by Muslim warriors in Andhra Pradesh. They moved from Andhra Pradesh back in the 1600s because the Mysore maharajah was a Hindu king who attracted well-known scholars to Mysore. The king would somewhat take care of them. He would give them responsibilities at the temple, five acres of paddy fields (rice) so the families would always have some food, and he would give them a small house in the fort of Mysore Palace so the families could settle down.

If you look at the records, we were from a high-achieving, scholarly family—Sanskrit scholars—and my great-grandfather was a textbook writer. The women were also educated. My mother went to high school, and because she married young, she didn't go back to college. My mother and Kumar Malavalli's mother were classmates in high school. My aunts were all very well educated. Of my mother's two sisters who have passed away, one was a scholar of Russian language as well as statistics. She worked in the Indian Defense Department in Delhi. The other was a professor of English at the university. Neither of those aunts was married; we would call them "spinsters." The youngest of my mother's sisters and her husband are research scientists, retired from NYU. Education was the top priority in our family, and our parents taught us how to discipline ourselves to get an education. It was expected that we would get a good education and good grades and be successful. My elementary school and middle school were public schools of about five rooms right in the heart of the market near my home. The teachers were just wonderful. There was good discipline and a lot of homework that my mother, who was a homemaker, helped me with. When I came home from school, I was expected to focus my time and know my lessons. I have an older sister who now lives in Holland and a younger brother who is an electrical engineer and was a classmate of Kumar's brother Shivaram.

The house where I was born was right in the middle of the Mysore market. I had many classmates who were from the merchant class—a lot of poor kids—but we had no differentiation because we all loved each other. We didn't see a class or caste distinction, even though our parents did. There were a lot of street urchins where I grew up. Our house and my dad's office were on the second floor. The first floor was shops, and the third floor had some tenement houses. I used to play soccer in the street with these kids from my elementary school. Cricket was played on the grounds of the town hall.

I started my schooling early. When I was four years old, I was in second grade because I was able to read and write well and understood mathematics, thanks to my mother's efforts in raising me. I completed my matriculation (twelfth grade) when I was sixteen. I went to college early; normally you would have been twenty years old. In those days, there were no entrance exams. I applied to various colleges and got a seat in the engineering school in my hometown so I didn't need to go away. I also got a seat in a college about two hundred miles away, but my parents preferred I stay in our town. In those days, you had to depend on staying in someone's house as a paying guest—there were no big dorms. Like in any middle-income family, my mother stayed vigilant about our education and kept an eye on what was going on. My dad was a busy lawyer attending to his office and the courts. My father became successful, and he built a home near the Lalitha Mahal Palace.

The high school was called Sarada Vilas High School. After I finished high school, I went to Sarada Vilas College for pre-university, and then I joined the engineering college at NIE (National Institute of Engineering), Mysore. I bumped into Kumar Malavalli in my third year of NIE; I think he came from another college. We hit it off with each other. The method of teaching in the college was so poor that I was bored and I really wasn't motivated. Except for a few professors, many of the teachers were ill prepared and used a set of notes they'd prepared ten years ago, so it wasn't very interesting. Outside of the college, I was interested in books and music and used to cut class to watch English movies. It wasn't until our third or fourth year of engineering school that we bumped into girls that were going to medical school. I think Kumar and I broke all the rules of the college. We'd go on day trips and try eating in hotels. Kumar had a camera so we took wonderful photos. We didn't do anything bad—we were just curious.

Kumar got an internship at a German steel factory in the north of India. After finishing civil engineering, I had an opportunity to work in a village. I joined my uncle's company to build miles of irrigation canals, roads, and bridges. We hired a lot of local people from the nearby village and built an irrigation canal and the dams and infrastructure needed to irrigate and provide drinking water. This was a very satisfying experience. The government of Karnataka encouraged graduating engineers to become involved in rural development and public works projects. After some time, I became disillusioned. There were lots of corrupt officials involved in the process. It made me mad that I was putting my heart and time into building the company, and here was this guy in the government asking for a 10 percent commission before approving payment for the work completed. After finishing the project, I thought that was enough. I started to work for an architectural engineering firm in Bangalore.

Muktha had completed her medical degree and was also working in Bangalore for about two or three years when we decided to get married. We were from different family backgrounds. Muktha was from an agricultural community, and I was from a Brahmin family. Our families weren't supportive about our decision to get married. This influenced me later in life. We were exercising our freedom of choice. Just because someone was born into another family or caste, that shouldn't be a reason not to marry. So this was one of the additional reasons we decided to go see the rest of the world. We spent a lot of time in coffeehouses with Peace Corps friends about our age and exchange students from US universities. We were impressed with those who left the US to go to small villages to help with teaching modern methods of animal husbandry, including poultry farming. We were curious to learn about this country (the US) that was sending their youth all over the world as Peace Corps volunteers. Who were these people who would leave their country and family to help improve the quality of life in rural India?

My maternal grandmother's side of the family was always concerned about helping others. My grandmother's sister was a social activist, helping working women who came from the villages to Bangalore to find jobs. She would build these working women's hostels as a safe and decent place. My dad was also keen on helping poor people and provided them with legal aid free of charge. Helping was a lesson we learned around the table. I would go to the town hall as a young student to listen to then prime minister Pandit Nehru speak. Gandhi was dead, but he was still a big influence. I learned from him to "be on the right path" and "speak the truth" about social justice. As a student, I could observe what he did in fighting for freedom from the British through nonviolence and his approach toward the concept of the untouchables.

India got independence in 1947, and I was just a year old then. Unfortunately, Gandhi was assassinated in 1948, and India became a republic in 1956. At home all of this was discussed in a positive way. Like most houses, we too had a portrait of Gandhi in our house. The atmosphere that pervaded our house was to do good.

We finally got our plan to go to the US. I told my mom, when she came to see me and Muktha off at the airport, that we would probably be back in a couple of years. We weren't sure whether we were coming back or not. We were curious about the Western culture and just wanted to explore. We were like explorers, not just exploring a foreign country, but also the culture and a way of living. We didn't have any idea that we were going to make it our life. I became so busy with the housing authority, and Muktha with her education and training, and then the children came along—and we just lived our lives here.

Yes, there was discrimination. We were looking for an apartment on Chamberlayne Avenue in Richmond. I'd see an ad and I'd call them up and say, "I saw the ad in the paper. We are looking for a one-bedroom apartment, and I am interested." The landlord would meet me to show the apartment and immediately tell me it was already rented. I thought, *Well, maybe it is rented and I was just late.* But this happened about ten times, and I started to understand there was something wrong. I'd go downtown to a department store called Miller and Rhoads to have my hair cut, and they would refuse to cut my hair. Discrimination was very much prevalent in the '70s. A couple of years before that, in the late '60s, the lunch counters in the department stores wouldn't serve blacks. Richmond was the capital of the South in the Civil War, and there were remnants of these practices still going on in the South. With the enforcement of civil rights laws, access to housing and jobs are improving, but there are still challenges in education, access to transportation, and jobs. With the current knowledge-based economy, Richmond is attracting young, diverse families, and there is a renaissance of the downtown area.

THOUGHTS ON IMMIGRATION POLICY

If I were to advise the government on an immigration policy, I'd remind them that this country has always attracted people who brought innovation and great initiatives for change and providing solutions. Every ten years, there have been wonderful technological breakthroughs. We need to attract those people who are curious, who want to innovate, to do research and provide new solutions. It's how we became number one in the world, but now we are failing. We have created boundaries to discourage people from coming to this country. Case in point—my nephew completed his MS in computer science at the University of Florida. It was quite revealing that he could get into a research program in a Swiss lab, but he couldn't find an opportunity to do research in *this* country, even though he was educated here. There may be call centers started in India, but as US companies have sold lots of equipment, manufactured here, to operate those call centers, there has to be a two-way street. We have somehow ignored these really big issues. If we can have an effective immigration policy, we can really grow the economy.

We need to look at education reform and immigration policy. Look at the various slogans different administrations have concocted about education, such as "Race to the Top" and "No Child Left Behind"—they don't have anything to do with outcomes. It should all be about choices and not slogans, just like in housing. People are worried that charter schools will leave poor kids behind. It all requires discipline and structure by the family. Look at some of the outcomes in the schools in Harlem. I had a good family life, but the family values in the Western world have been eroded. Families are under enormous stress. Just to get to work, one has to travel for hours, and by the time they get back home, there is no time for the kids. We see the latchkey-kid communities. We have to take care of our youth after school is out. They have to be engaged in a safe place. That's when most of the troubles occur. There is no teen pregnancy among the kids who have come to our programs. There is support for homework so they excel in school. There are sports activities and computer labs. We have to pay attention to what we take for granted during a child's formative stages. It has become the village that raises the children. Every house that we built has a front porch so the mother or a neighbor can keep an eye on the street. In the apartment communities we built, there are no remote parking lots. It is like the good old American city, with a hierarchy of public/private places—a public street/sidewalk, a porch, and cars parked in the rear of the house. The distance between houses is small so the moms can talk with each other. We have to build these types of communities without taking shortcuts to create profits. You can't just increase densities without paying attention to human needs. There is a cost to this type of development.

It is the same with transportation. There is a big disconnect between jobs, land use, and transportation. Jobs are in the outer ring, with people living twenty to thirty miles from the job, which requires them to invest a huge amount of money for transportation. With 40 percent of their income going toward housing and 30 percent toward transportation to an outlying job, there is hardly any income left to do other things. It's all so disconnected: jobs, health, transportation, and housing. It's time to pay attention to growing these mega-regions. We have to connect important centers of jobs with public transportation that requires less dependence on foreign oil and creates less carbon footprint. It is critical for the coming century.

MY LIFE TODAY

Eighteen months after retiring from the Better Housing Coalition, where I worked for twenty-four years, the Richmond Redevelopment and Housing Authority (RRHA) board was looking to fill the vacant CEO position with a new leader. They appointed me to help them on an interim basis. I couldn't say no, since I was concerned for the future of RRHA and very low-income residents. I wanted to create better choices and opportunities to improve the quality of life in public housing communities. My work reflects the vision and aspirations of grassroots leaders in our community to improve the quality of life of many low-income families who are trapped in the system. After six months, the board made me permanent CEO, which I have been for two years, and that has helped in attracting and retaining talent to build a strong housing organization. I have come full circle after four decades. I have been inspired by leaders such as President Obama and the late Martin Luther King Jr. to eradicate poverty, bridge the racial divide, and build trust in our communities. In January, on Martin Luther King Jr. Day, I make a habit of rereading Martin Luther King's letter to fellow clergymen from the Birmingham jail. It is a powerful, thoughtful, inspirational argument for advocacy of nonviolence and the pursuit of social justice.

EDITOR: From the *Richmond Times-Dispatch*, published April 28, 2014:

> "The first building honoring the former president and chief executive of the Better Housing Coalition, T. K. Somanath, was dedicated Monday. Somanath Senior Apartments, at 1208 N. 28th St. in Church Hill, is a three-story building with 32 one- and two-bedroom apartments. It also includes seven net-zero energy apartments, which opened a year ago in April, across the street. The 39 new apartments are part of the coalition's development at Beckstoffer's Mill Lofts & Apartments, which started in 2010 with a capital fundraising campaign that leveraged an estimated $36 million in community investments. The development, in a 10-block radius in north Church Hill, is made up of the adaptive re-use of Beckstoffer's Mill into 22 mixed-income loft apartments, the preservation of 56 affordable rental homes, 12 single-family for low-to-moderate-income buyers and the Somanath Senior Apartments."

KAILASH JOSHI, SILICON VALLEY

BORN IN PAURI, UTTARAKHAND, INDIA

EDITOR: *Kailash's route from the hills of northern India to becoming a general manager of IBM and eventually helping IBM return to India after decades of absence is extraordinary. Kailash is one of the founders of TiE and also the American India Foundation (AIF). His personal life philosophy is inspiring, and as a humble man he continues to advance the causes of equity, fairness, and philanthropy in both India and the United States.*

FROM INDIA TO THE UNITED STATES AND THE PRECIOUS EIGHT DOLLARS

My move to the US in 1963 was not triggered by a desire to migrate. Instead it was driven by the collective resolve of my graduating class members to earn PhD degrees from US universities. Ours was a transitional generation, as the prior generation of Indian students went to England for further studies. Only fifteen years past independence from the British, our generation in 1962 was projecting the massive opportunities in India for engineering and technology in the coming years

Kailash Joshi
(photo courtesy of Kailash Joshi)

and wanted to be well prepared. The US was deemed to be the preferred destination for this purpose.

In 1962, our class of twenty-two (males only) was completing degrees in metallurgy from [Indian] Institute of Science (IISc), one of the most prestigious schools in India. Most applied to top US universities and some to UK schools, and more than half got into the PhD programs. My objective, like that of my friends, was to secure a PhD degree, return to India, and become a professor. In reality, after the PhD degree from Cornell University, I decided to get some experience, and then went back to India to get married to Late Hem Lata, and we became parents to our beautiful son, Monty. This all happened in a span of eight years, and we found ourselves attached to the US rather comfortably, in professional, family, and emotional terms.

In the '60s, getting a US visa was not a problem, because the number of Indians traveling then was very small, and those wanting to work and stay overseas were even fewer. So in quick succession I went from being a student to a green card holder.

There were some interesting factors surrounding my decision to go to the US for graduate studies. First, no one in my extended family had ever taken this route. Our circumstances were modest in financial terms, but very rich in education. My family did not have resources to fund my US education. I got scholarships, assistantships, and eight dollars from the government of India. Why only eight dollars? Well, India had a chronic shortage of foreign exchange during the '60s, '70s, and '80s. The country had a major imbalance between exports and imports, including massive food imports. But India encouraged its youth to go abroad for advanced education. They said, "We love you, but you are on your own. So we will hand you eight dollars for a taxi and wish you good luck." Incidentally, these days any Indian citizen can ship out up to $300,000 per year for investments, etc. So, there has been a dramatic change.

Among fellow Indian students in the US some picked apples, others did dishes in the cafeteria, and so forth. People have different stories. I did a part-time job in the library, for example, and also had teaching assistantships. If you ran out of money, your buddies would lend you some. We helped each other out under an honor system. At Cornell I had an old Rambler car for which I made eight keys and gave them out.

I told my friends where I parked it, and they could take it any time they needed, as long as they left a note for me and put the gas back in it. So it was a shared car. We had a good buddy system. If someone needed to travel, like going to India, we would pool our money and send them off. The loans were always paid back.

I grew up in the Garhwal hill region of India in Uttarakhand in the north. It is a beautiful region with 70 percent forest coverage, rivers, and lakes. It is a heavenly countryside, about three hundred miles north of Delhi. Our elders were in education. Incidentally, in June 2013 this state suffered one of the most devastating floods, which affected over one million people.

My grandfather was superintendent of schools, and my father was a teacher of English in a high school. So, education was in our blood, and just about everyone in my family was driven to achieve the highest education they could get. But our hill terrain was harsh when it came to facilities for education and health care. In fact, motor roads connecting my hometown of Pauri were built around the year of my birth, and electricity reached my home when I completed high school. So prior generations had to venture far away to the cities of the plains for education and somehow manage things within their meager means. In my particular case, my inspiration and support was my maternal uncle, I will call him RB, who was a civil engineer. So, after high school, I left the hills to go to the city of Meerut, where I stayed with Uncle RB, my aunt, and their five children. There were a few other cousins also staying with them for studies.

We went to school for nine months, and for the summer we would read books, prepare for the next year, and goof off with friends. We mostly played outdoors, climbing trees, playing football in the streets. For us childhood was nothing but running around and playing. We were a close extended family system of cousins and friends. We would only come home from the outdoors for evening dinner. We were a close-knit group, but would also fight like all siblings. For school we would have some form of uniform and very strict teachers. You studied for six to eight hours and came home. My father taught English so he would converse with me in English. Our home language was Hindi and a local dialect call Pahari, so we used three languages freely at home. Our mother carried on the spiritual dimensions for our family. My parents were Hindu. There was an altar at home; we went to temples only on a few occasions. We were told to do our own reading of religion and thinking, but my mother showed us about prayers (puja), and you followed along. It was a typical Hindu family living.

I received my first degree in physics, when I lived in my uncle's house, and then went to Bangalore and got a second degree in materials science. My school, IISc, was very demanding and competitive for admissions.

The biggest highlight of IISc was that it attracted students from all over India, with different languages and backgrounds, and everyone was top of the class. You now had to be differentiated among students who came from top universities. The nature of competition drastically changed for us. You had to be really good and work extra hard to stay at the upper level. Unlike the high school days, you now faced a bigger league of talent. Well, someone would still end up at the bottom, and you sure didn't want to be there. We had no tutors; you worked extra hard—more diligence in the library, less playtime, more serious homework and discipline. In homework and term papers you added extra meat on it. You had to show your teacher you really knew your subject and were a bit different. Your whole perspective on excellence and competition changed. With only a hundred people from all over the big country of India, you were in a whole new pool of people. We made good friends and have maintained our relationships over all these years. Some of them are professors at top universities, and some retired from national laboratories and manufacturing companies.

MASTER'S AT WASHINGTON STATE AND PHD AT CORNELL

I got admitted to Yale University, and at the last minute they changed the US defense grant that I was expecting so I couldn't go there because they canceled the scholarship. So now I had this entire year ahead of me. I could not apply until next year. So I applied for a job in India as an instructor of an engineering school and taught for a year at a college in the north. It is a prominent school now in the north. Having been academically successful in India, it was very easy to get used to the US system. We knew how to compete, and the books and authors were also familiar. I applied again, and this time Washington State University came through first. Washington State University (WSU) was a land-grant university with a strong agriculture faculty. So, there were many more students from India and Pakistan in those fields than engineering. The American diet was straightforward. I wasn't a vegetarian, but I had never eaten beef in India. I decided to experiment with beef for some years and then gave up.

I got my master's at WSU after a year. In 1964 I subsequently joined Cornell University and completed a PhD in the emerging field of materials science and engineering. What baffles me in hindsight is how I left my home country for the promise of America without the slightest concern or contingency plan if things did not work out. Strangely enough, all the wise men and women of my extended family enthusiastically supported this, without even a whisper of any inherent risks. America of the '60s was a land of unquestioned opportunity to many in India and around the world. So optimism brought me to America, and hard work and luck brought results, as I had collected four degrees by age 26: two bachelor's, one master's, and one PhD. I was on the research faculty at Cornell for one year and then joined IBM in 1968.

TRAVEL TO THE UNITED STATES AND
SPENDING THE EIGHT DOLLARS

When I first came to the US, I landed at Portland, after two days of flights on Boeing 707s. When I landed, I felt my whiskers from the travel so I thought I should get a shave. I wanted to look my best for fellow students who were going to receive me at Pullman Airport. So I walked into the airport barbershop, where the barber politely asked me to sit on this big chair. He took me through a methodical treatment of hot towels, shaving cream, and two rounds of razor shave. It felt great, and why not? It is America after all. I figured I would have paid 25 paisa for a shave in India, so with the dollar exchange rate it would probably be 25 cents now. So still feeling great, I thanked him and asked how much I should pay. He said, "That will be four dollars even." My jaw dropped a bit, but then I also remembered reading how one is expected to add 15 percent tip on all services. I gave him a five-dollar bill and asked him to take $4.60. So, sadly, within hours of landing in the US, my net worth had shrunk from the memorable eight dollars to $3.40 that day. My thoughts shifted to *I need to be very careful in these spending decisions now.* It was a month until I got to college. I was going to live in a dormitory, so they said I could wait to pay until I got paid. I got a room, all the books and food, and a maid to change our sheets. Life was good, and when the checks came in I paid for it. It was beautiful luxury for about $180 with three meals a day in the cafeteria. It was an easy adjustment. I just had to study hard.

MARRIAGE AND THE IBM YEARS: MUCH LEARNED AND ACCOMPLISHED

Just before joining IBM I went back to India. I got married to Hem Lata, a remarkable lady who would be my partner, guide, and support for over forty-one years. I knew her through our family connections, but not in a romantic way. Her family and mine were known to each other in mutually positive ways. There were discussions about getting married. We consented, and plans began for an arranged marriage. Hem and I were blessed with one son, who gave us three beautiful granddaughters. Hem had a master's in English literature. We started our life together when I joined IBM in 1968 as a staff engineer. In my first job I was assigned to a dream project called ACS—or Advanced Computer System, a liquid-cooled computer under the legendary Gene Amdahl. Gene directed three small groups located in Endicott, New York (where I worked); Poughkeepsie, New York; and Menlo Park, California. After a couple of years I moved into management. I liked working on technologies, but working with people appealed to me even more. My career took off in a positive direction and at a good speed.

I was assigned to various functions, including manufacturing and semiconductors. I liked managing product development efforts most. I was associated with the creation of IBM's first fax machine and the first laser printer. I learned that most of our cost curves we weren't very realistic. And further that we weren't tough on ourselves for achieving competitive cost targets. At IBM the volumes were never a problem. The first year we launched a laser printer, in 1986, that product brought me one billion dollars of revenue in the first year, which amazes me even today. At IBM you could do that because it had the resources and the market.

IBM had a very good system for people management and succession planning. There was the "Early I" or Early Identification program. When young professionals joined, middle managers would begin to identify individuals with good leadership qualities and ownership attitudes. This list would evolve through various levels of management. There were the future directors and vice presidents of the company. For example, when I was general manager I had fifty such Early Is to mentor out of a ten-thousand-employee pool. That is how IBM grew its executives and probably does to this day.

Well, come to think of it, I too was given that opportunity with Jack Kuehler, who became IBM president. I "carried his suitcase" for six months. With Jack I learned two things. Jack did not take notes; he remembered everything. So I decided I would do the same. To this day, I strongly depend on my grasp and memory and do not necessarily write things down. From Jack, I also picked up the way to relate to people in personalized ways. For example, while flying to IBM locations, he would learn things about the wives and children of people he was going to meet. So, as we got off the plane, Jack would start his conversations with the receiving executives with subjects like the colleges where the children are studying, a wife's health, etc. Everyone thought that was amazing, and the visit would be off to a great start. Sadly, Jack passed away a few years ago.

In 1980, I moved to Tucson, Arizona, to manage manufacturing of storage, tape, and high-end printer products. In manufacturing I learned about a different mind-set: people dedicated to high quality and work ethics. They are very special people. They have insights that are almost never tapped. When I came to the Tucson plant, I did not park in the management parking area. Instead, I parked my car in the back of the factory and walked through the factory to my office. As I walked there were all these employees, many of them middle-aged ladies who would whisper to me, "Let us show you something, there is something wrong here." So now I was loaded with facts before I even entered my office. My team now could not tell me "all is well" during the management meetings since they knew that I knew a lot, so we spent time in constructive discussions. I therefore learned that factory workers have valuable insights that don't get tapped for various defensive reasons.

The US manufacturing dominance eroded primarily because of the cost of labor. When you have a big difference in cost, such as the wage gap for the same job, the whole dynamic changes to a new reality. India is experiencing this in software development. The fact is that over the very long haul the whole world will equalize. But between now and then there will be winners and losers in various markets, driven by cost considerations.

After Tucson I became the laboratory director at IBM, in Lexington, Kentucky. This is where most (Lexmark) printers are designed, and it had about a thousand engineers for typewriters, home PCs, supplies, and printers. I led this laboratory for two years and then went on to become general manager. It was a profitable four-billion-dollar business and running smoothly. Recently a large investment was made in automation, so very high-volume products could be built and shipped worldwide. Japanese companies were our fierce competitors and a benchmark to meet or exceed. My time was especially devoted to people management, manufacturing quality, zero defects, inventory, management, customer satisfaction, technical support, and keeping headquarters in the loop.

BRINGING IBM BACK TO INDIA

After five years at Lexington, in 1989 I was told that my time in the field was over and I would have to consider going to headquarters in Armonk, NY. I did not like this prospect, as I did not find it very appealing to look out the HQ window and contemplate problems or solutions in isolation. When they learned of my displeasure, I was invited to meet the senior executives, who tried to convince me that the HQ route was the only and the best thing for me at that time. At one point a senior executive asked what would I rather do if I had my choice. To this I said, "I don't know, but perhaps I could take IBM back to India after a long absence." Now, that wasn't something I planned to say. I didn't expect the question. They didn't want to lose me. I wasn't being outrageous, but in the back of my mind it had bothered me that IBM had left India in the 1970s and had never even discussed going back to this huge market. IBM left because of the adverse political situation. He said, "What makes you think you can do it?" I said, "You have never had a senior executive on your team who could do this, and I'm here now and can possibly succeed." He called Ed, the Asia head of IBM in Tokyo, whom I had known well, and told him, "I have Joshi in my office, and he has this crazy idea of going to India." Ed said, "I love it." So, I went on to set up an office in Singapore, and I would camouflage my work because I didn't want the media in India to know about IBM's efforts to come back. I had a small staff and would travel to India on Mondays and come back on Fridays—mostly Delhi. Coincidentally, one of the most senior bureaucrats was my brother-in-law, my wife's older sister's husband. Because of him the sensitivity of the visits worked out. His bureaucratic colleagues would not want to talk with me as an IBM executive because they were very bitter. Instead, he would invite them home, where they would talk to me as a relative of their colleague and friend. That made for a very open dialogue and discussion of possibilities for IBM and India.

I also learned details of why IBM left in the 1970s when the Indian government changed rules about 100 percent ownership, but there were also rumors about IBM selling old and new equipment, and the price differential was a problem. They felt IBM was taking advantage of India. In this mix, IBM and Coca-Cola were asked to lower their ownership to a 51 percent majority, and both companies refused and left.

As the bureaucrats began to engage, we told them, "Look, the times have changed, and the markets need to be opened, technology introduced, and jobs need to be created." We told them that, if allowed, IBM could do some software development and also develop the market for its products. In the meantime the India IT companies were also getting stronger. Tata had a joint venture with Unisys, and Infosys had just sprung up. We also engaged consultants, who recommended that it would be wiser and better for IBM to enter as a joint venture and later decide how it wanted to grow. We did further research and decided that Tata would be the best partner, and we entered as a 50 percent Tata/50 percent IBM company. Eventually, after eighteen months of discussions and difficult issues, such as the import of parts and royalty payments to India, things were resolved. We had this JV (joint venture) with a small team from IBM and Tata in 1991.

At that time I had decided to leave IBM, and thought this was a good time to do so.

It is ironic that I get more joy from this experience than I did at the time. IBM India is now wholly owned and has 150,000 employees. The success of IBM being so tied to IBM India is something no one had anticipated then.

Intellectually I look at my life now and find myself in a seamless state of mind. It does not matter the least to me whether I am in India or the US, as I find myself equally at home in both circumstances. But I know the understanding and approach it took to get IBM back to India required someone of Indian cultural background to understand and approach the matter sensitively. All the negotiations required knowledge of the culture as well as an empathetic view of the other side. I worked with the top secretaries and Dr. Manmohan Singh, who was the prime minister [from 2004 to 2014], and Chidambaram, the finance minister. These were the personalities responsible for the opening of India. IBM's re-entry in the 1990s coincided with India's opening up. In the final analysis the proposition was seen as mutually beneficial by all concerned. During all negotiations, I never experienced any suggestions of bribery or unlawful exchange of funds. None of my team ever said that this was ever asked of them. In fact, contrary to what one hears, even today, as I go back and forth for 50 years to India, not once has anyone ever asked me to pay a bribe.

AFTER IBM

After leaving IBM, I moved to Silicon Valley. I decided to sample some start-up activities so I joined a video telephony start-up, and unfortunately it was short-lived and didn't work out. I explored some other opportunities and decided to go into semi-retirement for a while. In big companies one requires strong people skills to get things done. I quickly found out that in the start-ups it is the ability to take charge and roll up your sleeves that counts more than the bedside manners. That is a big distinction. In large companies, as an executive you have support staff. Here you have to be innovative and efficient yourself. Therefore, I tell individuals that they need to understand these differences while considering change. I now found myself in a consulting and advisory role, mostly with small companies. But I didn't want to chase jobs. I realized I was interested in nonprofits, and that was how TiE got started.

ORGANIZING TiE

TiE was serendipity. One Mr. Vittal, a senior Indian government secretary, who had also helped us with the IBM approvals, was coming to the US, and I wanted him to meet me and also others in Silicon Valley. So, my late wife and I set up a lunch meeting and invited the who's who of the Silicon Valley Indian community. About a half an hour into the gathering, the Indian consulate general told me that Mr. Vittal's flight was delayed and he might not even show up. I told the group—bad news and good news. The bad news was that he might not show up, and the good news was that we were all there and we could use the time to get to know each other. We went around the table talking. One of the guys said this was a good idea, as we had not met before. We went around telling each other about ourselves. We decided to get together once a month for a dinner where individuals would take turns in telling their life stories. Mr. Vittal showed up late, but by the time he got there we had accomplished something very significant. This became TiE—twenty years ago. From there a small team of volunteers began organizing monthly dinner meetings. And in the spring of 1994 we had the first TiEcon. We planned on two hundred people, and seven hundred people showed up. In 2012 we had the twentieth TiEcon, with roughly four thousand attendees. There are over sixty chapters around the world and a whole lot of mentoring and start-up activities.

THE AMERICAN INDIA FOUNDATION

I also helped found the American India Foundation in 2001, while serving as president of TiE. There was a big earthquake in Gujarat, India.

I along with the TiE team announced that we would raise four million dollars for the victims. My TiE colleagues said, "You are running TiE. Why do you want to do this?" I said I really wanted to because the need was so huge and time was of the essence. At that time Bill Clinton, the US president, had just left the White House. He got a call from the prime minister of India, who asked if Mr. Clinton could get some Indians together to help. Clinton called ten people—and I was one of them—to come to New York for brainstorming. I had been with President Clinton to India as part of a delegation so he knew of me. He asked the group what each one was doing about the earthquake because it was a big disaster. He told us about his chat with the prime minister. As we went around the room, it became clear that we in Silicon Valley were the only ones doing anything at that time. As it happened I had already made the announcement, and Kumar Malavalli, a prominent philanthropist, had pledged one million dollars to us. That gave a big push to our campaign. President Clinton said this was great and suggested that we make this a permanent foundation. So he went to the blackboard, and we came up with the American India Foundation (AIF) name. All the attendees liked it. He offered to become the first chairman of this new foundation, and I assumed the interim role as founding president. Within a month we had a successful fund-raiser with President Clinton attending and raised a record amount of over five million dollars. We then took President Clinton to India and also made sure to select the right NGOs. Lata Krishnan took over as president, and she has in these ten years raised about a hundred million dollars. She has done a wonderful job. My big company skills came to be used in this effort. I was able to organize a complex effort and transition it with due processes. When you want to do things just for yourself, people run away from you. However, when the purpose is clear and your interests are not embedded in it, others will support you.

OTHER PHILANTHROPY AND MENTORING

Now I run an educational foundation, the Foundation for Excellence (FFE). It provides about twenty-five hundred scholarships each year to medical and engineering students in India who are in the top 15 percent of performance curves and the bottom 10 percent of the economics scale. It is an amazing program that nurtures brilliance. We want to scale it to be about ten thousand before the year 2020. We are now also encouraging the graduates to start giving back. In its nineteen-year history, FFE has awarded over thirty-three hundred scholarships.

I have also been an advisor for a visionary program to establish 911-like emergency services in India using 108 dialing. This program now covers over three hundred million people. I began an ambitious project whereby, in collaboration with a major Japanese technology company, we plan to establish a for-profit modern network of medical teleclinics, bringing affordable, quality diagnosis and treatment services to people in rural areas globally, beginning with my native state in India.

As part of my other engagements, I offer free mentoring to professionals, entrepreneurs, and companies, where mistakes I made are featured alongside lessons I learned. Through many years of dealing with people and problems, I also became convinced that there is a great need for online tools for people to deal with problems at work and the resulting dissatisfaction that affects the health and family lives of the large majority of working people around the world.

ABOUT THE GRANDCHILDREN AND THE FUTURE

If I were asked by my grandchildren and their peers what it takes to give back to society, the first thing I would say is, "Develop the attitude and skills in YOU that can enable you to do things for others." Without that you cannot engage and sustain such efforts.

Now that I have three granddaughters, I have also begun to think about the gender demographic changes around the world. Women are rapidly moving into leadership roles everywhere with doors opening for them like never before. So, I have developed my important list of "three things to do" for young girls. First, they need to master the balance sheet. Men typically manage the financial decisions without the collaborative participation of the women in their lives. I tell the girls, "Don't let that happen to you. You should be at least an equal in every financial decision of the family." Balance sheet knowledge is a good vehicle to get there. Second, participate in martial arts. You have a physical handicap and always will as a woman. So you should develop the skills and image of a strong person that no one treats lightly. The third requirement is to have command of a second language. People respect you for this, and you become a better person as you appreciate diversity and other cultures through the medium of the languages you know.

I find the greater roles for women around the world in all spheres a very positive shift for humanity. There is an inevitable power shift under way that is built more on capabilities and fairness. It is hard to believe now how half of humanity had been left out of participating and contributing in the fullest way until this awakening occurred. But that sad story is now changing. My grandchildren's times will see much more equity and fairness in the treatment of women and other neglected segments of various societies. That will also make them stronger and more influential as mothers and partners. Their children will most likely also be more generous and kinder. Most decisions they will make will also be sounder, we hope, for a harmonious world.

GURURAJ "DESH" DESHPANDE, BOSTON

BORN IN DHARWAD, KARNATAKA, INDIA

EDITOR: *When one lacks access to a proper education, where does the motivation come from to learn on one's own? With help from his mother, Desh took control of his own education and became one of the top-ranking students in the state of Karnataka. Desh applied his self-motivation to his studies at IIT, during graduate study in Canada, and eventually in the US, where he founded several networking companies. Now his work is to encourage self-motivation in others in the interest of creating positive change, both in social engagement and in entre-preneurship. Desh's story demonstrates how people can improve their own outcomes and their communities regardless of a lack of perceived opportunities or resources.*

EARLY CHILDHOOD

My whole life has been full of serendipity. I grew up in a very middle-class family with a lot of value placed on education. The family had absolutely no international exposure. Both my father and mother were educated. My father was a graduate of Benares Hindu University and became an engineer, but there were no jobs for engineers when he graduated. Therefore, he became a government officer. My mother went to the university, which was rare for women those days. It wasn't common for a woman to be university educated. I did not always go to good schools. Some of the schools were really bad because my father got transferred to different places frequently. Staying home and studying by myself was a big part of my early education. My mother was a great motivator and tutor throughout my schooling.

I grew up in Karnataka, India. My schooling was checkered because I went to lots of different schools. We started off in good English-language schools in cities. However, as I was entering fifth grade, my father got transferred to a small village called Sankeshwar. We lived in that village for four years. I switched over to our native language, Kannada, as the medium of instruction. Those days, very few people in villages spoke English. Because I spoke English and because I'd done my previous schooling in very good schools in cities, compared to everyone else in the village, I was a superstar. Most of my classmates from that village school did not even graduate from high school, let alone go to IIT. Many years later, I had an interesting episode. After I got married in 1980, my wife, Jaishree, and I were taking a bus from Hubli to Kolhapur. Sankeshwar is on the way. When the bus stopped at Sankeshwar, Jaishree and I got off the bus to stretch our legs, and I also wanted her to see the small village where I'd studied for four years. Soon after we got off, a porter yelled, "Gururaj . . . Gururaj." All my classmates in Sankeshwar knew me as Gururaj, which is my official name. I did not recognize him right away, and after we started chatting, we connected. Jaishree was, of course, surprised that my classmate got only enough education to qualify to be a porter.

In ninth grade, we moved to a bigger city, Belgaum, where I went to a good school, even though the medium of instruction was Kannada. When I was in the tenth grade, my father got transferred to Bangalore, and I switched schools again. Unfortunately, the school was terrible. What happens in Bangalore is that they are forced to have at least one Kannada-language class or they lose their government grants. After the seventh grade, if you got more than 40 percent marks, you would be in the English-language section, but if you got less than 40 percent, you would be in the Kannada-language section. I was a Kannada-language student and was only allowed to enter the Kannada-language section.

The first day of class was almost shocking. The students were terrible. They were gangsters with zero interest in education. So I never went to school. I bought the textbooks and studied at home. Finally, when I wrote the final exams, I was not only top in the school but I had secured a rank in the state of Karnataka. A lot of the motivation for me was my family and wanting to do well. After tenth grade, I went to a very good college for pre-university [eleventh grade] called the National College in Bangalore. I was a very motivated student and excited to be in a good college.

Desh leaving India, 1973
(photo courtesy of Gururaj Deshpande)

We lived in a small house, and there was a water tap in the house, but we wouldn't get water there. There was only one tap for the entire street, in a pit where you could get water. So in the morning you had to go and get water from this tap, along with everyone else on the street. People started lining up for water at five a.m. We carried our bucket to the tap to fill a small tank in our home for the daily supply of water. So there was always a long line, and this chore took a long time every day. One day, I discovered that the tap started flowing with water at two a.m. So for the remainder of the year, my older sister and I would wake up every day at two a.m., go fill up our water tank, which took only about twenty minutes at that hour, and go back to sleep and get up and do our studies. When you do things like this, there is a big sense of accomplishment and ownership. In hindsight, you could ask if it had an impact on our studies; I don't think it did. These situations built our confidence, gave us a sense of pride, and made us very disciplined to do well in school.

SERENDIPITY: HOW I LANDED AT IIT

Usually, in tenth grade you write a state exam, and I was among the top two hundred students in the state of Karnataka, so I qualified for a national scholarship of 100 rupees a month, which was a great deal of money. The year that I graduated, they made a rule that I could only get that money if I studied basic science and not engineering. Because I wanted to get the scholarship, I had made up my mind that I was going to get a bachelor's degree in physics. However, during the pre-university course, my friends were writing an entrance exam for Indian Institute of Technology (IIT). It was only a few rupees to write the exam, so I wrote the exam as well and didn't think much about it. I finished the academic year, and for summer vacation, I went about 150 miles away from Bangalore to my uncle's home. Back at home, my father would take all the mail to his office from home. He was opening the mail one day, and one of his colleagues saw the envelope with Indian Institute of Technology on the return address. His colleague said, "Wow, you got a letter from the Indian Institute of Technology." My father replied, asking him what that was. The letter said that I was ranked eighth in South India and I should come for an interview. My dad's colleague said, "Wow, your son should go to IIT, which is very difficult to get into." So my father sent a telegram, as we did in those days, and it said, "Come home immediately—stop." I immediately cut short my vacation and came back to Bangalore. My dad took me to IIT Madras for the admission interview, and the rest is history.

Going away from home to IIT was not traumatic for me, but it was for the family because we were a very close-knit family. I had a brother who was thirteen years younger. He was four years old and attached to me. The family missed me a lot, but IIT was very exciting for me. Our family had not traveled much. Meeting students from all over India and other countries such as Ceylon [now Sri Lanka] and Malaysia was an eye-opening experience. The variety of people and the beautiful campus kept everything exciting.

SERENDIPITY: HOW I LANDED IN CANADA

In 1973, I was twenty-two, in my final year at IIT, and companies would come for recruitment. I had a job offer for 500 rupees a month from TELCO, a Tata company, and my plan was to take this job. But in my final year, I had taken a course from a professor from the University of Alberta, in Canada, and one day after class when I was chatting with him, he suggested I apply to universities in Canada. Frankly, I am not

Desh's PhD graduation in Canada
(photo courtesy of Gururaj Deshpande)

sure I even knew where Canada was located. He suggested I apply to a few colleges for my master's, so I applied to a few universities with no idea of actually going. A few months later, much to my surprise, I got a letter from the University of New Brunswick offering me a full scholarship. I didn't know what to do with it, and I brought it to the professor. He encouraged me to go. I told him I had this great job in India. He said the travel would broaden my horizons and I could always come back to a job in India. This was the trigger for me to go to New Brunswick in Canada.

In those days, it wasn't common for students to go abroad. Out of 250 students graduating from IIT in 1973, there were three of us who went abroad. Landing in Canada was very similar to going to IIT; it was someone else's idea.

I had to borrow money to travel to Canada because they don't give you a scholarship for the travel. My father had to borrow the money, around 7,000 rupees, from his life insurance. This was a big decision for the family. They had to sacrifice quite a bit. His income was 600 rupees a month, so it was almost a year's income to pay for the travel. The scholarship in Canada was generous enough, and I had a very simple lifestyle that allowed me to save enough money and repay my father's loan within a year.

I left India with eight dollars, which is all the foreign exchange you were allowed from the government of India. I flew from Bombay [now Mumbai] to Frankfurt, and then we missed the flight to Montreal. The airlines put us up in a hotel in Frankfurt. It was quite fancy and even more so since I had not been in a hotel before. That was a real treat. From there they flew us to JFK, bused us to LaGuardia, and then flew us to Montreal. In Montreal, we missed the flight again, so they had to put us up in another hotel, and from there we went to Fredericton [in New Brunswick]. Some student I had corresponded with was supposed to meet me at the airport, but they didn't come. So I took a cab and had to use about three dollars of the money to reach the university. But as soon as I reached the campus, I had a place in the dorm and had a meal plan, and it was really fairly smooth.

I came in September of 1973, and everything was such a thrill and so different from what I had seen before. In India, I graduated in computers but had never seen a computer in my life. At the university, there was the big IBM machine that I could use for programming. There were other students from India, so we had a nice community of friends. It wasn't a very competitive environment academically, like IIT was, and once again it was easy to be a superstar. I got my master's in two years, and the professor I worked with, Dr. Eugene Lewis, was going on sabbatical to Australia for a year. He said, "Hey, I am going to Australia, so why don't you teach my classes for the year until I get back. You could be a rich man and then go back to India." That sounded like a great deal for me. I remember I made $12,000 a year, which was a great deal of money in those days. I had an apartment and a car and saved lots of money, so it was a big thing. I taught the microwave classes and learned that I loved teaching and got ranked very high at the end of the year. So I became convinced that being a professor was my calling. However, you cannot be a professor without a PhD. I decided to go to back to India for three months on a vacation and then start my PhD at Queen's University [in Kingston, Ontario].

In those days, life in India and the North American life were very different. I had been away for three years, and it was exciting to land in India after all this time. I got to eat homemade pickles that I had not eaten since I had left India. My family was very happy to have me home, and I had a royal welcome. I spent three months having lots of fun and then returned to Canada from India.

Going for my PhD was a done deal, and I packed up my things from New Brunswick and moved to Queen's University, and started the PhD program. Because I had taught, they asked me to do some part-time teaching, so I was a pretty rich graduate student, relatively speaking. My PhD didn't take that long—only three years. I worked on data communications rather than microwave engineering. My professor, Dr. Paul Wittke, was very encouraging and inspiring and a good mentor. I chose to do a PhD because I wanted to be either a researcher or a professor. I graduated at the end of 1979.

SERENDIPITY: HOW I LANDED IN TORONTO

After completing my PhD, I went back to India for a vacation and got married to Jaishree. Jaishree also studied at IIT Madras, although we never overlapped, as I left in 1973 and she went to IIT Madras in 1973. After graduating from IIT Madras, Jaishree worked in Bangalore for the National Aerospace Laboratory and Indian Space Research Organization. We got married and moved to Canada in 1980.

There was a struggling small company in Toronto called ESE Ltd., which had excellent technology. At that time, the state-of-the-art practice was to communicate at 1,200 bits per second on a phone line. ESE had found a way to transmit 9,600 bits per second, which was very high-tech. But the company was not doing well financially or in marketing the product, which is a common Canadian problem. They were good technically, but the company was going under, and the head of engineering, Dr. Peter Brackett, had to quit and came to teach at Queen's University. Peter's family was in Toronto, and he came by himself to Queen's. In practical terms, he was a bachelor and I was a bachelor, and we got to know each other well. In the second half of 1979, Motorola bought the struggling company. As soon as they bought ESE, they asked Peter Brackett to come back as VP of Engineering, and he did. Three months after he left for Motorola, I completed my PhD, and Peter asked me to join him. Because I knew Peter so well, I decided to go to Toronto and join him. It was a garage shop operation of twenty people. However, from 1980 to 1984, we grew rapidly to four hundred people and $100 million in profitable revenue. There were three of us who drove the growth—Peter, myself, and the CEO. Dr. Peter Brackett was the best boss I had in my career and a great coach. In 1984, I realized that I could do this corporate work. Initially I was the key engineer, but I quickly became an engineering manager, and I got to do a lot of business development. Motorola pretty much ignored us as a small company. Motorola had bought another company called Codex in Boston. Codex had bought our company, so we used to work with the company in Boston quite a bit. They were happy that we were producing all these products because our sales meant revenue for them as well.

Before this experience, I had no practical experience in business. I was a PhD graduate who could write papers and big equations. Building the Motorola business in Toronto was a tremendous experience. Every year I was doing things that I had never done before. This personal growth was not only for me but for everyone I hired into the company as well. It was very exciting to be a part of an entrepreneurial journey. By 1984, I had forty people working in my group, and they enjoyed working with me. I was a good salesman, and the salespeople in the US liked taking me to their companies on sales calls. I visited many companies, including Ford, GM, IBM, and DEC. I discovered that I had a good management style and a good sense for business. Before this experience, I thought I was hard-core techie.

In 1984, when I looked back, I said, "If I can do this for Motorola, I can do this for myself." I wanted to start my own business, and Jaishree agreed. There was no venture capital in Toronto, so the choices were either Boston or California. These were the only two places in the world that had this concept called venture capital—a new practice where an entrepreneur came up with an idea and a venture capitalist would fund that venture for equity in the company. I thought I would go to California. Motorola had also purchased a company called Four-Phase Systems, which was really struggling. Bruce Hanson, an executive at Codex, was made CEO of Four-Phase in Cupertino, California. I had a good relationship and credibility with the executives of Codex because I had made money for them. I contacted Bruce and asked if he had any opportunities for me in California. He assured me he did. I interviewed, he gave me an offer, and the real-estate guys showed me a house to buy. So we planned to move to California. However, a couple days later, I got a call from another executive at Codex. He said he had heard from Bruce that I was moving to California. He told me not to go because Four-Phase was a broken company, and I should move to Boston and come to Codex. So we ended up in Boston in 1984.

FIRST START-UP IN BOSTON

We moved from Toronto to Boston on an intercompany transfer L-1 visa. Jaishree was not allowed to work with that visa. However, she could go to school if she wanted. She went to Boston University to complete her master's in computer science. We had our second son soon after we came to Boston.

It took three years to get my green card, but during those three years, Codex was working on a new division for system integration. They felt that in addition to selling just their products they should offer system integration with products from other companies. I was one of the three directors they hired to build this new business. It was a great concept, but it never worked because the company could not accept that competitors' products could be better than theirs. I traveled and met many customers. It was also the time I wanted to start something on my own, so it gave me time to understand venture capital. There weren't that many entrepreneurs in Boston at the time. There was Ken Olsen of Digital Equipment and Edson de Castro of Data General— maybe a dozen of them at most. Whenever they spoke, I went to listen to them. Slowly, I built my network of people. In 1987, I decided to do something with a colleague at Codex, Bob Machlin. We both put in $10,000, and he quit his job, but I couldn't quit mine because of the visa process. So every morning we would meet at his house at four a.m. We would work for three or four hours, and I would go to work while he continued to work on the company. He would take just a bit of the $20,000 to live on for six months while we developed the business plan and spoke with VCs. That was my hands-on experience in a start-up ecosystem. But in 1987, the stock market crashed, and it was difficult to raise the money. Machlin's wife, Debbie, got pregnant, and his family couldn't go forward without a salary. Therefore, Bob had to take a job.

SECOND START-UP IN BOSTON

Three months later, I received my green card. Because I had met with many people during the failed start-up, I had a bigger network of people in Boston. I met Frank Bruns, an executive from a somewhat successful company, Proteon Networks, who wanted to do a start-up. So I started working with him and left Motorola to start Coral Networks. Frank had worked with Proteon, which was a token ring networking product company. We came up with an idea to do a Cisco-like product, but coming at it from the high end. Cisco was a very young company at this time. At Codex, I had called on Boeing and other large enterprise companies and understood that LANs were popping up everywhere. These networks grew organically and were not controlled by MIS (management information systems) groups. LANs did not have redundancies and backup, and they had performance limitations. The large companies told us that if we could make a product with the attributes of redundancy, backup, and performance, they would be interested and would pay a good amount of money for these products. Frank, a supersmart VLSI chip designer named Vic, and I came up with an idea to process packets in the hardware and started Coral Networks. Our design could process data packets ten times faster than what Cisco was selling. We felt it was a fantastic opportunity. But those days we still couldn't get venture funding without being off the payroll for a year, which seemed to be the test of whether you were committed. My wife was working, we had two small children, and I had been off the payroll for about a year.

Finally, we hit the jackpot. We got three million dollars in funding from fairly prestigious venture companies Sevin Rosen and TA Associates. I got on the payroll, and my wife quit her job. But unfortunately, three months into the company, Frank and I had a serious difference of opinion. This went on for a few weeks. I remember one day I was driving to work, and I stopped at a gas station, called my wife, and told her it was best if I quit. I couldn't see building a company with two partners who didn't get along. I did not want to be the person who hung around and kept saying, "I told you so, I told you so." I told Frank that I was going to leave, and in some ways I think he was relieved because I was a thorn in his side. I left. We disagreed over the approach. As we started designing the product, we found achieving a performance five times better was easy, eight times was doable, but it was pretty hard to achieve ten times. In my practical approach, five times was pretty good, and I wanted to optimize the time to market. My partner was more of a technical macho guy and wanted to achieve the full performance. Unfortunately, he spent $18 million developing the product and took three years and missed the market window. The company was sold for peanuts to SynOptics. But in some ways, the decision that I made to leave, although it was difficult, was the right thing to do. I couldn't stay at a place where I couldn't contribute. Here was this little Indian guy, and he was working with this veteran executive from the industry. My leaving the company didn't cause a big wave for the company. However, it caused a big wave for our family. When I left the company, there was no severance. My wife had just quit her job because we had two little kids at home. Neither of us had jobs. We had used up our savings. The others who went to IIT with me and were in the US were now executives in big companies and were having a good life. It was difficult, but it never felt hard because it was something I knew we wanted to do. So I regrouped, and six months later I got seed money to start the next company.

THIRD START-UP IS THE CHARM

Mentally, I visualized the future. I asked myself what is the next thing the world needs in data networking, and I focused on that thing; it was wide area networks (WANs). The concept sounds simple, but actually it was pretty profound. When I looked into the telephone business, all the phone networks, in the early days, were built just to connect companies. Slowly more phones got connected. By 1990, there was no phone in the world that wasn't connected to all the other telephones in the world. When you look at computers in the late 1980s, the networking protocols were generally proprietary and built by individual companies, such as Digital's DECnet, which was built for their own productivity. The concept of the Fords, GMs, and other companies pulling their vendors into a bigger network was bound to happen. My big bet was that every computer would connect with every other computer in the world just like phones. This meant two things had to happen: (1) networks could no longer be private, and (2) to build a public network, you needed a data switch and not a telephone switch.

Based on this idea, I started Cascade Communications. My idea for Cascade Communications was all about building packet switches for public computer networks. This turned out to be a big hit with the Internet coming along. We carried 80 percent of the Internet traffic in the backbone of the network by the time we sold the company in 1997. The customer base changed. Previously, data communications equipment was sold to private networks to build their networks. Cascade Communications started selling the data communications equipment to telephone carriers to build public computer networks. In fact, the venture guys would not fund Cascade because, before the 1990s, the carriers were a monopoly and weren't willing to pay any margins. We experienced deregulation, and lots of little carriers popped up everywhere. When a new carrier comes into the market, he looks for a technology advantage. Our competition in the early 1990s was Siemens, Lucent, and Nortel. They sold telephone switches for $10 million apiece, and they would add some ability to do data, and said they could do the same things as we were doing. We designed switches just for data, with no phone connections. This enabled us to perform ten times better for ten times less money through packet switches. Instead of making a computer behave like a phone call and pushing data through the phone lines, Cascade started a new revolution. We went public in 1994, with huge revenue growth. We started the company in 1990 with one person, and by 1997 we had a thousand people—so that was quite a ride. To fund the company, I worked with Ed Anderson, who was a new partner at Alex Brown Ventures. I had spoken with him about the company I abandoned in 1988. He got quite excited about my idea for Cascade Communications and wrote a check for $125,000 to seed the company without a business plan. I took the next six months to write the plan and we raised $3 million, and with that the company got built. Without the seed funding, the company probably would not have happened. I wanted Cascade to be a large company, and in 1997 an opportunity came along to merge it with Ascend for $3.7 billion, which was a lot of money. I had become chairman of the company, and Dan Smith was the CEO.

Until 1997, when we sold the company, I knew very few people in the broader community. Whatever time I had outside of business, I spent it with my family and playing with our kids. It was a narrow life with just our own family and the business. After we sold the company in 1997, I got out of Cascade and had no regrets. I then started TiE's Boston chapter and got to know lots of people, including entrepreneurs whom I was mentoring.

My parents came in 1984 to visit us from India for the first time. From then on, they visited us fairly regularly. My mother passed away four years ago. My father is in his nineties and lives in India. My parents obviously didn't know the market and technologies I was involved with. They knew the company was doing well. We lived a very simple life in a small three-bedroom house, even when the company went public. They liked the fact that we had our values, including how we raised our children. My parents were proud about us cooking and eating together, and all of that, fortunately, did not go away with the company's success.

THE NEXT BIG HIT

After Cascade Communications went public and we had money in the bank, suddenly I realized that I could get up in the morning and not have to work for a living, and I could do anything I wanted with the financial freedom. I used to run meetings from home and mentor entrepreneurs. I was a popular mentor for hundreds of entrepreneurs in the Boston area. In December of 1997, several months after we sold the company, I met two scientists/engineers from MIT, Eric Swanson and Rick Barry, who had a deep understanding of fiber-optic technology. Together we saw a big opportunity. We founded a company in 1998 called Sycamore Networks. The opportunity was to bring the optical networking technology to wide area networks. In the late 1990s, Cascade, Cisco, and others spent collectively about a billion dollars a year on quality of service (QoS), where you put more important packets ahead of lesser-value packets in the network. The bandwidth was very expensive across wide area networks. It would cost a million dollars a month for a 45 Mbps connection from Boston to London.

Desh Despande
(photo courtesy of Gururaj Deshpande)

The optical technology was magical. On one single fiber, you can shine a laser beam and blink it 10 billion times per second. You can get ten billion bits per second on one laser beam and on one single fiber. You can then put two hundred of these laser beams of different colors on the same fiber. That was an enormous amount of bandwidth. It is like going from oil-rationing days to finding new reserves where oil is unlimited. So we found a way to unblock the entire network. We looked at the market and found that if you wanted a connection from New York to Chicago or California, it would take you six months to get the connection, from the carriers to provision, and it would be very expensive. We developed the technology to get the big bandwidth and came up with an architecture for intelligent optical networking, where you could cut down the provisioning time from six months to six weeks to six minutes to real time and also bring the cost way down. It turned out to be a big hit. Sycamore Networks was born.

The timing was perfect. We started the company in February 1998 and started shipping the product in 1999. That is when the carrier and stock markets were booming. The fifth quarter after the company was founded, we started shipping the product. The quarterly revenue growth was $10 million, $20 million, $30 million, $60 million, $90 million, $120 million, and $150 million. In mid-1999, we went public and very quickly had a market cap of over $40 billion. There were many companies emerging that had access to fiber. If they built these networks, Wall Street was valuing them highly. They could easily raise money from Wall Street and wanted to buy as much product as we could ship.

Sycamore was valued so handsomely that every venture capitalist wanted to fund a Sycamore knock-off. Also, all the large companies, like Siemens, Alcatel, and Nortel, started investing heavily in optical technology. There were 250 optical start-ups, and all the large companies like Lucent and Nortel said, "We've been building these companies for one hundred years, and how can a little company like Sycamore have more value than we do?" So they started to invest funds in optical also. Suddenly the demand went down, and the supplier technology capabilities were way over what customers would need. If technology cannot keep up with what you need, then the technology has a huge premium. But if technology overshoots what people need, suddenly it is a commodity. So everything became a commodity.

ANOTHER TRANSITION

In 2000, I changed everything again, after realizing that I had been an entrepreneur for twenty years. My wife and I decided to start focusing on our foundation. I didn't want to be an entrepreneur or a CEO anymore. I became a non-executive chairman of Sycamore and got off the payroll. I started getting involved with one for-profit and one non-profit organization each year. When I got involved with a for-profit company, I was typically a non-executive chairman and usually a large investor in the company. I had a good run with several companies, including Cimarron, Airvana, A123 Systems, and Tejas Networks.

I was invited to join the board of MIT in 2000. When I looked back at my life, I found being an entrepreneur was an amazing opportunity. Most of the companies we started in the 1970s and '80s were based on the core technologies that came from Bell Labs. By the year 2000, there was no more Bell Labs, and the center of gravity for idea generation had clearly moved back to the universities. The US taxpayers spend about $50 billion a year for innovation and new ideas. What motivated Jaishree and me was to see if the innovation at universities could generate more opportunities for entrepreneurs, so that more entrepreneurs would have opportunities like the ones we had. Places such as MIT, Stanford, and Caltech were already doing a better job than anyone else in the world. But the big questions were, could they be doing better, and is there a process that all the other universities could use to bridge innovation to the marketplace?

We took a bold step and gave $20 million to MIT to set up the Deshpande Center for Technological Innovation. The core idea was to change the practice of innovation. There are about one thousand faculty at MIT. About fifty of them like working on ideas that are driven by basic science and curiosity. These are the people who get Nobel Prizes, and their efforts have a big impact in the long term. However, the majority of the faculty is driven by impact. They want to cure cancer, create clean water, or provide food security.

The practice of innovation is roughly where engineering was fifty years ago. Engineers designed a product, and then companies hired sales and marketing people to sell it. Some products were successful in the market, but most of them never sold. Now you would never do that. Engineers never design products without extensive knowledge of the market and input from likely customers. The best innovation practice today is that the professors conduct research, the best among them are patented, and the technology licensing offices at the universities try to peddle them. Very few patents ever get commercialized. We wanted to change this model.

The new model we came up with is the realization that Innovation + Relevance = Impact. An idea will have an impact only if it is directed to some burning problem in the world. How do you connect relevance? If a professor and his students have an idea and they are interested in impacting the world, then we connect them to the marketplace up front. As they research the problem and bake the idea, the idea is more likely to be relevant to the world and have a natural pull in the marketplace. This has been a very successful program. We have funded about 120 research projects at MIT, and about forty of them have become companies. This has now become a national model.

DESHPANDE-LIKE CENTER AT THE NSF

Later, I cochaired a council to further President Obama's efforts on innovation and entrepreneurship. The dean of engineering at MIT, Subra Suresh, was picked by President Obama to be the director of the NSF [National Science Foundation]. The first thing he did was ask me if they could do a Deshpande-like center at NSF to have a bigger impact with NSF research grants for translational research. Together we worked out a program that became Innovation Corps (I-Corps). To get Congress to approve the program, we had to make it a public-private partnership. My wife, Jaishree, and I gave $1 million to the $7.4 billion NSF budget to launch the program. The program became successful very quickly. It became so successful that it has now become a part of the line budget and does not need any private support.

With the success of the MIT Deshpande Center, other universities started calling me and wanted to have a Deshpande-like center at their universities. To help other universities, we started the Deshpande Symposium for Innovation and Entrepreneurship for Higher Education in 2012. The first year we had eighty people show up for the symposium. It then grew to 150, 250, and 350 attendees and continues to grow. We now have people from one hundred universities attending the symposium annually, and the network continues to grow.

We set up the Deshpande Center at MIT in 2002. After we saw the initial success at MIT, my wife and I wanted to take on a major project in India. The first idea was to duplicate the MIT center at IIT. However, we felt that social innovation was needed in India more than technological innovation. After we spent some time thinking about it, we realized that the equation we used for technological innovation gets turned around for social innovation. For technological innovation, it is Innovation + Relevance = Impact. However, for social innovation, it is Relevance + Innovation = Impact. Technological innovation always starts with an idea that the world has not seen before. However, social innovation starts with a deep understanding of the problem itself, and the new idea that you bring to solve the problem does not have to be patentable or have a big competitive advantage. To implement this idea, we came up with a concept called the Social Innovation Sandbox and started the effort in 2006.

THE SOCIAL INNOVATION SANDBOX

The Social Innovation Sandbox is based in our hometown, Hubli in Karnataka, where my dad lives. The Sandbox embraces five districts. About ten million people live in these five districts. It is large enough to have all types of problems but small enough to create a critical mass of activity. After eleven years, it has scaled into a major program, and we are very pleased with the results.

The philosophy of our foundation has become fairly simple. There are three types of people in the world: some are oblivious to everything around them, some see a problem and complain, and some see a problem and get all excited about trying to solve it. The only difference between a vibrant community and an impoverished community is the mix of the second two types of people—those who complain and those who want to do something about a problem. In impoverished communities, problems become chronic and get deadlocked. People try a little bit to solve them and give up. They then feel victimized and helpless, and the only thing they can do at that time is complain. Complaining becomes the dominant culture in these communities. Unfortunately, the political leadership becomes very good at articulating the miseries of these people and fueling the emotions. As a result of this, we have reached a steady state, where the people in the impoverished communities are supposed to sit around and complain, and others are supposed to solve their problems. Governments, think tanks, and foundations spend a lot of resources trying to solve these problems. Most of the programs don't work because the solutions are not originated by the people who need them. Therefore, our foundation focuses on converting complainers to problem solvers. This is the main idea behind the Social Innovation Sandbox, and it is producing very good results.

We have come up with several programs to get people to become problem solvers. We have a program where four college kids come together and pick a problem to solve in society. We now have five thousand college kids running around doing something or another. The idea with this program is to give young men and women a taste of what it is like to take charge and make something happen when they see a problem. In fact, they all wear a T-shirt that says, "Complaints Start with They. Solutions Start with I." Once people get a taste of being a problem solver, they don't choose to go back and become a helpless complainer.

We run a residential four-month-long training program for young men and women to be entrepreneurial in several domains. We graduate about two thousand students every year. We are building a three-hundred-thousand-square-foot campus and will be graduating five thousand students every year. About 2 to 3 percent of them start their own organizations. Others become a valued human resource for both for-profit and nonprofit organizations. So far, we have not had a graduate who has not been hired. I am always surprised with this program as to how, within four months, you can change the mind-set of a human being. This training program creates the capacity to scale solutions in the Sandbox.

We are also working with fifty social interventions that organizations have proposed. We try to build these organizations the same way one builds large companies. Some of these interventions have scaled in an impressive way. For example, many children in India go to school hungry. So one group said they can solve the problem if they use advanced engineering, engineer the supply chain, and use advanced accounting and logistics. They built a kitchen in the Sandbox that serves 185,000 hot midday meals every day to schoolchildren. They use local produce and serve local cuisine, food that children really love. The process has been optimized, and the meal costs only 12 cents. Thirty dollars feeds a child for the entire year. We only serve government schools, and the government gives us the $15 that they would have spent otherwise. We raise the other $15 to feed the children from thousands of donors in India and the United States. This program has now scaled to serving 1.6 million meals every day. We made this program a part of the Clinton Global Initiative six years ago. During the tenth anniversary of the Clinton Foundation, they had to pick one program to visit, and they picked this program. I went with President Clinton to India to show him the program. He was simply blown away with the scale of impact of the program. This is a typical reaction from any visitor who has been to one of these kitchens.

We are working with another program called Agastya that teaches science to rural schoolchildren. This program has also scaled to a million children. We have several other promising programs being nurtured in the Sandbox. The basic idea is to have a group of passionate people come up with a solution and then provide them with help to continue to polish the solution and find a financial model to scale it. India has 1.2 billion people, and it needs solutions that are very cost-effective and scalable.

About six years ago, our projects in both technological innovation and social innovation were enjoying success. Our original thinking was that the US needed technological innovation and India needed social innovation. We started rethinking that idea. We realized that the US needs social innovation and India needs technological innovation. We decided to bring the social innovation program to the US.

Six years ago, we brought the program to the towns of Lowell and Lawrence in Massachusetts and named it Merrimack Valley Sandbox. Over the last six years, we have seen it have a noticeable impact on the towns. We have now refined that program and call it EforAll (Entrepreneurship for All). This program is applicable to about three hundred impoverished midsize towns in the United States. We have now taken it to three other towns: Fall River, Bedford, and Lynn. We are hoping that in the next year or two, we will have optimized the program and then will take it across the nation.

About five years ago, we set up the Pond Deshpande Centre at the University of New Brunswick, Canada. This center works on promoting both technological and social innovation. More recently we set up the Dunin-Deshpande Queen's Innovation Centre at Queen's University. As of January of 2017, we are setting up the Gopalakrishnan-Deshpande Centre at IIT Madras.

After seeing all these centers in different countries and contexts, we have come to realize that innovation and entrepreneurship are very powerful tools, and they are equally powerful in improving the lives of those who live in vibrant communities as well as those in impoverished communities.

KANWAL REKHI, SILICON VALLEY

BORN IN RAWALPINDI, PAKISTAN

EDITOR: *Kanwal defied the odds by getting an IIT education and acquiring a master's degree at Michigan Tech. He humbled himself by earning money as a busboy and night watchman in Chicago, and absorbed hard lessons from jobs that vanished literally overnight amid changes in America's competitive mainframe and minicomputer industry. He learned self-reliance from his experiences as well as how to broaden his portfolio of skills to go from entrepreneur to CEO. He became not only an early angel investor but a lifelong teacher to emerging entrepreneurs through his founding of TiE.*

I came to the United States in 1967. I purchased the $8 from the government of India and saved it for my travel to the US. The $8 was all you could take out of the country because the rupee wasn't convertible. Not many people from India were allowed in the US until 1965, when the law changed through the support of President Johnson. The Hart–Celler Act changed the way quotas were allocated by ending the National Origins Formula that had been in place in the United States since 1921. It all goes back to the Soviet *Sputnik*. *Sputnik* was put in space by the Soviets, who were trying to beat the US into space. The

US was sure they were ahead of the Russians in everything. Russia put up *Sputnik*, and then they got the first man in space. *Sputnik* was a real wake-up call for Americans, who wondered how this could happen. We knew about this panic in India. The US stepped up the efforts for the space program in 1958 and 1959. Kennedy was elected in 1960, and in one of his key messages early in his presidency, he committed to putting a man on the moon and bringing him back. This acknowledged that the US realized it was behind the Russians. The government decided to open immigration for technical talent, and this meant India because China was still Communist, and the Chinese were not welcome as immigrants. Taiwan was in turmoil, and Europe was still rebuilding after the war, so immigration favored India.

The US in the '60s was on top of the world. It was before the major part of the Vietnam War. The US loved many things about India, such as Mahatma Gandhi and stories from the 1930s and '40s. The US knew India was a democracy and had gone through several elections. There were actually very few democracies at the time. Even though Nehru aligned India with the Soviet Union, when Nehru died the democracy continued on. There was this sense of superiority felt by the US, helping the poor people from the Third World. We were happy to get the help, and people would say this very openly. The US was helping the Europeans, and even with the alignment with the Soviet Union, the US was still helping India. The US and India had aligned by 1962 and 1963 because the Sino-Indian War was when the US used India and Tibet to spy on China.

We knew in India that immigration was being eased to come to America, but we didn't know the full story until much later. With the open immigration, engineers and scientists started to come to America. I was in IIT Bombay going to college, but US universities were opening up to Indian students doing their master's degrees and PhDs. This was a big shift. You could apply for a visa once you graduated and come to the US to study and have the visa in your hand in only two months. I got a student visa, which was the only viable method to come here for study, because if you were in India and wanted a work visa, it would take many months to a year demonstrating that you had a job and could support yourself, and after this, the process would take many more months. This wasn't possible. But when you came to the

US on a student visa and finished your education, it was easy to receive a green card. Almost everyone did this.

The other part of the equation is that the Vietnam War was happening, and thousands of people were being called to the draft every month. Universities were having trouble filling their graduate schools because the draft took the student candidates away. This made an opening for students from Iran and India and even Taiwan, although the Taiwan numbers were small, since it's not that large a country. The sun, the stars, and the moon aligned for students from India. Industry was booming in the US, while the country was undergoing a crisis in confidence. There wasn't any shortage of jobs in the US in the '60s, so you had no concern about proving you weren't taking someone else's job. That happened in the '70s. And immigration wasn't that large, not as it was later. The visa preference system was for technical people, which is how many of the people from India came. In IIT Bombay, there were about three hundred students in my class in all the engineering disciplines (civil, chemical, electrical, and material) and only about six women in that group. Perhaps one of the women came at this time, and maybe a few came in the '70s. Indian families would not have allowed women to travel on their own. People who came in the '60s went back to get married and brought their wives back with them.

A DIFFICULT TIME TO IMMIGRATE AND THE DECISION TO GO TO MICHIGAN TECH

It was a difficult time to immigrate, as there was no support system. You didn't know many people, if any, so you were on your own. You did whatever you could to survive. I knew no one, but Indian students had our connection to the US. Our destinations were the universities, and we knew how to get there. I got my degree at Michigan Tech in Houghton, Michigan. Everyone knew that was where the Norwegians and the Finnish went to school because they were used to the cold climate. It was a big change for someone from Bombay.

I did know someone who had gone to Michigan Tech. It was the cheapest of all the colleges I applied to, as I was on my own financially for the first semester/quarter. My family paid the airfare plus tuition, and I had the $8. There was an arrangement through the airlines

Kanwal in New York City in the fall of 1967
(photo courtesy of Kanwal Rekhi)

that you could get money. Airlines would sell you tickets for a slightly higher price than the actual price, and then they would rebate you the difference in cash as soon as you landed on the other side. Air France especially did this. They would sell you a ticket worth $500 to $600 and you paid $750. When you landed in Paris, you received the $150 difference. They knew that they had to do this. I didn't use it, but I knew others who did. They paid you cash or you later received a money order. The French did things like this, and Air France was the most popular airline because of this aggressive program that they did to try to increase ridership.

The government of India allowed you to pay your tuition in advance because you could only carry so much money out of the country, so we wired the money from India before I came. The rupee wasn't convertible at the time, so money transfer was difficult. When I arrived, I was set for one quarter with the funds from family and friends. Michigan Tech promised me financial aid if I did well. We helped each other; a friend's brother who was in the US sent me $100. Every dime had to be accounted for. We didn't even buy a cup of coffee because that would be a waste of money.

Michigan Tech was a very technical school at that time, with the College of Mines and other colleges, and it still is technical and has a small student body. There were about five thousand students at the time; now maybe it is seventy-five hundred students—it hasn't grown much. The Michigan School of Mining was its original name, and in the late 1950s it changed its name to Michigan Tech. It was and remains a rigorous school. I still return twice a year to meet with students and faculty, lecture, and remain very engaged.

TRAVEL TO A VERY NORTHERN CLIMATE

I flew from Delhi to Paris on Air France. Planes couldn't travel long distances in those days, even though it was a 707, so the route was Delhi to Tel Aviv to Rome to Paris to London to Montreal to New York and on to Detroit. In between flights, there was half a day here and there, and I had no money for a hotel, so I would go into town and come back to the airport six hours later. From Detroit I took a bus to Houghton. There were two of us from India on the bus; I knew the other man from IIT in India. There were several other people on the bus I didn't know from Africa, perhaps Nigeria.

It was late September, and it was very cold. It was colder than I had ever felt. I wasn't prepared with warm clothes because there were none in Bombay, and Michigan Tech was aware of this. The bus arrived in Houghton in the middle of the night (two or three a.m.), and the Greyhound would drop you at the side of the road. If you had no one to greet you, then you were lost. But Michigan Tech knew about this issue, and they had people that would meet the bus every night. They would be standing there with jackets, coats, or blankets for those who got off. They took us right away to their homes. It was such a kind thing. After a few hours of sleep, they took us to town to buy clothes and then dropped us off at the dorm. I got a heavy jacket for $5 and paid maybe 75 cents for gloves. It wasn't that expensive. I used those items for two years. Now they would cost a hundred dollars. I purchased them out of the $8 I had from India.

The university had a receiving point where we checked in. They had made arrangements for us to stay in the dorm, even though it was five days before school started. The staff made us feel welcome and they took care of all the details. Food was provided at the dorms. I was raised a Sikh so I had eaten meat and wasn't a vegetarian. It was very inexpensive for both the food and housing, and the $200 tuition was already paid from India. We were only allowed the $8, and that was all I carried. Somehow I had arranged to have another $350 available when I arrived—I don't remember how. This covered all the expenses, which all together came to about $1,000, including the plane fare, tuition, room, and food. There were 5 rupees to the US dollar (now it is 62 rupees to the dollar), so it was 5,000 rupees—a great deal of money in those days. For my father, 5,000 rupees would have been five months' salary, and when I left he gave me part of his salary. I had to make it with just that money.

THE MASTER'S PROGRAM AT MICHIGAN TECH AND BIG LIFE CHANGES

During that first semester, I did well. I was in electrical engineering working on my master's and had no specialization requirement. The master's program had none of the classes that we were familiar with, such as power and motors. For the master's we had control systems, logic design, transistors, and computer system design. There was a belief that there was nothing more that could be done in power systems, AC, or motors, so they were only addressed in the undergraduate curriculum. It was good that we were studying the new concepts, such as control theory and logic design, but since the underlying concepts were the same as what we studied in India, it didn't take us long to master the subjects. We took what we knew from our studies in India and applied it in a new way. Logic design is another form of mathematics—just applied in a new way. I was comfortable in less than a month in all the subjects.

The master's was a two-year program, and during that time, of course, I could not go back to India. When you left, you said good-bye to everyone because you never knew when you were going to see them again. You never sent a telegram because you would give someone a heart attack, since it always meant bad news. There were postal grams that took six weeks one way, so this meant several months' turnaround. There was no phone at home, so you didn't telephone anyone.

Almost all of us IIT students came to stay in America. There were no jobs in India, and there were definitely no jobs if you got your master's in the US. There were no design jobs in India at this time, and the government owned all the industry. In India it was basic work, and they imported the items they needed for the basic work. A PhD was another consideration for staying in the US. There were no examples of people who came back to India. Immigration to the US started in 1965, and I came in 1967. I had my master's and saved my original $8, and I was twenty-two years old.

It was a very, very big change for us to come to America. Food was different. Language disappeared, as there was no Hindi being spoken. No Bollywood movies. The sports were different—I had to learn about hockey. Houghton is maybe fifteen thousand to twenty thousand people, so it is a small town compared to Bombay. I stayed in the dorm with my friend from Bombay. There were about thirty students from India, as some were at Michigan Tech before I came. When I arrived, a professor looked at me and said, "You are from India, and you are going to have trouble because your education is not up to snuff." Nobody knew anything about Indian education at that time. He continued, "I just want to make sure you don't fall behind, and I will give you all the help you need." He showed me how to use the phone and told me how he could help me. After three or four weeks, he gave a shotgun test [pop quiz] and I aced it. He told me in his office, "First of all, I want to remind you that we don't cheat in America." I told him that I didn't cheat. He said, "No one should be acing this test, because we haven't covered the material yet." I told him that the ideas were very simple to understand. The next time he gave us the test, he stood behind me for the full hour of the test. He said after, "If you are cheating, you are very good at it." He was watching all the time. He had stereotyped us. Americans were very sure of themselves because they had put a man on the moon and done all these things. There was this sanctimonious and patronizing attitude. And yet they were very helpful. I don't think any professors ever behaved this way after 1970, because it wasn't just one person who did extremely well, it was person after person after person. They learned what education in India meant. We were smart, and we picked things up easily. The professors thought no one would be teaching these ideas except in American universities, but that wasn't true.

The assumption of low expectations meant we didn't have much pressure on us. We took advantage of those low expectations. No one in the US knew that we had such an aggressive education program in India. We didn't experience the Indian competitiveness in the US. By my second quarter, I had done well enough to get financial aid, although it was a small amount. We didn't buy textbooks, as the library had enough books, and graduate students had the first right to them.

That entire quarter I spent maybe $20 on everything. I had my jacket, gloves, and hood, so I bought very little else.

RESPONDING TO HELP WANTED SIGNS IN CHICAGO FOR THE HOLIDAYS

During holidays, the university arranged for us to go home with local families because the dorm was closed. They would pick us up, and we could see about life in American homes. This is the patronizing part, because they always believed we could never be in such a situation back in India. During the long Christmas and New Year's holiday, I decided instead to go to Chicago to work for two or three weeks. I stayed at the YMCA for $4 per night and I could make $20 a day. I returned to Houghton with maybe $300. These were menial jobs: doorman, bus-boy, and other service jobs. I looked for Help Wanted signs and got these jobs daily—it was day labor. Almost every business had these Help Wanted signs. They would ask if I was available the next day. I said yes and got the job, sometimes two jobs.

We knew about the YMCA from India, as almost every city had a YMCA, and I knew it was the cheapest place to stay. It was functional. I probably wouldn't stay there today, but even with a shared bathroom down the hall, it worked fine. I took the bus down to Chicago and back to Houghton. I knew after this experience that I would survive in America no matter what. I could earn some money, live on a fixed budget, and learn how to manage my affairs. When I arrived in Chicago, I had $6 in my pocket. With the YMCA being $4 a night, I knew I had to do something right away. I got the dishwashing job and a free meal, and they offered me food, such as donuts, to take home for the next morning. I left that job that day with $10, so with the $2 I had, I now had $12. I could survive another two days in Chicago without a job. But I would get another job and get another $8 or $9 ahead. Every day we'd talk about how long we could survive if we didn't get another job. I improved my discipline and focused on saving money. There was no money to spend on movies or entertainment. When I could, I would get two jobs or two shifts. In the three weeks I was in Chicago, I didn't take even one day off. I knew any money I saved would make my life easier. Financial aid was there, but it was minimal and only paid for tuition and the dorm. Now I had enough cash to have some life. I could buy an ice cream or coffee, which I wasn't able to do before.

THE INDIA ASSOCIATION AT MICHIGAN TECH

Winter quarter, a few more Indian students came, so we ended up forming an India student association of about thirty people. There were about a half-dozen Indian professors at Michigan Tech. Many Indians came to get their PhDs and got married and stayed to teach. They would invite people for an Indian meal. With the club, we would get together to cook once a month. The ladies would supervise us, but we would do the work. We also discovered that churches were very open to us using their facilities. As long as we cleaned up, they were very welcoming. There was one church we latched on to for our meals. We got food and spices that were close enough for our use. We got curry powder, turmeric, and other things that we could use. You wouldn't get the same items as you would in India, but it was enough to make the food and have a good gathering. There was always someone who was good at singing, so we sang songs and talked, in addition to eating.

We felt an affinity for the Iranian students at Michigan Tech. They were like us, although they were richer and had a nicer lifestyle than we did, because the Iranians had oil. In terms of academic achievement, they were peers and sometimes ahead of us. The second quarter was a tough quarter physically, with a hard winter and lots of snow, due to the lake effect, and the temperature was down to -20 or -30 degrees Fahrenheit. The sun never seemed to come up. We were young so it was an adventure. I tried to learn hockey, but I never seemed to understand it, although I went to watch it and I went to football games. Sports were where the students congregated. I played ping-pong and later, at twenty-three or twenty-four years old, I learned tennis—first in New Jersey and then in Florida—and have played it ever since. The schoolwork got even easier. Our confidence improved with the comfort around language skills. The school calendar went from September to December and then January through May.

In May, I returned to Chicago for the three months of the summer break. I went back to the same places, and my day jobs were a bit steadier. I kept trying to get jobs in engineering firms. I took a day off every week or so to look, and I looked in the newspapers. Every day you took a day off you lost $30, and yet I hoped to get some technical job. I did find a factory job as a semitechnical job and worked in the hotels at night. But the factory was still a low-level job. The factory made aircraft parts. You picked up the items from the assembly line, did some spot welding and testing, and then put it back on the assembly line. It wasn't quite unskilled, and I went from $1.25 per hour to $2 per hour, so I made more money. At the end of the summer, I had $2,000—that was a lot of money. The university didn't know I had made this money, and I was doing a lot of work for the professors as a teaching assistant and part-time research assistant. One of the professors tried very hard to get me to do my PhD, as he had gotten his at the University of Wisconsin, and encouraged me, because I was sharp, to keep going for my PhD. I got the admission papers but decided it wasn't for me to spend three to four more years studying and then become a professor and earn $10,000 a year. I had a job in New Jersey, which was for $11,000 at the end of my master's. Why would I want to spend four more years in academics and get paid less money?

MY FUTURE WAS COMPUTERS AND LOGIC DESIGN

It took me four quarters to secure my master's in the spring of 1969, with my degree in electrical engineering (EE), but at that time I was heavily into logic design and computers. I fell in love with computers, and this was at the time of PDP-8 and the PDP-11, which was just announced that summer. The university had an IBM 360, an IBM 1620, and old Raytheon machines, and there were other companies that had products, such as Honeywell. It was a time when CDC (Control Data Corporation) was at the top of their game. I took programming classes and did fairly well. I became an expert after my first quarter, but that was easy because I had no social life. I had my evenings free and spent them at the computer center. I took all the hardware courses, but software I learned on my own, such as FORTRAN, COBOL, and PL/1, and ALGOL was just coming on as I finished. I was becoming very confident in programming, and I really liked it—and being competitive helped. Engineering is more than just engineering; it is logical thinking and building on first principles. By the time I left Michigan Tech, I knew I was well suited for the coming changes in technology.

Nineteen sixty-nine was the year we first put a man on the moon. Right after that, the world changed. There were no plans by the government to do anything other than a few missions. NASA had no plans, and they started to wind down because they had enough hardware and people trained to put *Apollo 12* and *13* into outer space, and nothing else was coming after. NASA was a large employer of engineers, and they not only stopped hiring engineers but they started to lay off engineers. The NASA contractors were also laying off engineers. Now there was a glut of engineering people, and the Vietnam War was changing, and a half million people were being drafted. The years 1969 to 1971 were very bad years for engineers in the US.

TOUGH TIMES IN THE JOB MARKETS

I went to my job in New Jersey as a design engineer in a minicomputer company. Right after I got to the job, Digital Equipment Corporation announced a new PDP, and DEC knew they had a winner. The other minicomputer companies knew they were in trouble so they started to lay people off. My company was in big trouble, and I only had the job for seven months before I was laid off. I went for an interview with Digital in Maynard, Massachusetts. It happened that when I went to the interview in Maynard, it was one of the biggest blizzards in the history of New England. My flight from New Jersey to Boston was canceled, but I didn't want to miss the interview so I took a bus to Maynard. I went for the interview the next day, and the guy doing the interview was stuck somewhere else so I wasted that trip.

I went for a job interview from Boston straight down to Florida with Systems Engineering Labs (SEL), which was the main supplier of real-time computers to NASA and was eventually acquired by Gould. What a difference the environment was in Fort Lauderdale. I landed around eleven p.m. and it was about 89 degrees. I was bundled up so it made me ask myself what I was doing up in New Jersey. They offered me a job as a hardware engineer, and I accepted and moved to Florida right away. The green card required for me to work was very easy to acquire. I finished at Michigan Tech in about April or May and applied for the green card, which required a degree. It took just three to four weeks after we went to the US immigration office in Sault Ste. Marie— which was at the Canadian border, about 130 miles from Houghton— to get the card. That was all it took—from start to finish about four weeks. Now it may take ten years.

The green card was in my hand before going to New Jersey. Six to seven months after I started the SEL job, I got laid off a second time because of the downsizing of NASA. I did have a job offer from IBM in the New York region before taking the SEL job. I reapplied to IBM, but they had blacklisted me. They sent me a letter saying that I would not be hired by IBM "for life" because I had turned them down without sufficient reasons. I saved that letter. No one would write that letter any longer.

Next I got a job at RCA Computer Systems, which was located in Cherry Hill, New Jersey; Boston; and West Palm Beach, Florida, which was up the road from SEL. RCA laid me off in another six or seven months. RCA had an IBM-compatible mainframe machine, with a business strategy to have IBM 360–compatible machines at 10 percent better performance at 10 percent less cost. That was their slogan. RCA was always ahead in technology. They were the first ones to use transistors and the first to use chips in building computers. Then IBM moved from the 360 to the 370, with all the software programs compatible but selling for 40 percent to 50 percent less. It was much better and cheaper, and the RCA business dried up overnight. RCA shut down as their sales went down to zero, and they immediately laid off about eight or nine thousand people. This was my third layoff in two years. When I went to Florida, I had also gone to interview in Los Angeles, with a company called SDS, Scientific Data Systems, which was eventually acquired by Xerox. I had been to California for just one day, and now I was in the middle of nowhere (Florida), with thousands of laid-off engineers.

RCA set up a nice office to assist our job search by helping us do our résumé and providing us with a copy machine and other support. I applied for a job with Singer-Link in Sunnyvale (California), which was in the defense business; they had contracts and needed hardware. This was 1971, and Silicon Valley was in a rigorous start-up mode. The RCA job fair gave me the introduction, I sent my résumé, and Singer Link flew me back for the interview. RCA really tried to help me.

EXPANDED FOCUS FROM ENGINEERING
TO BUSINESS AND CUSTOMERS

After my third layoff, I realized that I could not rely on employers for jobs, and jobs weren't something you could depend on. I also became aware that I had to pay attention to the other side of engineering—to the business and the customers. Were the customers happy, and was the company profitable? I knew I had to prepare myself for a broader background. If I got too specialized, what would happen if the need for that specialty went away? I broadened my horizons and gained more expertise in software, systems, and the business. Jobs are not forever, and you have to find your own way. If you put your life in someone else's hands, then there will be problems. I tell people I am glad I got the three layoffs so early in my life. With my new job, I estimated I would be okay for about a year and started taking classes at Santa Clara University and Stanford. Santa Clara University had an early-bird program from seven to nine a.m. before I went to work, and companies paid for these courses. Stanford also had enhancement programs in business and technology, and these were moneymaking courses for Stanford. They weren't for a degree—each course was a stand-alone— and I took these classes for six years. Singer-Link paid, and I chose courses in finance, business law, and marketing, but mostly software.

My job was going well, I had several promotions moving up the technical ranks, and I was a star performer. It was now the mid-to-late 1970s, and I noticed that people who came and worked under me were being promoted into management. After this happened a few times, I asked my boss why I hadn't been promoted. He told me I was an asset, a backbone of the department, so they couldn't lose me. I asked him who made more money, and he told me the management, and that I made the maximum the technology position allowed. Even though I was feeling very sure about my job, and life was good, I was very aware of how others were determining my future, including how much I should be making.

BECOMING AN ENTREPRENEUR

So I asked myself, why do I have to work for someone? A person I trained left to become an entrepreneur. He was smart, but I figured I was smart too and I could do this. There weren't many Indian entrepreneurs at this time (1980 and 1981). Indians had gone into real estate; it was the type of math we understood, especially back at that time. With depreciation you could avoid taxes, and you could buy the houses with cash because you weren't paying taxes yet—you were building equity. I decided to strike out on my own as I had four rental houses at the time and managed the cash flow from the house rental income. I eventually sold the houses, one at a time, to support my entrepreneurship. I had done my analysis to know when the time was right for each sale and how to shelter any income.

Nineteen eighty-one was a watershed year with the IBM PC. The initial networking standards of the Ethernet were announced that year as the future networking protocol. I looked at the Ethernet specification and understood that the world was changing and needed to be networked and that maybe there was an opportunity in this area. I very quickly realized that my training as a logic designer had prepared me to design anything. The new generation of engineers and products required LSI computer chips, which were being made by AMD and Intel. What if I designed a board and could apply these off-the-shelf chips? Excelan was the earliest company in Ethernet networking. The actual Ethernet protocols had to be designed into the chips, and there were none available. In 1972, there were adders and multiplexers and better and better building blocks that you could put together. Today there are no logic design people outside of the chip companies. People who were building the functions had to put together a microprocessor, an SIO, and an Ethernet chip. I designed an Ethernet chip on a board, and it was followed by building a Multibus board, a VME board, and a Q-bus board, so we had boards for every market. We were the first networking company in 1982 that offered Ethernet connectivity on all the computers, and we sold about a million boards.

FOUNDING A COMPANY: EXCELAN

I was one of the three founders—the technical founder. The CEO cofounder was later sacked by the board, and I became interim CEO. The third person was a software expert. I loved being CEO, and we turned the place around in three months, after initial struggles. The board brought in a permanent CEO because we were doing so well and we could go public. There was a fear that, because there were no Indian CEOs, Wall Street might not like an Indian to head a company. The argument used with me was whether I wanted to be rich or be a "proud CEO." I told them I wanted to be rich, and so they brought in this guy and it was hard to watch. He was also let go by the board a few months after the company went public, and then I became permanent CEO. The board finally saw the difference in how I built the company and sharpened the market positioning. I brought marketing to the company, and I raised pricing a hundredfold. I turned out to be a brilliant marketing guy, which meant positioning and pricing and value propositions. There was no experience base in pricing software. Companies know how to price software now. We had software at $60 a copy for the PC, minicomputer, or mainframe—it was all $60. Hardware we knew how to price. It was easy because if it cost us $300 to build a board, with a 60 percent margin to the end user, you put the price at $2,000 with a 50 percent discount to the channel and 10 percent to the customer. We sold both direct and through the channel.

SELLING SOFTWARE: UNBUNDLING
HARDWARE AND SOFTWARE

Software only—how do you price it? There was no software industry. At the lowest level, operating systems were priced at $60 to $70, so we charged that price. I tell entrepreneurs today that there has to be value pricing, which means value to the customer. I looked at DECnet, from Digital, who sold the bundled products at $29,000. DEC's pricing was $29,000 for the VAXs and maybe $18,000 for the MicroVAX. I didn't have DEC's brand or reputation, so I just decided to price at half of what DEC charged. I bundled everything the customer needed for $14,995. The issue was that the customer could buy his or her own software, so we also sold hardware separately. But I did offer bundled pricing. I was creative in my approach, and it changed the business. The person they brought in as president, a senior person from HP, asked me why I was charging so much money and gouging the customer. I found the HP and IBM senior guys didn't have any financial sense about business. HP had established the value system, which made some profit, but it was very soft. We were competing more aggressively in the market. The CEO got into trouble because he couldn't drive the business. The stock was going well, and it made sense for the board to make the change, as there was no excuse left. In the beginning we had some OEM (orig-

Kanwal with Bill Gates
(photo courtesy of Kanwal Rekhi)

inal equipment manufacturer) business. We had thirty-five OEMs and sold them the software at $60. Apollo Systems and the workstation world would OEM from us, but they only took the margin and we had to do all the work—and they never priced it right, even in that world. We suggested end-user pricing and gave them 35 to 40 percent off that number, which made them happy. We found this to be an unsatisfactory business. It takes six months to make an OEM sale and contract, and then you had to teach them how to sell, with no revenue—and this was nonsense. Our market also changed to direct to customers, with most of the hardware from Digital's PDPs, VAXs, NCR towers, and others. Customers could even buy DECnet direct from DEC, at a much higher price.

Most of the time we sold fully bundled solutions. I even did the ads myself for the technical publications. There were three ads: one ad showed a VAX, a UNIX machine, and a PC, and it showed how we solved the networking mess. It was a clear and simple message, including a money-back guarantee if you didn't like it. The same ad was put in *PC* magazine, with the PC in the middle and the VAX and UNIX machines by its side. The PC was the center of the universe in that ad.

We even promoted with our satisfaction guarantee that we would fly someone out to help them. Fortunately, there were enough margins to cover this cost. Our plan supported 10 percent of the customers requiring help to be satisfied, but we actually only had less than 1 percent of customers request services to meet their satisfaction with the product. It became a very profitable business very quickly.

Prices never were a problem. I learned never to sell on prices but instead on value and solving problems. Then you need to make sure you have good customer support to make them happy, and I knew whether they were happy or not, as I always spoke to customers directly. I had a fast-talking VP of Sales who always had a list of twenty reasons customers wouldn't buy at a certain price. I asked him how many boards he was going to sell that year, and he said ten thousand. I did the math for ten thousand units and showed him the business couldn't survive. I asked him, if he had a "blowout" year, what would he sell, and he said twenty thousand. I reminded him we had fifty-nine engineers that we had to meet payroll for. I told him that we couldn't operate at the prices he was suggesting because we couldn't even pay the engineers. He was very upset with me and told me that I was approaching it as an engineer and that is not how the world works. I told him I would be out of business if I followed his plan, and I would rather go out of business trying my model. He told the board that I was crazy, and the board sided with me. I eventually fired the guy. I moved the software pricing from $60 to $600, and the pricing stood. No one complained. Too low a price can represent low functions. Software prices went up, but the bundle was $14,995. I gave a 15 percent discount for buying direct. Software prices went up a hundredfold. When they bought a second or third time, it was proof that the buyer was satisfied. A repeat buyer is real proof.

I created the ads myself because the agencies had fancy ideas. I was selling to engineers and needed to show in a simple manner that we were solving problems. We showed how we offered everything they needed. The pricing and positioning made all the difference. I became aware how we could sell technology, but customers needed to solve problems on their own terms. If we were solving problems, we didn't have to worry about price. I became CEO in 1985, and in 1986 they brought in the new guy to take us public. We did very well and went public in February of 1987. Sales flattened after we went public, but the market crashed at that time also. The CEO they brought in was let go. In the fall of 1987, I took over, and Novell acquired us in the summer of 1989. Novell approached me, but it was like flirting. Microsoft and Novell both approached us. We had $60 million in revenue by the time we merged with Novell, and we had a sense that networking would be integrated into future products, and we would have to expand our business. The area we wanted to expand into was already taken by Cisco. Cisco had become the wide area network (WAN) company.

INCREASING MY SKILLS PORTFOLIO
IN RUNNING A COMPANY

The skills you need to become a good start-up entrepreneur, and to prove that you can solve problems, are different skills than what you need to expand a company with financial, marketing, sales, and distribution requirements. I ran Novell for three years, as their CEO was sixty-seven or sixty-eight years old; all his lieutenants had gone and he was very detached. I started as the president, and all the staff reported to me. All the same problems manifested themselves again. Novell was a Mormon company, and the Mormon Church felt they were losing control when we moved the headquarters from Utah to California. I used to fly from the Bay Area to Utah three times a week. We moved the company to Silicon Valley, but they required us to move the headquarters back to Utah. The Church wasn't a shareholder, but they still had control, and I owned 2 to 3 percent of the company. The Church leaders went through the CEO Ray Noorda's wife and encouraged her to get him to go on a mission, which he had not done and which was expected of Mormons in good standing. He had gone to war instead of a mission when he was young.

A non-Mormon as a CEO wasn't going to happen with the Church influence, so they split it into a California company and a Utah company. I ran the networking units as we had bought a UNIX company from AT&T. They brought in John Young, who was CEO of HP, to be on the board, as he was a descendent of Brigham Young, one of the founders of the Mormon Church. The Church brought in several senior guys from HP who didn't work out, including Bob Frankenberg, over me and another guy from within the company. Around 1996, they brought in Eric Schmidt, the last of the CEOs, who was a technology guy from Sun Microsystems, to run Novell. He ran into the same problems with the Church. Eric got hired in Utah, but he brought the company back to California. That didn't sit well with the Mormon Church. Novell was in Provo and had acquired WordPerfect, the word-processing software company.

I left in December of 1994. I knew that Novell wasn't going to make it; they weren't speaking about business any longer, just internal issues. We didn't spend time talking about our next move or similar discussions. We owned UNIX and the TCP/IP networking company. Nineteen ninety-four was the peak of the company. Eric tried to turn the company around. They had brought in another guy as CEO who worked for me at Excelan, and I was shocked as he was totally out of his element. He lasted about a year before he was fired. Eventually Novell was sold to Documentum.

BUSINESS IS BUSINESS: AN ECONOMIC ARRANGEMENT

The lesson I learned was that, even though I had people I didn't want thrown to the wolves, there was nothing I could do about it. Business is business. It is an economic arrangement. They keep you until they don't have business any longer. You need to work for someone as long as it is profitable for you personally. I hoped that I could help the people because I didn't want them to suffer, but they were going to suffer anyway, and I stayed a year longer than I should have. I wasn't passive. I was on the board and spoke up and had big issues with them. They didn't understand that the hardware and software would deconstruct and that eventually there would be the software business. It wasn't easy dealing with Young, who was twenty years older than I was—a former CEO and chairman of HP, and a high-ranking Mormon. He and the board didn't understand software as a business. We had some messy arguments. I left in peace but felt it was such a waste to see what happened to a company that had good talent and products, good positioning, and everything we needed. CEOs also change. Sometimes they are sharp and a solid business driver. Sometimes they do foolish things. Sometimes they overstay.

It was time to move on, and I thought I was going to take some time off, but then I started The Indus Entrepreneurs (TiE), where I volunteered my time. It was a place to go to, and my wife didn't want me at home. She had her space, and TiE had an office where I would go. I re-engaged with entrepreneurs. They would drop in for basic advice, and I discovered I liked being a coach. I was just reading newsletters and magazines, and people would drop in for advice on issues such as how to price things or how to handle a situation. Without realizing it, I engaged with many, many people that year. I would send them to VC (venture capital) friends that I knew, and they would always turn them down. I realized it was the same thing again—they were being turned down because they were Indians. People like me, and some of the other guys, were seen as outliers and some sort of freaks. The Indian brand (in 1995) wasn't established yet.

ANGEL INVESTING AND LAUNCHING TiE

I started to invest as an angel investor in 1995. I first invested in seven companies, and they all did well. I liked the ideas and the plans, and I had the money. I didn't expect high returns, but one company was acquired after one year, and I did well. I never looked back and was having fun. I did this investing for about ten years.

The view of the Indo-American as a successful entrepreneur steadily changed. Suddenly we were no longer the freaks and outliers. There were first two people, then three people, then ten people, and then it kept rolling forward until it changed completely. They had mentors, and suddenly TiE became the brand to help these people. TiE may not be needed for the same reasons as when it was started, but in 2015, 4,800 people showed up for the Silicon Valley TiE conference (TiEcon), and it is well run. TiE now has become self-perpetuating, and it is a nice platform to volunteer for. Some VCs tried to recruit me, but I no longer had any interest in working for anyone again. I no longer have the stress I did, and now I do what I want. My life doesn't change whether I make more money or not. I have probably mentored more than two thousand people, and I get e-mails from people I don't remember, who write and tell me that what they learned from me was useful. Last week a person came up to me and told me that he still lives by the rules I gave him, especially about pricing. You acquire wisdom and knowledge over a long period. It is tested, and if you share it freely, and if it becomes absorbed and becomes a value for others, you haven't lost a thing. I never hear from people who didn't make it, but those who I have had a positive impact on come forward and tell me. You can do everything right in life and in business and still fail—timing may be wrong or the competition changes. Even if one person succeeded because of my help, I am pleased. I can look at many people in the Valley I mentored, and I am proud of their accomplishments.

CONTINUING COMMITMENT TO MICHIGAN TECH

I have been involved with Michigan Tech for about fifteen years. I didn't go back for about twenty-seven years. I also engaged with my college in India. Michigan Tech wanted to connect to the Valley. Dave House, of Intel, is also from Michigan Tech, and some other graduates who are in Silicon Valley go back twice a year. We need to focus entrepreneurship in the world beyond this valley. I recently flew three students from Michigan to Silicon Valley, and they were just blown away. Michigan Tech started an Entrepreneurship Club and has made tremendous progress since we were there. These three students were leaders in that club, and they were undergrads. The idea is to get their eyes and ears open. Everyone in that area has come to believe that the dream job is working at GM or Ford. It's only now true that people working in automotive companies need to have high technology experience.

*Kanwal on the bridge to Rekhi Hall
at Michigan Tech University*
(photo courtesy of Kanwal Rekhi)

The Wadsworth Society of Michigan Tech is for large donors, and I am a member. Wadsworth was one of the early pioneers at the university. The main dorm is named Wadsworth. When I first returned about fifteen years ago, I was on the board of advisors to the president. I asked the president in a meeting who his customer was. His response was that he was running a university and they didn't have any customers. I replied that everyone has customers. My explanation of a customer is that their success and happiness is your success and happiness. A customer is somebody whose interest you have at heart, because if he succeeds, you will do well—actually, even in a marriage you have a customer. Someone you need to pay attention to. He finally responded, "Ford and General Motors." I queried, "What if they go out of business or go bankrupt?" His response, "Surely you don't mean that—they will never go out of business." I assured him that ANY company could go out of business. I encouraged him to define his customers as his students. "Their success will help Michigan Tech succeed, and your job is to be sure these students are prepared for any job out there, not just with GM and Ford. You need to start thinking differently, rather than help-ing them toward working in only one industry."

I don't do five-hundred-person lectures at the university. We meet in smaller groups of fifty to one hundred people in several meetings and also with professors. Professors think so differently, and I want to broaden them too. I bring students back for TiEcon and for meetings with Apple and Google and show them this world. They leave with a level of excitement. The faculty comes out here twice a year to show them the future of America.

THE FUTURE OF SELF-RELIANCE

You can't do now in America what we have done historically with low-end manufacturing. There just isn't enough value added. If you don't add enough value, you won't have enough to pay the costs. The facto-ries will use robots, because it will keep the cost lower. If you go back to the start of the industrial revolution, machines took away jobs—with a machine you don't need that many people. It was true then, and it is true now. Here is one story for perspective: In the 1960s, there was a professor of economics who was a big fan of China and Mao Tse-tung, and he went to visit China. They were going to build this massive dam in the Yangtze River. A million people were building the dam with shovels and baskets on their heads. The professor looked at Mao and asked him why he didn't use machines. Mao said, "This is an employment scheme." The professor replied, "Oh, I thought you were building a dam. If this is an employment scheme, then why don't you just use spoons instead of shovels?"

As we created more machines, more robots, and more software, unemployment hasn't substantially shot up. A 5 percent unemployment rate is considered full employment. If you are a full-employment economy, you can't do anything new because everyone is already employed. What happens as you become more productive and efficient is that you lay people off, and these are the people who go off and do something new. You create surplus labor by using machines and efficient processes. We have gone from 60 percent of people on farms in the 1900s to 2 percent of people on farms. But unemployment didn't shoot up. As you take people off what they are doing and implement processes that are more productive, you free up those people to do new things that weren't being done before. If you have an economy with all the people making all they need and consume, such as food, you will have a subsistence economy. More productive people create more quality-of-life jobs, such as insurance, banking, and travel. You convert the economy from hard goods to soft goods and services. Of course, you can only eat so much food and buy so many washers and dryers. You can consume an almost infinite amount of services.

I encourage professors to make their students self-reliant. Don't focus them on a job. Get them to think about the basics and enhancing their skills. What is it that they need to do differently? What is not being done today? Entrepreneurship in Silicon Valley is possible because we have surplus people. The notion that somehow everyone will be unemployed when we implement robots is a nonsense notion. The skill levels have to change, of course. It is your own job to invest in yourself. You have to because it is a free market setup, where everyone is a CEO in his or her own life. You have to have a safety net because people who are laid off from jobs are the ones who are the least able to adapt to new jobs. You have to not depend upon a job or anyone for your livelihood. Everyone has to think in terms of "What is my next move?" In this valley, a marketing person from the '90s would find that marketing today has almost nothing to do with the skills you needed at that time. Now you have social networking, CSM, and other online activities. Events and programs like we used to do don't exist in the same manner. Sales have changed too. This has always been true for engineers, but other professions are facing the same issues. It is the philosophical question of who is responsible to keep up the skills of the workforce. Either you have the Russian- and Chinese-style planned economies, or you say you are free people and you must advance yourself.

MY ORIGINS AND FAMILY

I was born to Sikh parents in Rawalpindi, Pakistan, which was on the northwest frontier. Pakistan is on the Indus River, which used to be the traditional border of India in the flatlands. Beyond that are mountains, and Rawalpindi is on the north side of that. During the partition in 1947, when I was two, our entire family, as Sikhs, had to move to India—it wasn't safe to live in Pakistan because the divide was based on religion. Pakistan didn't say that people who weren't Muslim had to leave, but they made it very difficult for those who wanted to stay. India didn't interpret the partition based on religion. India said, "Everyone is welcome to stay here." At the time of the partition, about one-third of the population of India were Muslims. Indian Muslims didn't feel compelled to leave, even though many did leave. India has the second-largest population of Muslims in the world. India's constitution supports a secular government. Pakistan was organized because people wanted an Islamic country. Britain had a simple divide-and-conquer strategy—they didn't have the numbers, so they had to pit groups against each other. I suppose if I were them, I would have done the same if I didn't have the numbers. At the time of the partition, there were less than one hundred thousand English people in India ruling three hundred million people, and they couldn't do so by force. What happened, in my opinion, was once the British decided to leave, they acted like they wanted out immediately—they wanted out yesterday. Muslims wanted a homeland, and the British said they would have it. A million people died in riots during all the changes. Sikhs coming back to Punjab in India told stories of sackings, burnings, and rape. On the India side of the line, there was the same. There were no innocent people. They were both nasty to each other.

My father was in the army during the time of the partition and went to war. The army had a very orderly split. They transported army people to Pakistan if they were Muslims and brought the Hindu and Sikh army people to India. Right after the split happened, they immediately fought the war for Kashmir. The British ruled about two-thirds of India. The other one-third of India was ruled by maharajahs, as princely states. The British, as part of the Freedom of India Act in Parliament, said that people had to state which side they wanted to join, including the maharajahs. They couldn't opt to stay independent. Maharajahs who were in India chose to stay in India, and those in Pakistan chose to stay in that new country. But there were two very large states—Kashmir (a maharajah state) and Hyderabad (which was bigger than England in size)—that wanted to stay independent. Hyderabad was in India and was a Hindu majority state with a Muslim ruler. Kashmir was a Muslim majority state with a Hindu ruler. So everyone chose between Pakistan and India except for these two states. They thought they were large enough to stay independent. They protested to the British about how they sold them down the river. When Pakistan tried to take Kashmir by force, the maharajah said he wanted to be part of India, and the Indian Army moved in immediately. They threw the Pakistanis out of most of Kashmir. It has been sixty-eight years since the partition. Both Pakistan and India have a fight based on principle. The majority of Kashmir is Muslim, and India doesn't support segregation based on religion any longer. There eventually has to be a soft, open border because Pakistan has one-third of Kashmir today. There is no reason for Kashmir to be part of Pakistan, except for the claim of being Muslim. For them it is based on principle.

Because my father was in the military, we moved very frequently. We finally settled in a city named Kanpur, which is a large city in northern India in the state of Uttar Pradesh. The family stayed there, and my father went to his postings alone. At the time we left Pakistan, there were four children, and eventually there were eight of us. I was number three of the original eight children—seven boys and one girl. There are now several of us in the Bay Area. In India, my father had his father and mother living with us plus a couple of his sisters who were later married in the fifties. My grandfather died in 1958. In India, a woman's family would rather die than live with the daughter. Your son has to take care of you. Daughters belong to the husband's family, and you cannot have any financial dependency on the daughter's side. My eldest brother went into the army very quickly because it was a stable and respectable job. He went to a junior college and went to the military academy at NDA (the National Defense Academy in Pune) and became an officer. Another brother attended IMA (the Indian Military Academy in Dehradun). My father started out as a soldier and went to war in Egypt and North Africa. When he came back, he had visions of being a master sergeant, the top of the non-officers. He went to war at age twenty-four and came back at age twenty-eight—he was, at that time, the most senior noncommissioned officer.

When the partition happened in 1947, the army split, the British officers went home, and my father had the opportunity to become a lieutenant in the army. Being an army officer and senior bureaucrat was a very big deal because it was a very stable job. I don't remember him being at home very frequently. My mother was not educated, yet she was very sharp. My grandfather was paralyzed due to a stroke, and he wasn't able to move. My older brother, the second one, wasn't disciplined, but he was sharp, and he became an army officer also. I was, by and large, on my own. I had no one to help me with my homework. I did it myself, with no supervision by an elder.

EDUCATION

I went to a Sikh school because they are very committed to education. There were boys' schools and girls' schools, and they were side by side. Those were considered very good schools. I was good in school and wanted to be an engineer. In the 1950s, radio was available and news was common. *Sputnik*, the transistor radio, the atom bomb—they were part of our world, and I thought about being an engineer. I had no mentors and was very self-reliant. Fortunately, I was able to mentor my younger brothers and sister. Unfortunately, I did not have any teachers that I connected to or who inspired me.

I had a speech impediment, which I still do, and I was very quiet. No one could see me. I may have seen myself as sharp and a good learner, but others would say that I didn't speak well and wasn't physically strong. My brothers went into the army, and that made others proud. I was not in the army. My father didn't see me as army material. He saw me as someone who was physically weak and not capable. He just hoped I would find something to do with my life. I didn't fit his characteristics. I was a reader and had access to books. I became the man about the house because my mother was running the house alone, my father and brother were in their army postings, and the brother older than me was sort of a goof-off. He wasn't responsible in any way. I was the helper, did the shopping, and managed the household. My mother needed someone to help her, and I was dependable, reliable, and sharp enough to do it. I was her partner in running the household.

My first language was Punjabi, my second was Hindi, and then English. By the time you were in high school, the science and math curriculum was in English, and IIT was all in English. You weren't able to speak English, but you were able to read it. English became the basis of your learning, and Punjabi and Hindi were something you did in your community. I went to the Sikh school until tenth grade. I didn't have a formal education for the first five grades because we moved around so frequently. My grandfather was only partially paralyzed at that time so he could teach me. I learned math, which is something every Indian is good at. When we settled in Kanpur, my father took me to school for the first time. They tested me for this and tested me for that, and they put me in the fifth grade. But the problem was that I was not that old for fifth grade, so when I finished tenth grade, I was only fourteen years old, when it would be standard to be seventeen. So I couldn't go into IIT because I was too young and had to wait.

THE IIT DECISION

Going to IIT was advertised in the papers, and I wanted to be an engineer, so I thought I would go to IIT. No one knew that I even applied. I took the tests and I was selected, but no one knew before that time. My father didn't even know what that meant. I told my father that I got accepted into IIT, and he asked me what IIT was. I told him that it was an engineering school that the government of India had set up. His response was "Oh, the government of India has set up these schools. Are they free?" I said, "There is a nominal tuition of about $100 a year, essentially free education." He said, "Your brothers went to schools

Kanwal at IIT, 1967
(photo courtesy of Kanwal Rekhi)

that were free and we didn't have to pay. So what kinds of schools are these? When you come out, you will have a job?" I told him no, that it wasn't certain that I would have a job. His response was "You go to school for four years and you aren't even certain you have a job? What is the matter with you?" He was upset paying for four years, and I wouldn't be sure I would have a job. He said that going into the army meant I could have a job and a pension for life. How could this make sense? Then he went into the office, and even though he was an officer, he was old for his rank. He had senior officers younger than him, but he looked up to them because they were smart and more educated. He told them that he didn't know what the matter was with his son wanting to go to this IIT school. One of them responded, "He got into IIT? He must be really smart because no one gets into IIT without being really smart. My sons have tried and none of them has been accepted at IIT." My father, for the first time in his life, could be proud of his son, who was doing better than the sons of people he looked up to. So he came home all puffed up and said, "Attaboy" (for the first time). It was interesting to watch that none of the other boys had previously wanted to associate with me, but now that I was going to IIT, I was somebody. I chose IIT Bombay because it was the New York City of India and where the action was. I stayed in the dorm, which everyone did. My parents and family were proud of me.

Once you get into IIT, you discover very quickly that everyone is smart. They are all the best in their classes, and they are proud of it. To have a slight advantage, you had to be ten times smarter because everyone was smart. It was an environment that was very competitive and very high energy. I didn't have quite the discipline that the others did who went to private schools, as I went to public schools. There was no money for private schools with all the people in our home. The students were well rounded and into sports, but you learned to hold your own. I still have one of my best friends from my IIT days—Bhopi Dhall, who lives in Dallas. We met at IIT the first day, and even fifty-two years later, we remain friends.

IIT was a great equalizer because all the smart kids made it hard to stand out. The best and the worst weren't that far apart. It was highly intellectual, and I was in a rarified community of the chosen few in India. There were about five IITs with a total of two thousand students across India, which at that time had about five hundred million people. Our peer group would have been maybe seven million people. The campuses were set up with American, British, German, and Russian help—and you knew you were in a different world. There were many professors who had done overseas work and come back. I got into abstract programs very early. There is the abstract part of electrical engineering called field theory, which includes things such as electromagnetic waves and is hard to understand from the beginning. I really was attracted to it and understood it early. The professor of that course was surprised by how quickly I could understand and adapt.

I was a loner because of my speech, in addition to being shy. I was shy about my speech all the way up to the time I became a CEO, when I realized there was something that I could do about it. So I hired a speech therapist—an old woman, about eighty, who was also a music teacher. One of my VPs knew her from his church. She would spend about two hours a day with me. I spent a year with her and got more adept, but I dropped it and I regret I didn't keep it up. Once I knew I was speaking to the analysts in New York and they understood me, it made a difference. I was even recognized by Wall Street analysts one year as the most credible executive who spoke clearly and was effective communicating with them. This was shocking because there weren't that many Indian executives dealing with Wall Street.

After four years of IIT, I went to Michigan Tech. By the time you finish IIT, you know that going to America is where the action is, where the computers are being invented, where all the interesting projects are happening. If you want to be part of that, you have to go to America.

Being a loner and going to IIT made me independent. While at IIT, I only went home once a year because Bombay [now Mumbai] was about a thousand miles away from my home. My father finally made it clear that he was proud, although we weren't close. When I went to the US, I didn't think I was going away forever, but I didn't go back for six years. My mother and siblings were able to come to America, although my father passed away in 1974, before I became successful. He did meet my wife, Ann Douglas Holt, in 1973. They got along very well, and that was the last time I saw him, as he died about six months after I left.

FROM PEN PAL TO MARRIAGE AND FAMILY

I got married in the US and was one of the few that didn't go back to India to get married. I am still married, for over forty-five years now. Ann Douglas Holt was my pen pal, and she lived in Connecticut. Parker Pen had a pavilion in the New York World's Fair in 1966, and they matched up people to be pen pals. It was the first Match.com. They had people all over the world they were matching. We wrote each other back and forth for years. I was working in Fort Lauderdale and had never met her, even though we wrote for over two years. We poured our hearts out to each other because we thought we would never meet. Ann was from a broken family with generations of divorce and alcoholism. She was the oldest child and had lots of responsibilities, including a brother and sister. Ann broke out of the dysfunctional life by going into the Air Force and getting away from a selfish mother. She was in Texas for her assignment as an Air Force nurse and wrote that she could meet me in Fort Lauderdale. We met, and I said, "This is wonderful—let's get married." I told her to take her time deciding. We did like each other. I was gone from India three and a half years and only had letters back home every three or four months, so I wasn't going back to India for an arranged marriage. I proposed in May, and she told me in October that she agreed to marry. We only saw each other twice—the second time when I went to Texas to meet her. Ann and I got married in a small Protestant church in Fort Lauderdale, about a month after I got laid off. The military would give you a hardship discharge if you were more than fifty miles from your husband at the nearest Air Force base, and this was the case. We married in March, she moved out in April, and we both

Kanwal with Ann, 2015
(photo courtesy of Kanwal Rekhi)

had to start new lives. I did get the job at RCA that made it fine for some months. She was a vocational nurse and got a job right away. Later, living in Sunnyvale, when we had moved to California, she got a job that wasn't very well paying. We didn't have an arranged marriage, as I said, but the reason arranged marriages usually work is because your parents know you best. They can find someone compatible and can filter out distractions. We have one son, Benjamin, and one daughter, Raj-Ann, named after my mother. Ben lives in Santa Monica and is in the Hollywood and Bollywood connection business, and currently he is based in Mumbai. Raj-Ann lived in Delhi for a while, as her husband works for the State Department. Ben and Raj-Ann spent lots of time in India before they came back to reside in the US.

THOUGHTS ON EDUCATION

If I were going to give advice to parents about educating their children, I don't know what I'd say, but I do speak to both American and Indian students all the time. My basic message is learn to become self-reliant. You can't depend on jobs; don't put your destiny in someone else's hands. I tell them the story about being laid off, and looking back, it is what set me free. I strongly believe the modern corporation is a temporary phenomenon. One hundred fifty years ago, everyone worked for themselves. As the industrial age began, the economies of scale came into play with building structures; keeping machines going twenty-four hours a day required companies of sufficient size. If you don't need capital, there is no economy of scale. The whole structure was driven by economies of scale and productivity. The problem with that model is that when you become larger, there is inefficacy of internal communication—the left hand doesn't know what the right hand is doing.

As you become more information oriented, there is less value in building things than in managing things. Software design moved to India, and organizations became much more virtual; virtual organizations don't need economies of scale. I can have a company manufacture one item, and next time I can choose from other suppliers. Look at Uber and how many employees there are. Not that many—but there are drivers all over the world. Look at the financial return per employee at Facebook, which is in the several millions of dollars range. But these companies don't employ that many people. Ford and General Motors get a low return per employee. You can see that the guys who start these companies get all the wealth and you become just an employee. And you are putting your trust in the wrong people. With the information technology you can become a well-rounded person. Don't specialize. If you get a master's or PhD, you will be specialized and can make some money at that time, but that specialty can be totally out of date tomorrow. Be generalists and learn this and that.

EDUCATION PHILANTHROPY AS A PASSION

My philanthropy passions are education—mainly Michigan Tech and IIT. I also keep them connected besides being my charity. I haven't been an active Sikh, but community and public service is an area I still engage with my family once a year, serving and preparing food and cleaning up. The TiE phenomenon continues through my lifelong teaching and mentoring. I taught my siblings how to ride a bicycle and how to drive a car at a very young age. I brought all my brothers and sisters to the US starting in 1976, and the last of them came in 1991. I continue by mentoring their children. My brother is still the oldest male, and we honor him as head of the family—the front man at family gatherings.

REFLECTIONS ON BEING AN ENTREPRENEUR AND CEO

As I look back on my career, the time I think I was at my best was in 1985. We had a company we started in 1982 that was in trouble. I was VP of Engineering and another guy was CEO. We lost more money than we budgeted. The CEO was fired, and that liberated me. When he got fired, he wanted me to leave. But I was also starting to see him as the problem. I spent three months totally on my own, with no help from anyone, to rethink the business. It was the first time I was on my own, and it was a terrible situation. As a board member now, I don't like rationalization or explanations, and I want to see clearer planning. I am a strong believer that people in charge must be on top of things, with good explanations and knowledge of why they will succeed. Most of the CEOs I work with now I have mentored, so I am familiar with them. I tell the women not to complain but to look at the journey the Indian male has made and use us for inspiration. We had no one believing in us or giving us a break. You just have to stick it out. Indians were seen as very good "techies." It was like they perceived us as having this gene that helped you write the software, or the mathematic gene—a

Kanwal Rekhi
(photo courtesy of Kanwal Rekhi)

singularly one-dimensional person. They thought we didn't know how to sell, market, or do the numbers on the finance side. The funders would ask us why we wanted to do something we weren't good at, and say that we should just stick to being an engineer, where we would be good, instead of wanting to be an entrepreneur. They didn't believe we should go outside of being engineers and offered no encouragement and no mentorship. You couldn't speak to anyone about it, and if you did, they would ask, "Why are you doing this?"

My experience in 1985 taught me I would do better alone. By the time they found a CEO, the revenues were shooting up, and the board was happy but didn't understand what was happening. The board wasn't a partner with me. Once the numbers started happening, they did recognize that I had turned the place upside down. They brought in the new CEO, but they also didn't want to lose me. And I had to remember the question of whether I wanted to be rich or to be CEO. What if the IPO failed because we had an Indian CEO? It's like this today for women going through the same changes we did. TiE was effective because the early organizers realized that we had no one to turn to; we were all in the same predicament, and it shouldn't be this hard to get funding and support. The Indians were good raw material, and with a little bit of help, they blossomed. The ratio for women in technical areas has improved a bit, but it is still around 20 percent. One major issue is that math is not seen as a critical asset for most people and especially for women. This isn't true for everyone, but the population of women with math backgrounds has to be larger.

I have always seen myself as a firefighter, from the time I was a child helping my mother at home. When I worked for Singer Link, I was a firefighter. Whenever projects were in trouble, they put me on the team. By the time I left Singer Link, I understood that I could get to the bottom of the problem and distill the problem to action. This relates back to my lifelong self-reliance. I got tagged as a person who could get things done. I had a simple mind-set: the company is in trouble, we have run out of cash, the CEO has been there six months, and without tons of money we will go out of business. I could make a difference and learned to solve these problems because I didn't see anything but upside. We were already on the downside. With time and money, we had to make things happen. In my case, I had to will myself to succeed. I may not have been the smartest engineer or marketing or business person, but I had the confidence to pull it all together. I was action oriented, even in the face of odds against me.

THOUGHTS ON IMMIGRATION

I do think about the immigration strategy for the US. When a child is born in the US, it takes over twenty years of investment and education for that person to become productive. If you bring an engineer here from India, he or she is productive from day one, is paying taxes, and is more likely to be an entrepreneur. Yes, he or she is part of the end of the bell curve in India separated from the major population. The US was very racist in its immigration policy, for a long time not wanting to admit Asians. The Indians weren't allowed to own land in California. Canada was open for Indians, and they came down from Canada. In 1910, Asians weren't allowed to own land. They were mostly farmers and frequently married Mexican women, so there is a large population of mixed marriages. Now they are very rich farmers and some of the richest farmers in America.

Indians weren't allowed to become citizens until the late 1940s, and yet they had been here for two generations. Right after that, one of the people from India, Dalip Singh Saund from Southern California, was elected to Congress from 1958 until 1962. He was a professor of mathematics at Berkeley and was later elected a judge. In 1958, US immigration was based on the ratio of the existing US population. So if there were 30 percent Germanic people, you gave out 30 percent of the green cards to German immigrants. If the population from a country was low, you were only allowed fifty people. India was allotted fifty persons in 1958. They didn't count anyone that wasn't a citizen. Then the Russians launched *Sputnik*, and the government went crazy believing we had lost the space race. So in 1965, the basis of first preference for immigration changed from country of origin to qualifications. That is the moment that immigration for Indians changed, because of our technical background. I brought my brothers and sister to America through the family unification program in the 1980s. But that was closed and later opened in the 1990s. The 1990s saw the largest number of immigrants coming to America, more than in any other decade, based on some principles that aren't entirely clear. It must be about basic economics, and with the demographics changing in the US, things will change. America is the way it is because it attracted the best and the brightest, not just because of the circumstance of birthright. The US got trained manpower and got productivity right away. Technology distinctions now don't matter the same as they used to. Competing with the Chinese now requires a very different model than competing with the Russians did in the 1950s and 1960s. There will be continued cycles of change.

M. R. (MADHAVAN) RANGASWAMI, SAN FRANCISCO

BORN IN CHENNAI, INDIA

EDITOR: *M. R. is the last of the early mover immigrants[†] in these stories. His career is a sampling of law, marketing, sales, and company-building experiences. He motivates the members of his vast network to become agents of change. He continues giving back through his leadership, supporting environmental sustainability stewardship programs in global corporations and organizing the India diasporas in the United States.*

I first thought about coming to the US to study while living in India. My background is kind of different from many of the folks who came to Silicon Valley. In those days, Indians typically went to IIT, came here to get a graduate degree in computer science or engineering at an American university, and then went to Silicon Valley as a developer or a programmer. That used to be the path. But in my case, my initial studies in India were in accounting and commerce. I didn't quite like that program, but I did get my bachelor's degree in it. A lot of people in my

[†]*See the graph in the Introduction, p. xvii, for further information about early movers.*

family were lawyers: my father, my uncle, and both of my grandfathers. With so many in my family being lawyers, people suggested maybe I should go into the legal profession. So I ended up in law school and did a couple years of it. I found I didn't like that either, but I managed to get a degree—a two-year degree called a bachelor's in general law. As I was completing the program, India was faced with many social issues, and the government was clamping down on rights. This was called in India at the time an "emergency." And I thought, what do lawyers do when human rights are curbed? So I was disillusioned as well.

About that time, my eldest brother was visiting from the US. He was the first one in the family who went to the US to go to college in the 1950s, which were the early days of Indians coming to the US. He was an engineer. When he came back to India in 1975, he asked me, "What are you doing?" We were talking about my career, and he said, "Why don't you come study in the US?" His mentioning this idea to me put the bug in my ear that maybe I should go to the US and get an MBA. I thought, *Maybe that's a good idea,* and I started looking into colleges at that time. I got here in 1976 and got into Kent State University [in Ohio] to get my MBA.

Everyone leaving India in 1976 was under the $8 rule. If you were a student, the government of India really didn't give you much to assist your education. Eight dollars is typically for tourists. You say you're going for eight days, and they say, "Okay, you get sixty-four dollars," or whatever. For students, I think it was the bare minimum—it wasn't much. I remember that my brother slipped me a hundred-dollar note when we were at the airport in India. He put it in my pocket, and I remember thinking, *Wow, this is cool.*

My brother's friend picked me up at the airport in New York. Then I took the Greyhound bus to my brother's house, which was in upstate New York, and spent a few days there, and then took a bus to Cleveland. I got my start in the US this way.

While getting my MBA, I was initially kind of interested in marketing. Then I met a professor who was really good on the operations management side, so I ended up taking extra courses in operations management. Basically, at the end of my MBA I was just a generalist. I didn't take any courses in the typical things that you would expect in the tech field. At that time, my thinking was that I would come to the US to study and I'd go back to India. Then, once I was nearing completion, there was something in those days called a practical training visa, where any foreign graduate was allowed eighteen months of work experience in the US. I said, "Okay, maybe I'll do the eighteen months and then go back." Then the next step was after the eighteen months, maybe I should get my green card and then go back. It was basically postponing of the decision, which ultimately led to me never going home.

M. R. at immigration
(photo courtesy of M. R. Rangaswami)

I grew up in Chennai, and I come from a middle-class Brahmin family, also known as TamBrahms. My dad was in government service, and my mother was a homemaker. She got married in the old days, when my dad was, I think, eighteen and she was twelve, though the marriage was unconsummated until she went to my father's house when she turned sixteen. So she didn't complete her schooling. I think if my mother were a modern-day woman, she would have been the CEO of a company. She was very smart, had tremendous willpower, and could get people to do things. In today's world, she would absolutely be very successful in business. I was the youngest of seven. It's a large family, and so my mother had a busy time raising the family. She didn't have time to do anything else.

My dad was a gold medalist in mathematics and became a lawyer, and then he was in government service. He did different things and became responsible for the imports and exports of products in Chennai for that region. He then went into diplomatic service for a while and was part of the Indian High Commission in Sri Lanka and was responsible for the trade relationship. The family all lived in Sri Lanka. I already spoke Tamil, although English was my first language, so living in Sri Lanka wasn't a problem. I learned Hindi in school, and I can speak it, read it, and write it.

The boys in my family all completed college, but my three sisters were pulled out when they got married. This was usually the case with girls in those days. In the 1940s and the 1950s, when my siblings got married, it was the norm and tradition at the time that the boys got educated and the girls did not. I was born very late, so most of my brothers and sisters had already left the house. I was the baby and the last. There was only one brother and I at home. My father did not reach sixty and passed away when I was ten years old. He was forty-nine or fifty when I was born, and my mom was forty-four. I had the same parents as my siblings, not a stepmother or stepfather.

I attended a Catholic school, English-language, and then a Catholic college. I went to Loyola College, which is one of the top schools in Chennai, and then to law school. It was all English-language. In India, the system's quite different than in America. They teach to the syllabus, and you make sure everybody can understand the basics and everyone is prepared to do a lot of work to get through the exam. So you were basically taught to the syllabus and to do well in exams. So very little thought was given to thinking, debating, and discussing. That's the style even today in most Indian schools.

I played some sports. Obviously, any kid in India plays cricket. I also played field hockey. I would say I was a typical kid. Nothing out of the ordinary—I guess I was just a regular kid. I loved watching movies, and in India you get English movies, in those days, six or twelve months later, and they'd be highly edited because of the censors. It was definitely a big thing for me to go to movies in English, Hindi, and Tamil. Tamil movies, right after Hindi, are the second-biggest movie industry. It's huge.

COMING TO THE UNITED STATES AND KENT STATE

My brother, living in the US, didn't come home to India for a long time—he couldn't afford to. The conversation with me about immigration was a conversation on one of his very first visits to India. There was no correspondence, no communication at all—it was more sitting down and chatting. It was definitely not planned. I came to study in 1976, and it wasn't as big a deal. But it was different, because Chennai is a hot and humid city twelve months a year. And when you come to the United States and go to Ohio, it's completely different weather. The change in climate was huge. I'd never seen snow or any of that winter weather. I came in late August, I think. But soon it was November and December, and in those months it was snow, ice, and all the problems that go with it—sliding on ice and falling down. I think one year I was there, it was the coldest winter ever reported, and another year it was the snowiest winter. So it was a pretty brutal experience, especially since, during winters in northeast Ohio, you don't see the sun often. I remember we had a sun watch, and it was day twenty and we hadn't seen the sun! I think it was eventually twenty-nine days before we finally saw the sun.

In those days, calls to India were, I think, three to four dollars a minute. So you could maybe make a call once a month for a couple of minutes. You had to scream into the phones because Indian phones were so bad they couldn't hear you, so you'd end up shouting to be heard. Those were the days!

I think I was prepared for college, and it wasn't super hard or super easy. I was prepared to do a good job. Food was definitely a challenge: the big issue for me was that I was a vegetarian, and, at that time, it was pretty hard to get veggie food, unlike today. I had to cook my own food because even the cafeterias wouldn't have many vegetarian choices— mainly boiled peas and carrots. But I really enjoyed the atmosphere, the environment, and making new friends. I would say it was absolutely a fabulous experience being at college. In those days, there weren't that many Indians in the United States. There was an international students association with an office where there was a staff person who could help us, and it was fun going in and meeting other foreign students as well. But I also made a lot of American friends, so I didn't really need to be in that environment for long.

I first tried to live in the dorms, but I did not like the experience of shared toilets and all the communal living, as I just wasn't used to the American style. I had a friend, another Indian guy who also didn't like the dorms, so within a couple months we found an apartment and moved out. We did our own separate cooking, because the other guy ate meat. For the rest of my time at the university, I lived in apartments and had different roommates. My sister-in-law in New York got me all the spices and other ingredients that were difficult to find in Ohio. I learned just a little bit about cooking at home and a little bit with my sister-in-law before I came down to Ohio; the rest was improvisation. I wasn't a great cook, and I didn't aspire to be a great cook. I learned how to do my own laundry. Somehow I managed to get by without learning how to iron.

One of my jobs at Kent State was in janitorial services, and one of the assignments we got was to clean the locker rooms of the Cleveland Browns and to clean all the urinals at the stadium, so I did things to make a living that I'd never done before. I managed to survive and had jobs with janitorial services throughout the year, cleaning toilets, changing light bulbs, and cleaning carpets—whatever was required. I had to finance my own college, and I took a loan from my brother initially for the first semester and then managed to get a research assistantship. From then on, I was okay for funding for the two years of my master's.

I was in the economics department, and I worked with an economics professor who was doing a lot of econometric modeling. It was quite interesting to do research and get involved in a topic I didn't know much about. It was useful to broaden my skill set, but I really wasn't interested in going into research or teaching. One of the things that I wish I had done more is really meet more with external companies and organizations. I didn't know how the world worked. When I give advice these days, I say maximize and leverage everything you can with the placement center in college or get a mentor. When there is an external guest speaker, go visit with them, get to know them, get advice. I never did any of that; I was too naive at the time. I went to classes and did all the work, but I never really did all the other things that one needs to do. I didn't have a mentor who told me to do all these things. If I'd had a mentor who gave me all that advice, I'm sure I would have followed it.

Looking back, the challenge with MBA programs is that the practical element was missing. I think colleges these days are doing a lot more than just case studies. Now they're getting you into a company for a while, immersing you in the real-world experience. I could've used more on-the-job training. I'm very involved with Kent State, and I just went back this past year and did a talk on entrepreneurship and mentorship. I do what I can to get the school better known, and now the program's doing really well.

The whole concept of marketing was interesting to me so I took some classes and I liked it. But really my whole education, when you look at it, was complete exploration and trying to figure out what I liked to do. I didn't like accounting, I didn't like law—so then I was trying to figure out: Was it marketing? Was it operations management? I really didn't quite know. The professor who I did my research assistantship with was quite helpful. But I was more of a generalist. I've always been a generalist, not a specialist; even now, I do many different things and never really focus on one thing. I guess that's the story of my life.

There was a practical training visa at that time, but there were hardly any jobs when I graduated at the end of 1978 and into early 1979. There were no jobs in Ohio because the steel industry and related industries were being shut down. I had a friend in Texas, and people told me there were jobs in Texas. I went down to Houston, and within two weeks I had a job. It was good that I had my operations research–type experience as I got into a manufacturing company. I was in the area that they called scheduling and production management. So I managed to get in; even though I was highly overqualified up front, I still impressed people enough to give me a job. I initially really enjoyed what I was doing. But at some point you realize manufacturing is a dead-end job, and that there's only so much you can move up to in management. That's what led me to get some advice. The company had sent me for some training, and there was a consultant giving the training. I ended up having a conversation with him and talking about how I was using computers in manufacturing and asking him for advice as to what the future would be. He's the one who said I should go to Silicon Valley. I suppose that with my background in using computers, and since I had an MBA, he for some reason thought I should go. It was just free advice—go to Silicon Valley. In 1982 there was no Internet or anything, so how do you find out about this mythical place? How do you just go to Silicon Valley? I went to the library, did research using microfiche on some old newspaper articles, and then, finally, I also found a list of software companies. I proceeded to just write all of them.

FROM THE GREEN CARD TO THOUGHTS ON IMMIGRATION POLICY

I got my green card in 1982, and I could have applied for citizenship in '86 or '87, but didn't. I was traveling more and more, and back then the Indian passport made it difficult because you had to get a visa for every country you went to. You had to FedEx your passport and apply to get a visa. It was 1994 when I gave in and decided to get a US passport. Congress keeps talking about comprehensive immigration reform. Some in Congress talk about doing different parts of it separately. What I would ask people to do is to consider the legal immigration part as much as they consider the undocumented part. There are so many Indians who come here legally; they've applied for green cards for their close relatives, and those are backlogged for years and years. If these people are applying legally, why do we back them up ten or twelve years?

The second thing is, people like me who come here to study should have the opportunity to study and stay and not be sent back. Give visas to people with a master's degree from overseas or those who come for a master's program in the US. These people are pretty good at figuring out job creation and jobs, and the work that goes with it. I think we should give anyone with a master's degree a green card.

And the third type of case is the H-1B visa. This is a legal form of immigration—and it is important to really make sure that this program is expanded and robust, even though there are politicians calling for the program to be shut down. It's crazy, because even today there are so many start-ups we work with that can't get enough people with technical skills. You often have to go for someone who's overseas. I think it's a capitalistic thing; when supply equals demand everything will be okay. I'd ask Congress to look at these three types of cases: family immigration, giving graduate students green cards, and allowing skilled workers from overseas. I think a lot more attention is being paid to getting amnesty for the eleven million undocumented workers. I would really ask people to pay as much attention to the legal part of the equation.

SABBATICAL

I wanted to take some time off, so I decided to take a sabbatical between my manufacturing job and going to Silicon Valley. I'd never done the whole backpacking experience around Europe, so I did that for two months and then went home to India and spent time with my mother and siblings. I arranged it such that two weeks before I came back, my sister-in-law in New York mailed out all the letters I had written to these companies. It was all organized—she mailed them out, and I came back and waited for the phone to ring and also made calls. One of the companies called me and said, "Hey, we liked your background and we'd like to interview you. Can you come out to California?" This company was looking for someone to be the first quality-assurance person for a business application. They were looking for someone who had used computers in business and for a user approach to a program. They flew me out and hired me, and that's how I became an accidental Silicon Valley person. The company culture was great, and one could make friends and do a lot of social things. I did not have an arranged marriage. When I was living in Houston, I met a girl I liked who was Greek American, and not Indian, and ended up dating her and kept dating her for a long time; we married later, when we were both ready to make a commitment.

THE ACCIDENTAL SILICON VALLEY LIFE

The company I joined was a start-up in those days called Madic. It is no longer in business. The typical Silicon Valley company does great for three or four years and then goes bust. The company's product was aimed at business applications for companies. Those days, they used to be called MRP, and now it's called ERP. The program was running on a weird operating system out of Prime Computer. We competed with DEC [Digital Equipment Corporation] and all the other big systems, but the software led the way to the hardware. I grew in that company from being in quality assurance to customer support, and then I went into sales and became a branch manager. I found a mentor who was the Vice President of Sales in the company. He saw something in me that

I didn't, and he encouraged me to come back to corporate, which I did and became the Director of Marketing. Then the company went bust.

I had a friend at Deloitte who said, "Why don't you come work for us?" So I went over to Deloitte for a couple of years doing management consulting. Then my mentor, who had been with me at Madic, went to a tiny company called Oracle. When he was talking to Larry [Ellison], the cofounder and CEO of Oracle, one day, Larry said he wanted to get into the applications space. He told Larry about me, and Larry said to bring me in. That's how I went from Deloitte to Oracle. I was at Oracle for four years. I joined when the company was doing $125 million. Every year, that doubled—so it was a phenomenal time—until it was a billion dollars of revenue in four years. I was brought in as the marketing manager and then became a director, and then Larry made me the VP of Applications Marketing, which launched the financial and manufacturing applications.

Oracle employed quite a few Indians, even at that time, and some in reasonably prominent positions in the company—mostly in technical positions, but none in sales and marketing. I guess I was one of the pioneers in the sales and marketing space. I can't think of any other Indians who had those skills and were in those departments at that time. When I first started at Oracle, we were in a small office, and my cube was outside Larry's office. We had to share cubes, so there were two people in my cube. They also didn't want too many people in the office. That was a great experience being outside Larry's office and being able to interact with him when he went by. I learned a lot, and he is such a smart guy. He picked up stuff so quickly that he was able to translate into his vision and put into practice. Now you can hardly get near him. In the '80s you met him all the time, and he was much more active in the company day-to-day. He was really inspiring to all of us, and we loved to be on his team!

By this time, America was my home. And my wife was from America, so I wasn't going to go back to India. Oracle required a lot of travel, but my work didn't take me to India—most of my travel was to Europe, especially to London and Germany. This was about 1991 and 1992. I traveled to speak with customers and the press. I could have stayed for a much longer time at Oracle, but I had the entrepreneurial bug and had the opportunity to do another start-up. It was time to leave, although Larry was not too excited about me leaving because he doesn't like losing people. I think I still have this in my memorabilia somewhere, but when I was leaving, Larry wanted to meet me, to convince me to stay, I guess, but he had gone surfing and had an accident and broken his shoulder, so he wasn't coming into work. We were communicating by e-mail. I saved an e-mail from him, which was very gracious, in which he said, "M. R., if you ever want to come back, the door is wide open." I saved it as my insurance policy.

FROM SILICON VALLEY TO ARIZONA
AND THE TRAVELING LIFE

When I left Oracle, I went to a start-up to do another ERP system. And this time the company was based in Tucson, Arizona—not even in Silicon Valley. We pulled up roots from the Bay Area, my wife and I moved to Tucson, and I got going with a company called Avalon Software. I was the chief marketing officer. The company was unknown, and my job was to make it known. I did quite a bit of traveling, analyst relations, and trade shows. The company did really well, and it grew very fast. It got venture funding and grew, and we were then taking Series B and C funding. At that time, some of the bigger PE [private equity] firms came in to talk to us, and one of them took a liking to me and said, "We really like you, but I don't think we're going to invest in the company." I stayed in touch with these guys, and they were asking who our competitors were. One of our competitors was a European company, and they said maybe I should go and talk to those guys. They called me six months later and said, "Remember that company—we funded them. Why don't you come be the chief marketing officer?" I was very loyal to the company I was with, but, by that time, the company was getting into a lot of trouble. Growth was slow, there were lots of issues, and you could see the writing on the wall. And so I had to make a really tough decision between loyalty and staying with the company all the way to the end versus going to the next opportunity. That was a tough decision for me personally, and it wasn't made lightly. At the end of the day, I knew this company was going to start selecting bankers and go public. I talked to a lot of people who said, "You don't get invited to the Super Bowl often. You don't get to do an IPO often.

You have to do something to put away some money because you haven't really done well financially, and you can't give up on it." So that's how I ended up switching after three years at this company in Arizona to a Dutch software company called Baan. We went to selecting the bankers, and it was the first time that Goldman Sachs and Morgan Stanley agreed to come together on an IPO.

I was commuting out of Tucson, as I didn't move. The headquarters of the company was in Holland and Menlo Park [California]. My weekly trip would be Tucson, San Francisco, Amsterdam, and back. I would do lots of trips like that. It was a great experience because I got to help with the S-1 filing and ended up doing the road show with the CFO and CEO. We did seventy presentations in thirty cities, thousands of miles of travel, including three continents. This was a global company, so we took the road show to Tokyo, Germany, London, Amsterdam, and all over the US. It was a great thing, because the first day of the public offering, the company's market cap hit a billion dollars. In those days, that was a huge deal. It was a rewarding experience but lots of travel—the first year I did three hundred thousand actual miles. I went thousands of miles without ironing, as I bought wrinkle-free clothes!

It was a fabulous job, but my wife and I were thinking of having a family, and I was never home. I would leave on Sunday, spend the week traveling, and come back Friday night exhausted. I needed to have a different lifestyle, so I made the hard decision to leave corporate life. I did leave a lot of money on the table, but that was not the important thing. I wanted to do something that was close to home and not travel so much. Within two months of me quitting the company, my wife was pregnant. At that time, a couple of people I knew were investing in a start-up, so I said maybe I should go look at that. I found another software executive who wanted to do the same thing, and we formed this company called Sand Hill Group and decided we would invest in start-ups. Little did we know, we were starting a new trend—angel investing.

ANGEL INVESTING

It was now 1996, which was way before the angel thing was even a big deal. We started investing in companies and decided we'd live the six months of winter in Tucson and the summer in Sausalito. We had the baby and we said, "Oh, you know, we only have a baby—we can camp four or five months here, six months there." We did that for a couple of years and did some investing. And then my friends at the *Wall Street Journal* heard about this and said, "You seem like you have an interesting life. We're going to put a reporter on you." Next, the reporter called me from New York and immediately started interviewing me, saying, "What you are doing sounds so interesting. Can I come and follow you for a couple of days?" This was now 1997, so I said okay, and I talked to my wife and she said it seemed okay to her also. So the reporter came out and spent two days with me and then decided there's an article here about being a pioneer in angel investing. I guess she thought *Wall Street Journal* readers would be interested in what was going on, so she wrote the story and sent it to the editors. The editors looked at it and decided this is not a Section C story—this is a front-page story. The result was it would be the lead story on the front page They couldn't tell me which day, but they then called me and said it was going to be in the next day's paper.

I was in Sausalito at that time. I got a six a.m. phone call from a friend who said, "Hey, your picture is on the front page of the *Wall Street Journal*!" And I said, "Really?" So I went down to the grocery store and bought the *Wall Street Journal*. I went to check out and the guy looked at it and said, "That's your picture!" I didn't realize the power of the media, and luckily the phone number listed was in Arizona. Believe it or not, that week I received over a thousand phone calls. I guess people were looking at angel investors and asking what angel investing is. All these types of requests came in, running the gamut from asking for money to giving me money. People would be calling to say, "I want to deploy five million dollars—do you want to do it?" And, on the other side, people were hitting me up for money. People saw the article and sought me out. I ended up doing a couple of those deals.

I thought this would just be some article on angel investing—I didn't think much of it. I wasn't looking for any publicity. So that got me my fifteen minutes of fame. I was famous—and once you become famous you get more famous, because then someone else finds out about you and says, "Hey, we're going to put you on the list of the twenty-five software luminaries of the year." All this stuff happens. I had fun with it.

We started Sand Hill Group to have a company so we could do our investments. It was not a fund. We would tell our friends, and they would put money directly into the company. We didn't take any carry or commissions. We didn't want to complicate life by starting a fund. We just found deals. We had a different model of working, which was to very seriously work with the entrepreneurs for the first six to twelve months. It was a serious effort of time as we were not just putting angel money into a company. So we couldn't do more than one or two deals a year. In twenty years, I've done forty deals. I devote the time to the deals, so I really don't invest a lot of money in a lot of deals. The first few years, we were quite active in all of the deals. I'm not as active in the deals anymore.

I've learned a lot of things about people. How do you judge people? How do you value people? How do you get to know people? I think the biggest part of investing is the people element. I may not care as much about the market opportunity or any of that; I think it's who are the people, can you work with them, do you like them, are they going to listen, are they going to change, are they going to persevere, are they going to tell you the truth? All these things come out over time. So that's definitely something important. The other thing is, it's a crapshoot. I don't think anyone is smarter than anyone else. In fact, my daughter says, "Dad, you should just put all these deals up on the wall and throw darts to pick one." I don't think you can be a great picker of these companies. I think it's luck. I've done well, but it's all luck. I don't think I'm smarter than anyone else.

It's good to have a second person, rather than be the sole person making a decision. My partner is someone who is very operations oriented—I'm more sales and marketing oriented. When we look at every deal, we look at it completely differently, and the only way we do an investment is if we both agree. It has to be both of us approving. If it's one-one, we pass on the deal. It involves quite a bit of back and forth and understanding people and the deal. We never rush into them; it'll take us two or three months. The way we go about trying to learn about people is, when we meet a new company, we give the people some ideas. If they agree, we tell them to go off, execute, and come back. Then we see if they come back and if they did what we'd advised. We learn if the chemistry is good, if they listen, and if they execute. We never rush and put money into a company. Some of the deals went away because they didn't want to wait for us, but that's okay. We wanted to do it our way. And by not having a fund, there's no pressure for us to invest.

Some of the deals you think are the good ones turn out to be disappointing, and the ones that are not doing well initially sometimes are the good ones. They always surprise you. I can't help thinking about the deals I missed. One of the deals I didn't invest in was Salesforce. Marc Benioff was a colleague of mine at Oracle, and when he was doing the deal, he called and said, "Hey, come take a look at the deal." We talked about it a little bit, but I was too busy to follow up and put money into it. Another one was Ariba in the early days. The CEO, Keith Krach, asked me to put money in the pot, which I thought was highly overvalued at $100 million. At the peak of the bubble, it was worth $40 billion. So a lot of those things, you say, "Man, I wish I'd done that." But for some reason or another you ended up not doing it. You always feel bad about the deal you didn't do or missed out on. I talked to friends, "Dang, we missed Uber!" And it's like, "Okay, you missed Uber." You always feel bad about the deals you didn't do. We do celebrate the deals that have been successful.

USING MY PEOPLE NETWORK TO EXPAND THE NETWORK OF AGENTS OF CHANGE

When I left my corporate job, I really had gotten to know a lot of people. My secretary at that time had all these business cards that I collected. She said, "Okay, before you leave, I'll put them all in binders." I left with binders full of these cards. I counted them, and I had four thousand connections. This was 1996. There was no LinkedIn—nothing.

I asked myself, how can I keep in touch with these people? E-mail was just coming about, and people were barely starting to go online. People said, "Have a party." I said I can't just have a party. So they said, "Have a conference." When I was a chief marketing officer, I ran all the user groups, user conferences, and user seminars. I loved meeting people and networking. I'm an entrepreneurial type of guy, so I thought, *Okay, let me start a conference.* I talked to a bunch of the guys in Silicon Valley who I deal with, and I said, "I want to do a conference," and they said, "Great." "And when I asked them if they could be on my advisory board, they said it would be fantastic. When it came time to invite them to the conference, they said no because they said there were so many conferences. They asked, "Why are you different?" They pushed me really hard. I started thinking, and suddenly one day I had it. I called my partner and said, "I've got an idea." And he said, "What?" And I said, "We're going to give all the money [from the conference] away." And he said, "What?" And I said, "We're going to give all the money away." So we created the first charitable technology conference. It was called Enterprise, and we started it in 1998. We invited the top leaders in technology, like John Chambers, Scott Cook, Ray Lane, Charles Phillips, and Hasso Plattner—all the recognizable names in the industry. I wasn't the keynote; rather, I was the organizer who pulled it all together.

Everybody had to pay for it. I remember John Chambers' [CEO of Cisco] secretary calling me the first year and saying, "You know John usually gets paid for these events?" I explained the concept to her, and she came back and said, "John would be happy to pay for your event." That first year we had a hundred people. They each paid four thousand dollars, played golf at Pebble Beach, and had a two-day insiders' event. We ran it for ten years and gave all the surplus away to women's and children's nonprofits: one local and one international. Over time we gave away over a million dollars. I started a foundation from the proceeds of the event called the SHG Foundation where we still have an endowment, and we still give money away to women's and children's causes each year.

The purpose was to get people to talk about enterprise software. It was only the CEOs of companies and the VCs—it was highly curated and exclusive. VCs were included because they were the ones who funded companies publically, especially larger companies. The CEOs could talk to these guys and ask them, "What are you funding? What kinds of companies can you buy?" The money was not the only thing. We would bring the nonprofits in to present, and they would walk away with more than money—mentors, advisory board members, and trustees came out of this. Great organizations like Room to Read and Build came out of Enterprise. Along the way, I also started a for-profit conference company in Silicon Valley, called Software, to cover the software industry. So the charitable one was called Enterprise and the commercial one was called Software. I did that for ten years, and then I also sold off my conference company—the commercial business.

ENGAGING FOR MY DAUGHTERS
AND ENVIRONMENTAL SUSTAINABILITY

We have lived in San Francisco now for close to twenty years. I have two daughters. In 2007, when they were ten and eight years old, I thought, "Gee, what do I do now?" I wanted to do something that they would be proud of, so I started thinking and talking with my network. One of my friends said, "Hey, everyone's invested in green tech and clean tech, and since you did such a great job with the software industry, why don't you do something in this space?" My entrepreneurial bug was still there. So I thought I'd do something good for the world, and I started talking to people. As I had built this huge network of people, I called up about sixty of them in the Fortune 500 world and started talking to them to see if they worked with start-ups and what kind of stuff they were interested in. And in that research that my cofounder and I did, we found that most of these large companies had problems in this space. So we ended up starting the Corporate Eco Forum (CEF). CEF is a membership group of seventy of the world's largest companies. Our members include Amazon, Apple, Disney, Ford, FedEx, Google, Nike, Unilever—you name it, every brand—and we deal with the chief sustainability officer of these companies and really look at innovation and best practices around everything from the green data centers to the supply chain to the office buildings and factories.

The CEF model is quite different. We don't start with an agenda—the members help develop it. Every member pays an annual fee, and everybody gets an equal seat at the table. We don't take any advertising, sponsorships, nothing—and nobody can sell anything. It's vendor-free, consultant-free, and sponsor-ship-free, so there's only one agenda, which is, can we get the

M. R. at Corporate Eco Forum
(photo courtesy of M. R. Rangaswami)

world to be a better place by large corporations doing good things? The peer group meets and talks to each other in person, and we do webinars, research reports, and such. There is a full team working on it.

My daughters come to the meetings; in fact, they speak—they've been speaking at CEF since, I think, they were eight or ten years old. They talk about their personal commitment to sustainability, and the members love it. They say that's really the highlight—my kids. As a result of this work, I gave up having a car for three years. We went from two cars down to one car, so we had to share a car, which makes things challenging, but we made that work. And recently, I had to try something new so I bought a Tesla.

We've done a lot of work around green data centers, making sure everybody understood the best ways to create data centers, and our members include Microsoft, Google, and Apple. We've got pretty much anyone who knows anything about how to do data centers, and they're willing to share best practices, which is really nice. We've also done work around natural capital. There's a whole summit around natural capital every ten years called the Earth Summit. So we went to the last Earth Summit in Rio de Janeiro in 2012 and took twenty-four companies who made a major commitment to forests, including Disney and Enterprise Rent-a-Car. All the companies who are members made a commitment to what they're doing with water and forests. We've also done work in something called the materials marketplace, which is a way for companies to get rid of all their waste. If you're disposing of a thousand tons of cardboard every month, you can tell people and someone else might pick it up. So we're doing all sorts of projects. We also give out an award in memory of my mentor, C. K. Prahalad, recognizing companies for their work. We do both the inspirational and also the practical. I've taken the program to India a couple of times, because they really need a lot of help.

There is a lot of benchmarking going on between companies. All our member companies have goals that they can measure. It's fairly scientific with the work that gets done now. I think it was Peter Drucker who said you don't manage what you don't measure. But people have started measuring their greenhouse gases and measuring similar things and making commitments to lower them. It's now a full-fledged function within these companies. The challenge is doing more. Always the challenge is doing more. And doing more good, that's the other challenge. Not doing less bad—doing more good. So a lot of conversations happen in our meetings, and I think it's all looking good, but we need to do it faster.

This sustainability involvement came about because I questioned how I could be a role model for my children. It was maybe a naive proposition, but it led to this. My daughters are now in their late teens. They've met with the executives of all these companies every year. It is hard to deal with the issues for women in leadership. My older daughter goes to a women's college, Scripps in Claremont, and the women's colleges have startling statistics. You find them much more sensitive and appreciative of what needs to be done. Putting girls out in these kinds of situations changes their own confidence levels, but also from the men's position, they are seeing more women being more confident to do things. I think it's going to take time; I think it's a process, but it's starting to change. And I'm much more sensitive to it because of this. Also in the eco space, there are a lot more women in our membership. I would say it's like fifty-fifty. Definitely, in that space, many more women are prominent and high positioned. It is changing in parts of large companies as well, but I think there's a long way to go. I mean, it's great that some of the companies have now said they've made the wages of men and women equal in tech. I'm funding a group of Scripps girls to come up to Silicon Valley to do a three-day business tour of all the tech companies. Because tech companies are looking for more women employees, I'm bringing the best girls from Scripps and introducing them to companies like Salesforce, and maybe they'll end up getting hired and get into the mix. I just funded that program at Scripps, as I'm much more sensitive to it now. It's still an ongoing process, and I guess you could call it a kind of a family business.

MOTIVATING BY EXAMPLE FOR EDUCATION

If I were going to influence America's education practices, having studied in India and here, I think something that melds the two systems is an important strategy. The Indian system is really good at the rote part of it, which is sorely lacking in the US, in areas as simple as multiplication tables. In India we have to memorize them. Here kids don't even know their multiplication tables, so bringing that discipline on one side and marrying it with the thinking and creative analysis and discussion-type approach that the American institutions have would be a good direction. In India, we never discussed anything in school. Here we have lots of discussions in schools on the latest issues—kids have discussions, which is very good. Somehow if we can meld the two—on one side, you have to do your multiplication tables, and on the other, let's talk about women's empowerment. It's going back to the basics. I think here the continuum has swung more to being the loosey-goosey stuff. And I think it has to be brought back to one where we kind of measure people on their math skills and science skills and do a lot more to bring back focus to that part of education. There's a big difference between public schools and private schools. We're fortunate enough to have our kids go to a private school. But that's a very small part of the population. The bigger challenge is, how do you get thousands of teachers to change their habits and parents to get the kids more motivated to do the core rote stuff, which is sometimes boring.

Parents have to motivate their children through examples. I mean the only way is to say, here are ten people who succeeded and this is why they succeeded. We can only inspire and motivate—we can't legislate. I don't think that is effective. I think it's more about inspiration. Giving them support outside of school is another criterion. We need to help them, because many of them may be struggling. Putting programs in place to get them better at what they have to learn outside of school is important. I think it's going to require a lot more than just putting in dollars.

My entrepreneurial spirit hasn't stopped. Seven years ago, I started doing pro bono work in India. I go once a year to Bangalore to cohost the largest technology entrepreneurship forum in India. I take a delegation of Silicon Valley leaders to India with me to do workshops and to speak in Bangalore. The event has grown, and in 2015 there were twenty-five hundred people at the conference. This is one way I was giving back to India, by doing this pro bono event in Bangalore.

ENCOURAGING THE INDIA DIASPORA

That led me to think about Indian Americans, and I said, "Okay, if I'm doing this for India, what am I doing here locally?" There are three million of us in the US, and what can we do as a force? Four or five years ago, I started thinking of this, and four years ago I made it a reality by bringing together one hundred leaders in the community from across the United States and saying, "What should our community do?" because we're single yet strong—1 percent of the population. We're the highest-earning demographic at $100,000 a year. The average American makes $50,000. We should be a potent source of influence, but when you look at our social and political influence as Indian Americans, it's zero. I made a benchmark against the Jewish Americans. They're 2 percent of the population. That said, they're only twice our size, but you look at their social and political clout, and it's extraordinary. So I said, "Why can't we be like them?" That's why I started an organization called Indiaspora. My late nephew came up with the name from the two words *India* and *diaspora*. Four years ago, I started convening a hundred leaders. We came up with three things that we need to do as a community. One is to raise our visibility. We need to encourage more people to go into politics, community service, and such. The second thing we need to do is to put out a call for robust US-India relations, because a lot of these leaders wanted to work with India as well. And then the final thing is for us all to give back more. So philanthropy is the third pillar. How do we not just give by check but through mentorship and providing services? These are the three goals of Indiaspora.

We were told that to get visibility, we have to be big in Washington. In 2013, we did a ball for Obama—a presidential ball. There were twelve hundred people. Senators and governors and congressmen and

M. R. and President Obama
(photo courtesy of M. R. Rangaswami)

others who came were saying, "Wow, where were you guys before?" And they started seeing us now potentially as a political movement and also as a source of money and everything else. More recently, we did Diwali in DC last year. We had fifty senators and congressmen come celebrate with us; we had twelve hundred people celebrating at the Library of Congress. We are now getting a lot more visibility in DC, which we need, but as a community we're also encouraging people to run for office. So this next year, we could have four people in Congress, which would be 1 percent of Congress, and we're 1 percent of the population. Right now, we only have one Indian American in Congress. So next year we hope to have four. That's a big boost. But the Jewish Americans have 10 percent of Congress. We need to learn how to get more. We also take delegations to India. I take a delegation of fifteen Indian leaders to dialogue with their counterparts about ways that Indian Americans can help India, whether it's in health care, innovation, entrepreneurship, or renewable energy.

What I like to do is bring people together—smart people. I like to bring them together over a set of issues that they can tackle, whether it's ecology or Indian Americans. Hopefully, I won't start anything else because anything I do takes a ten-year commitment. CEF is ten years old, so now I can say, "Good, I've done ten." I'll do more—I'm not going to stop—although I'm not planning on doing anything new because ten more years is a lot.

I don't usually talk about my family much. This is the first time I'm talking about my wife, Krisanthy. She's a professional musician—nothing to do with tech or conferences. She plays the cello with chamber groups and orchestras in San Francisco and, in the summers, at the Grand Teton Music Festival in Jackson Hole, Wyoming. Before I met her, I knew nothing about classical music at all. I first got introduced by hanging around her and then started liking it, and it's become part of my repertoire. On the other hand, I also listen to hip-hop with my kids, so I listen to all kinds of music. I love music, any kind of music. But one thing we decided to do when we had kids, especially since my dad died when I was ten, was that I said I was going to have a profession or a job that allowed me to work at home. So we both ended up working at home. I don't have another office; my office is my home. We brought up our kids together; we brought them up where we're both stay-at-home parents. My wife lets me do what I want, but we're both at home together so it's not like I'm gone. The last few years, as my kids have gotten older, I've been taking more trips. They go with me a lot. We're a family in motion. We've taken our kids to, I think, between thirty and thirty-five countries on holidays. I follow the academic schedule, so when they get spring break, I get spring break; when they get summer holidays, I get summer holidays. So we've been lucky enough to lead that kind of lifestyle, but at the same time I want to be sure that I do whatever I can to make an impact on society. I can do all these things because my wife is fully supportive.

I didn't think the concept of retirement was something I bought into—I didn't believe in it. I remember when I was thirty-five or so, my wife and I went to a financial planner, because our friends said, "You have to go to a financial planner! You don't have any planning!" So we went to this guy, and it's a pretty good anecdote, because he said, "So when do you want to retire?" And I said, "Forty." So he plugs this thing into his computer and it prints out this twenty-page report. And it says I've got to start saving like a gazillion a dollars a month in order to retire by forty. And I said, "This model is broken, because we're conditioned to retire at sixty-two, when Social Security kicks in." So the model was broken. And at that time, being in Silicon Valley, you think of crazy ideas. My idea at that time, at age thirty-five, was that I'm going to quit by forty. And I was one year late. I was able to quit the corporate life at forty-one. I haven't had a job since then, but the fact is, we're molded into thinking this way. I think we need to break the mold. I thought that way, and I was lucky that I was able to break it, but I would probably have still kept trying to quit corporate life even if I weren't forty-one. I would have kept trying for forty-five or fifty. But we're conditioned to think sixty-two is the time for retirement. So people go through this whole life thinking they're going to enjoy it when they're sixty-two, but they're old. So I think, why can't they enjoy it when they're forty? Being an entrepreneurial kind of guy, I go into new areas that I don't know, and that's how you learn all these new skills and ideas. Most people are afraid, so they won't do this or they don't have the resources to go and do it.

When I look at my life, there are three components. I look at my early life—studying accounting and law and the MBA—and all that is kind of an exploration phase in my life. I didn't know what I wanted to do. So I guess you could call it wandering, or you could call it exploration. And I had no clue what I was going to do with my life. And then you get into kind of the building phase, I guess you could call it. This is when you build experience, and you build wealth. That's when I was at Oracle and at Baan and all the other companies. You get into building wealth and building life. And then the final one is the giving-back phase, which is what I do with Indiaspora and all the charitable things I do. My only regret is not compressing the second phase and giving more back. I can say that these three parts of my life are in roughly twenty-year phases. I'm sixty-one right now, so I hope I have one more twenty!

APPENDIX

SUPPLEMENTAL INFORMATION ON US IMMIGRATION LAWS IN THE 1900S

In 1917 a law was passed that excluded immigrants from a geographically defined "Asiatic Barred Zone," which included all Asians except for those from Japan and the Philippines. (Japan had a voluntary pre-established limit on immigration, and the Philippines was a colony of the United States.) Chinese people were already banned from the United States under the 1882 Chinese Exclusion Act. Then, in 1924, the Immigration Act (or the Johnson-Reed Act) was passed. According to this act of Congress, visas would be doled out on a strict national-origins quota system. White immigrants from Northern and Western Europe received preference, while Jews from Southern and Eastern Europe, along with immigrants of African descent, were restricted. Under this new act, Asians from all countries were completely banned.

The United States immigration policy did not substantially change until the mid 1960s under President Lyndon B. Johnson.[1]

---

1. "Immigration Act of 1924," *Wikipedia*, accessed February 22, 2017, https://en.wikipedia.org/wiki/Immigration_Act_of_1924

Excerpt from "Special Message to the Congress on Immigration,"
January 13, 1965, by President Lyndon B. Johnson[2]:

Too often [our immigration law] arbitrarily denies us immigrants who have outstanding and sorely needed talents and
skills. I do not believe this is either good government or
good sense. Thousands of our citizens are needlessly separated from their parents or other close relatives. To replace
the quota system, the proposed bill relies on a technique of
preferential admissions based upon the advantage of our
nation of the skills of the immigrant, and the existence of a
close family relationship between the immigrant and people who are already citizens or permanent residents of the
United States. Within this system of preferences, and within
the numerical and other limitations prescribed by law, the
issuance of visas to prospective immigrants would be based
on the order of their application.

First preference under the bill would be given to those
with the kind of skills or attainment which make the admission especially advantageous to our society. Other preferences would favor close relatives of citizens and permanent
residents, and thus serve to promote the reuniting of families—long a primary goal of American immigration policy.
Parents of United States citizens could obtain admission
without waiting for a quota number. Transition to the new
system would be gradual, over a five-year period. Thus the
possibility of abrupt changes in the pattern of immigration
from any nation is eliminated. In addition, the bill would
provide that as a general rule no country could be allocated
more than ten percent of the quota numbers available in any
one year.

In order to insure that the new system would not impose
undue hardship on any of our close allies by suddenly

2.   "13 - Special Message to the Congress on Immigration," *The American
     Presidency Project*, accessed February 17, 2017, http://www.presidency.ucsb.edu/
     ws/index.php?pid=26830&st=immigration&st1=

curtailing their emigration, the bill authorizes the President, after consultation with an Immigration Board established by the legislation, to utilize up to thirty percent of the quota numbers available in any year for the purpose of restoring cuts made by the new system in the quotas established by existing law.

Similar authority, permitting the reservation of up to ten percent of the numbers available in any year, would enable us to meet the needs of refugees fleeing from catastrophe or oppression.

In addition, the bill would:

(1) permit numbers not used by any country to be made available to countries where they are needed,

(2) eliminate the discriminatory "Asia-Pacific Triangle" provisions of the existing law,

(3) eliminate discrimination against newly-independent countries of the Western Hemisphere by providing non-quota status for natives of Jamaica, Trinidad and Tobago,

(4) afford non-quota status to parents of citizens, and fourth preference to parents of resident aliens,

(5) eliminate the requirement that skilled first preference immigrants needed in our economy must actually find an employer here before they can come to the United States,

(6) afford a preference to workers with lesser skills who can fill specific needs in short supply,

(7) eliminate technical restrictions that have hampered the effective use of the existing Fair-Share Refugee Law, and,

(8) authorize the Secretary of State to require re-registration of quota immigrant visa applicants and to regulate the time of payment of visa fees.

This bill would not alter in any way the many limitations in existing law which prevent an influx of undesirables and safeguard our people against excessive or unregulated immigration. Nothing in the legislation relieves any immigrant of the necessity of satisfying all of the security requirements we now have, or the requirements designed to exclude persons likely to become public charges. No immigrants admitted under this bill could contribute to unemployment in the United States.

The total number of immigrants would not be substantially changed. Under this bill, authorized quota immigration, which now amounts to 158,361 per year, would be increased by less than 7,000. I urge the Congress to return the United States to an immigration policy which both serves the national interest and continues our traditional ideals. No move could more effectively reaffirm our fundamental belief that a man is to be judged—and judged exclusively—on his worth as a human being.

ACKNOWLEDGMENTS

I don't consider myself a writer, but I do consider myself an enabler of people telling their stories. I don't listen as a voyeur; I listen because there is a special intimacy that can't be replicated in any other manner when we just stop to listen about a person's journey.

There are many people who have introduced me to the value of storytelling. Our childhood family friend, Alex Moose, who as an Ojibwe elder, found our family willing to listen to his stories of learning from his grandfather the ways of hunting, harvesting wild rice, and the forest. Our mother eventually wrote out his stories as he told them to her, and she helped him make it into a book so the learning was not lost to the ages. I remember my mother writing down my grandfather's stories and still hear the part of the story when he said good-bye to his mother for the last time as he emigrated from Norway. He wanted his farewell to that life and land told by Magnus John Olson and not someone else. As a small child I listened to the stories from our great-uncle, Martin Olson, who also emigrated from Norway and became a US soldier in WWI so he could secure his US citizenship. There were stories of the rats and the mustard gas and the place of the storytelling, told in a darkened apartment with light peeking through broken blinds, which enhanced the tales. My dear friend R. Alan James read me the stories from Bonhoeffer while on a canoe trip in northern Minnesota when I was fifteen. He taught me so much about asking questions through our fifty years of friendship. For all these people, I am grateful beyond measure.

I believe I listened well and with enthusiasm to the technology parts of the stories due to my years at Digital Equipment and give my thanks to Dr. Donald Gaubatz, Tom Furlong, and Mike Nielsen, who supported my learning new technologies and the excitement of marketing their ideas even if I wasn't an engineer. Thank you to my dear friend Kumar Malavalli, whose story is written about in the introduction and then told again in his own words. We cross-taught each other marketing and engineering knowledge in our decades together. Hopefully if you are a technologist, you will find these sections of the stories interesting. If you aren't a technologist, you may have chosen to avoid those parts, although there is much to be learned.

Thank you to Mr. A. Pavan, who introduced me to the wonderful people in Minnesota whose included stories and impressive commitments to assimilation, community, and education are inspiring. These people give me hope that we can raise our vision for a shared humanity and enjoy the beauty of music and poetry of India.

Thank you to Judy Arnstein, my original editor. Hampering an editor by saying she couldn't change some phrases or spell out every acronym doesn't make their task easy, but she did it with grace. Thank you to the staff of Girl Friday Productions, who make it possible for self-publishers to get their book to market.

Thank you to Hugo Arevalo, the only person I allowed to read the stories before I started working with Girl Friday Productions, because he has an insatiable appetite to read every book in every public library that holds an interest. You made such a difference and boosted my enthusiasm to complete the book.

Thank you also to Kumar for opening up India to me and for introducing me to his friends and colleagues. Through my years of traveling in India and being with people of Indian origin in the United States and Canada I am so inspired by the culture, the history, and the commitment of people of Indian origin to make life better for so many others, known and unknown.

Thank you to my sister, Lana Mulder, who was my sounding board in my frustration to get the transcripts approved by the storytellers and on to the editor. And thank you to my dear husband, Thomas Barry, who never appeared to tire of hearing me repeat the sections of the life stories that I would haul out to inspire people at gatherings around our table or with friends and strangers in conversation. Thank you for the support that you offer in so many ways and for your encouragement to get the book available to the public.

Thank you to each of the people whose life stories are represented in this book. I trust that your children and grandchildren will appreciate that you participated so you could tell your story and it would not be lost to time and interpretation.

Brenda H. Christensen
Woodside, California

ABOUT THE EDITOR

Brenda H. Christensen is a marketing professional who has spent more than three decades in the computer and storage networking industries. She has worked in sales, marketing, and engineering at Xerox, Houghton Mifflin, Digital Equipment, Adaptec, and Brocade Communications and has spearheaded and co-owned a technology-conference business based in India. She is in the Storage Networking Industry Association Hall of Fame and is an adviser and on boards of start-up companies and nonprofits. As the grandchild of an economic migrant, she has always had an interest in immigrant participation in North American politics and commerce. She currently shares her time between Silicon Valley and British Columbia.